Albert Bushnell Lloyd

In Dwarf Land and Cannibal Country

A Record of Travel and Discovery in Central Africa

Albert Bushnell Lloyd

In Dwarf Land and Cannibal Country
A Record of Travel and Discovery in Central Africa

ISBN/EAN: 9783337307578

Printed in Europe, USA, Canada, Australia, Japan

Cover: Foto ©Andreas Hilbeck / pixelio.de

More available books at **www.hansebooks.com**

IN DWARF LAND AND CANNIBAL COUNTRY
A RECORD OF TRAVEL AND DISCOVERY IN CENTRAL AFRICA

BY

A. B. LLOYD

WITH INTRODUCTION BY
THE RT. HON. SIR JOHN
H. KENNAWAY, BART., M.P.,
PRESIDENT OF THE
CHURCH MISSIONARY
SOCIETY

146 ILLUSTRATIONS AND MAPS

This Book

I HUMBLY DEDICATE TO

MY MOTHER,

WHOSE SAINTLY LIFE AND EARNEST PRAYERS

HAVE EVER BEEN MY ADMIRATION AND SUPPORT,

PARTICULARLY DURING MY MANY AND VARIED EXPERIENCES

IN CENTRAL AFRICA

PREFACE

AS President of the Church Missionary Society, I gladly accede to Mr. Lloyd's request that I should write a few lines of introduction to his book.

He has been bearing his share of "the white man's burden" of ruling, civilising, and Christianising the "silent peoples," of whom John Bull carries no less than 350 millions on his back.

The duty is no light one, but it gives an outlet for the energies of our people, an object worthy of an Imperial race, of a Christian country, a call to put forth the highest qualities of the Anglo-Saxon character. Mr. Lloyd has been for four years and a half engaged as one of our missionaries in the grand work of helping to build up the Church in Uganda and the regions around it, within the confines of the British Protectorate.

It is a church whose foundations were laid by Bishops Hannington and Parker, by Mackay, Shergold Smith, Pilkington, and many others—a church rich in martyrs, now numbering more than 20,000 baptized members, besides catechumens and readers, with 15 native clergy and 1,000 lay Evangelists—a church self-supporting, possessing the Bible and Prayer-Book in its own tongue, and spending £1,500 a year in the purchase of books.

What hath God wrought?

PREFACE.

During his sojourn in Africa Mr. Lloyd has been witness of the stirring scenes of the Soudanese rebellion, which he assisted in repressing. He was privileged to close the eyes of his friend and brother, Mr. Callis, so early struck down in Toro, and to him was dictated the wonderful letter from King Daudi Kasagama to "The Elders of the Church in Europe," thanking them for sending teachers, and telling them that he wanted very much to arrange all the matters of his country for God only, that all his people might understand that Christ Jesus is the Saviour of all countries, and that He is the King of all kings.

To his *rôle* as a missionary Mr. Lloyd has added that of an explorer. Last year, when the time of his furlough had come, he determined to strike out a line for himself and make through Belgian territory for an exit on the West Coast. This brought him to the Pygmy Forest, where Stanley spent so much time, and reviewed the old memories of Herodotus.

Much progress has been made, even since the later of the two historians, and it speaks well that our traveller was able to make his way through the midst of Pygmies and cannibals, unharmed and unharming. The knowledge he has gained cannot fail to be of use to him when he returns to Uganda, and it will certainly be of interest to his readers, to whom I heartily commend his book.

JOHN H. KENNAWAY.

CHURCH MISSIONARY HOUSE,
SALISBURY SQUARE, E.C.

PREFATORY NOTE

..

THE writer of the following pages makes no pretensions to literary ability, and he intends this work merely to be a plain, unvarnished story, simply told, of life lived under many conditions in Africa. He hopes no apology will be deemed necessary for the imperfections which may appear in the telling of his narrative. The writing of such a book was far enough from his thoughts when he went off upon his mission to that benighted continent, and nothing would now induce him to do so but the conviction that the knowledge he has gained of unknown countries and unknown tribes should not be kept to himself. As one who has laboured, and still hopes to labour, among the helpless and friendless millions of the Dark Continent, his natural desire, if writing a book at all, would be to treat with missionary enterprise exclusively, and to establish and enforce the claims of the perishing heathen. But this is not what he has set himself to do in producing this volume. The other side of missionary life must sometimes be told, and to this task he has put his hand. It has been a difficult one, but however imperfectly it has been accomplished the writer simply asks that the reader will bear in mind that the intentions of the author are to introduce facts in such a way as to interest the most casual reader; and he is not without hope that it will in some measure procure for the dark, perishing millions of Central Africa an increase of sympathy from the Christian public of Great Britain.

INTRODUCTION

Africa—Past and Present.

DURING the past century no country has opened up to the civilised world in so marvellous a manner as Africa. Not many years ago the Map of Africa was almost a blank. The great desert and the Nile seemed to be the only natural features known. And yet, looking back upon the Africa of the past, we behold her greatness— the nursery of science and literature; the seat of an Empire almost as great as that of Rome, and one which contended with Rome for the kingdoms of the world; and we think of Egypt, the great stronghold of the early Church, with its archbishop and bishops, its churches, and its learning.

The old Egyptians of the bygone ages seemed to know more about the centre of Africa than did our grandfathers. There on the tombs of their kings, far back in the Sixth Dynasty, we get a record, not only proving the knowledge of the Egyptians of those remote ages, of a great lake at the sources of the Nile, but of the existence of the Pygmies. There is described on the tomb of Aswan how the King Mer-en-Ra sent his servant to fetch a Pygmy from the country of Punt by the lake Punt, supposed to be the source of the Nile, and it is recorded how that the

King Assa, five reigns earlier, is spoken of as having seen a Pygmy from this land brought by his servant.

This means that about 3,200 years B.C. the very centre of Africa was known to the then civilised world. The writings of Herodotus seem but as yesterday before such inscriptions as these; he, however, was called the "dreamer," and his account of the Pygmies dwelling near the great Mountains of the Moon was scarcely believed, and yet to day we know the truth of what he wrote.

The Portuguese will tell us of great cities built by them centuries ago in the very heart of Africa, and on the west there still remain traces of what once must have been a flourishing mission; and these traces may yet be found in the centre.

We speak to-day of the great explorations for the opening up of the Dark Continent; our proposed railways, increased trade, and our civilising agencies. But what is the true state of affairs? alas! it must still be called *Darkest* Africa. Thousands of square miles still unexplored, huge forests absolutely untouched, millions of her dusky sons in as gross a state of darkness as they were a thousand years ago. And this for all that more lives have been laid down for Africa, and a greater sacrifice of men to the enterprise of discovery than in any other land. The border is yet hardly touched. Civilised countries have been made the richer by her gold, and where is the recompense that has been paid to her? Her tribes are sunk in deepest depths of ignorance and sin, and alas! the white man's greed for her gold, her rubber, and her ivory has only deepened her guilt, for often it has brought within her domains drunkenness, lawlessness, and vice, and all this rushing in upon a defenceless people.

And still her hands are stretched out, and it is to us that she looks; to us—who have taken her wealth, and the blood of thousands of her sons, and who, in exchange, have given to her gin, and a handful of missionaries.

But the day is at hand, and darkest Africa shall yet be enlightened. Already from her very heart a tiny streak of light has commenced to glow in the British Protectorate of Uganda. Thank God! Britain's sons have planted the Union Jack in her very centre, not to suck her life-blood for the sake of her wealth, but to bring to her the priceless treasures of Peace, Prosperity, and Religion.

Africa shall yet hold up her head; her down-trodden sons and daughters shall leap into a new-found freedom, and the fiercest spirits that ever trod her burning sands shall be brought into complete subjugation; not by the military fort and the roar of cannon and the rattle of musketry, for it will require a mightier power than this to bring peace to this troubled land. That which has made our Empire what it is to-day—"The Word of God"—this is the power that shall transform Africa from the tenfold horrors of her millions and make her a land of peace.

We may make our railways and establish the claims of our nation and open up her dark recesses to our commerce, but if we Britons forget to send her that which has made our own land so great, then will the sorrows of Africa lay at our own door.

CONTENTS

PART I.

ENGLAND TO UGANDA

CHAPTER I.

ENGLAND TO ZANZIBAR.

The *Gaul*—Passengers—The Doctor as an entertainer—Musical talent, &c.—Lisbon—The Portuguese—Teneriffe—Sunday on board—Cape Town—We meet with friends—Algoa Bay—Durban—The Kaffirs—Delagoa Bay—Beira—Mozambique—Zanzibar—Hotel d'Angleterre—Change of plans—We secure porters, boys, &c.—"Mission boy"—We select donkeys—Universities' Mission—Ramazan—Tippu-Tib—Ready to start 1

CHAPTER II.

THE START.

Eleven hours in an Arab dhow—Waiting and whistling for the wind—Ashore at last—First night in Africa—A restless night—Final preparations—K'shimba—Reviewing our porters—Our first camp—Great oration by K'shimba—The lion's roar—Discomforts of camp life—Famine ahead—We send for fresh supplies—Dr. Baxter—A ministry of love—A pot of porridge—And what came of it—The power of an Englishman—Letters from home—Scarcity of water—The horrors of human porterage—Leopard in the tree—Lost in the forest 23

CHAPTER III.

GLIMPSES OF CAMP LIFE.

Under the tamarind tree—Refreshment for the cows—Hope deferred at Mbuzini river—The Wami—First real wash in Africa—Famine stares us in the face—Fever—Crossing river on African bridge—Tent left behind—The cook's story—Overtaken by Bishop Tucker—The wild ass—The Bishop to the front—Long solitary march—Kindly reception—Lions in the path—Mamboya—Hospitality in Central Africa—The "Mission boy" again—Practical Christianity—We split our caravan—The porters rebel—How we squashed the rebels—Peace making—Mpwapwa—Kisokwe—Famine and its horrors . . 41

CHAPTER IV.

CAMP LIFE (continued).

Wagogo thieves—K'shimba in distress—Trouble in the forest—The Martini rifle—Our hunting expeditions—When the boots wear out—Burungi, the land of plenty—Rains are upon us—Buying food—The Warungi—The warriors and my dog Sally—How troubles come—Irangi—A courteous reception—We tend the sick—The Governor as a patient—An African's gratitude—K'shimba turns up—He relates his troubles—Bwana Kitangi to the rescue 67

CHAPTER V.

THE LAST STAGES.

Farewell to Bwana Kitangi—Rains—Washed out—Floods—Swampy ground—The porter's slave—Sandawi—More troubles—Considered himself a dead man—A hostile people—Turu—Poisonous roots—Christmas Day—The Wanyamwezi country—Sickness—We reach Nera—Meeting with Messrs. Gordon and Nickisson—Carried in a hammock—Arrival at Nasa—Rest at last—Native cloth—Embarkation on Lake—Our canoes—Hippopotami—Ukerewe—Mr. Stokes—A narrow escape—The German Station—The stormy winds do blow—The Wasese—Crocodiles—The last day 84

CONTENTS.

PART II.

UGANDA. THE SOUDANESE WAR.

CHAPTER VI.

UGANDA.

PAGE

Our entrance into Mengo—The four hills of Mengo—Kampala—The British Government of Uganda—Troubles from without—Missionary occupations—Native customs—The Waganda—Woman's position—Missionary efforts Loyalty of the native Christians—Medical work—The chief dresser—Native industries—Iron-working—Wood-working—Pottery—Basket work—The bark cloth—The native market—Efforts to catch zebra . . 116

CHAPTER VII.

UGANDA TO TORO.

Experiences gained—Toro—Ruwenzori—A lay missionary's work Valedictory feasts—Obtaining porters—The boys—Mika's conversion—A leopard scare—The Mayanja—Mosquitoes—Mitiana—Crossing the Mpamujugu—Elephant country—Antelope steak—Forest glades—Elan—Sally, a distinguished guest Unfriendly Papists I nurse a black baby—Cow stealing—Fishing for breakfast—Mwenge Byakweyamba—The banquet—An embarrassing welcome to Toro . . . 139

CHAPTER VIII.

TORO.

Brief history of Toro Kasagama—Developments in Toro Liberation of slaves Ruwenzori, Mountains of the Moon—Attending the sick—I build a dispensary Wanted, a hospital—Leopards of Toro—A midnight scare Lions—The little hero—The Watoro—Toro customs—Teeth breaking Burning "Njoka"—Cupping—Drinking parties 159

CHAPTER IX.

A TRAMP INTO THE UNKNOWN.

Footprints of the lions—Snake in the grass—Ravages of the lions—A narrow escape Dry and thirsty land I meet the Captain The Soudanese guard—Following the compass Hunting water-buck

—Between heaven and earth—A fine specimen A picturesque camp—Elephants—Carving our way—Up a tree—Patience rewarded—Tropical vegetation—The Captain and I part company—We camp in the wilderness—Mount Edwin Arnold Mpanga river A hostile people Heathen sacrifice—Home again to Toro . . 176

CHAPTER X.

AT HOME IN TORO.

Climate of Toro—Brick-making—House-building—A tornado—A disaster The Government fort—Missionaries and the Government officials—A Christmas feast—The Mission garden—My first elephant—The Batatela rebellion—Adventures of a French priest Belgian officer takes refuge in British protectorate—Fort George attacked—A splendid victory—Death of Rev. John Callis—Lions again—A lucky shot 191

CHAPTER XI.

RAMBLES ROUND ABOUT TORO.

Visiting the craters A day on the lake—A bicycle experience—Lion in the path—Visiting Mwenge—The "Speed-away"—A swollen river—Exhaustion—Kindly help—Fever—I am hailed as a "rain producer"—I go to see Prince Matu—I overhear an interesting conversation—Sally to the rescue—A would-be assassin—To the Semliki Valley—A black man's gratitude—A magnificent view—Albert Lake—Hunting reed-buck I start for Mboga—Elephant hunt—Over the Mountains of the Moon—Fresh meat—Among the Bamba The hot springs—Crossing the Semliki—Elephant camp—A morning call—Alive with game—Mboga—Church history 207

CHAPTER XII.

SOUDANESE REBELLION.

Political troubles—Mwanga's flight—Major Ternan wounded—Mwanga's capture by the Germans—Uganda regents—A record journey—Major Macdonald's expedition Soudanese rebellion—Its causes—British pluck—Battle of Luba's Hill Murder of Major Thurston—Disarming the Soudanese in Mengo—Native auxiliaries—Night attack—Battle on the plain at Luba's—Some one has blundered—Reinforcements—Destroying banana gardens—Death of George Pilkington and Lieutenant Macdonald . 230

CHAPTER XIII.

SOUDANESE REBELLION (*continued*).

The Major leaves for Budu—Christmas Day in camp—The mutineers raid the gardens—Vigorous attack upon the Waganda camp—Mwanga's escape from Germans—Evacuation of rebel fort—I am sent to Ripon Falls—Attempts to blow up the dhow—Fort building—Rebels attempt to cross into Uganda—Indian troops arrive—All into Mengo—With Major Macdonald to Kabagambi—A responsible charge—A night scare—A brush with Mohammedans—Off again to the front—Rifle-stealing—A kind offer—More fighting—Severe struggle at Kabagambi—Death of Captain Maloney 252

PART III.

UGANDA TO THE WEST COAST.

CHAPTER XIV.

UGANDA TO CONGO FREE STATE.

Westward Ho—Uganda escort—An alarm—Blackened ruins—Elephants—My reasons for journey through Pygmy land—The Bishop's consent—Preparations for the start—Farewells—Escorts—The start—Violent earthquakes—Elephants again—A glorious sight—A faithless donkey—Sally submerged—An elephant hunt—Another snake story—Wakonjo village—Kikorongo—Chased by a hippo—Katwe—Hospitality of No. X. Company—Their loyalty 269

CHAPTER XV.

KATWE TO KILONGA-LONGA. THE GREAT PYGMY FOREST.

The boundary river—Lions—Meeting with the Belgian officer—We have a little hunt—Sporting yarns—Frontier settlement—Women slaves—Abundance of game—Traces of Mr. H. M. Stanley—Crossing the Semliki—Fort Mbeni—Preparing for the plunge—The forest—Its extent—Pygmy area—Vegetation—Clearings—Animal life—Rivers—Birds—Insects—Darkness—An Arab settlement—Cutting our way—Sakarumbi—Our camp in

the forest Elephants Wading through rivers—Red ants
Adventure with a snake—"A man-monkey!" Visit from the
Pygmies Friendly intercourse—Mode of Life A Pygmy hunt
 An attempt at photography An Arab chief—Tippu-Tib—
Kilonga-Longa . . 290

CHAPTER XVI.
KILONGA-LONGA TO AVAKUBI.

Kilonga-Longa or Mawambi—The donkey sold Gymnastics in the forest—A narrow escape—Falling trees—The Pygmies again—Renewed friendship—Bows and arrows—A Pygmy settlement—Pygmy women—Pygmy temples Fever—My black nurse—Elephant scatters the porters Wild pig—Snake adventure—Fishing—Crossing river on fallen tree—The guide kills an elephant A hungry panther—Two days through water—Pengi Canoes awaiting us—Socks *versus* stockings—First experiences on river Shooting the rapids Canoe men submerged—Canoe smashed up—A miserable night—Avakubi . . 318

CHAPTER XVII.
AVAKUBI TO BASOKO.

Houses Gardens Coffee—Rubber Ivory—Another start—A struggle for dear life—A great loss—Cannibals of the Upper Aruwimi—An anxious night—Another canoe swamped—Among the cannibals—Their dress—Their habits—The kola nut—Iron work Panga Falls Our warrior boatmen—We make rapid progress—"The European is coming"—Bangwa weapons—Choosing a tender spot—Mukopi—Gymnastics in the forest—A cannibal dance—Mupe—Cannibals and the bicycle—Banalya—A headstrong Belgian—I visit the cannibal chief—An eye-opener—What it will lead to—Basoko 336

CHAPTER XVIII.
BASOKO TO ENGLAND.

Captain Guy Burrows—Ten days' rest—The palm grove—Shooting our dinners—The steamer arrives—Mode of progress—Missionary friends at Upoto—The captain drunk—Stanley Pool Leopoldville—Kind friends—Catching the train—The saloon car—A strange sensation—Matadi—Kind hospitality—Boma—The Governor-General's compliment Cabenda—The mail-boat arrives—The lazy Portuguese—Getting passport signed—On board the *Loanda*—Lisbon—Sud express to Paris—Home at last—Conclusion 365

LIST OF ILLUSTRATIONS

	PAGE
A. B. LLOYD (PHOTOGRAVURE)	*Frontispiece*
PORT ELIZABETH MARKET HALL	7
DURBAN BREAKWATER, (SHOWING CHAIN GANG)	8
DURBAN TOWN HALL	9
BEIRA CANTEEN	10
ZANZIBAR	12
ZANZIBAR AFTER BOMBARDMENT	15
A PORTER. (WITH HIS LOAD)	17
WASUKUMA PORTERS	19
WANYAMWEZI PORTERS	27
CAMP LIFE	31
A MINISTRY OF LOVE	35
EAST AFRICAN MAIL CARRIERS	37
EAST AFRICAN HUT, WITH STOCKADE AND DEVIL HUT	39
CAMP AT MBUZINI	43
USAGARA LANDSCAPE	45
FAMINE-STRICKEN DISTRICT	47
USAGARA WOMEN AT HOME	50
SALLY	53
C.M.S. MISSION STATION, MAMBOYA	55
CHIEF OF MAMBOYA, WITH HIS SON AND WITCH DOCTOR	57
GERMAN ROAD, EAST AFRICA	63
GERMAN FORT, MPWAPWA	64
KISOKWE	65
UGOGO VILLAGE	69
GAME DISTRICT	71
RAINS UPON US	74
TREE FERNS	77
USAGARA QUEEN	80
WHERE AFRIC'S SUNNY FOUNTAINS	87
SANDAWI NATIVES	90
YOUNG OSTRICH	94
CHIEF OF NERA AND WIVES	98

LIST OF ILLUSTRATIONS.

	PAGE
C.M.S. MISSION STATION, NASA	100
KAPONGO, CHIEF OF NASA	101
NATIVE LOOM, USUKUMA	102
READY TO EMBARK ON VICTORIA NYANZA	103
UKEREWE, CHIEF'S ENCLOSURE	106
BOA CONSTRICTOR KILLED ON ISLAND OF UKEREWE	107
STORM ON VICTORIA NYANZA	110
VIEW ON SESE ISLANDS	112
WASESE FISHERMEN	113
DEAD HIPPOPOTAMUS	114
MENGO	117
INTERIOR OF MENGO CATHEDRAL	118
MISSIONARIES' HOUSE, NAMIREMBE	119
INTERIOR OF MISSIONARIES' HOUSE	120
KAMPALA	121
THE FORT, KAMPALA	122
MWANGA AND HIS PARLIAMENT	123
HIS OWN COBBLER	124
THE HOSPITAL, NAMIREMBE	128
DR. ALBERT COOK AND STAFF	129
EFFORTS TO CATCH ZEBRA	137
ON THE ROAD TO TORO	143
PAPYRUS SWAMP	146
UGANDA LANDSCAPE	148
ROAD-MAKING, UGANDA	149
ROAD THROUGH UGANDA FOREST	150
HEARTY RECEPTION, TORO	156
KASAGAMA, KING OF TORO	160
QUEEN MOTHER OF TORO	161
A DISTANT VIEW OF MOUNTAINS OF THE MOON	163
SICK FOLK	165
TORO DISPENSARY	166
KING'S HILL, KABAROLE	168
THE LION KILLER WITH HIS SPEAR	171
TYPICAL TORO HUT	173
C.M.S. MISSION STATION TORO	175
A TYPICAL ROAD	177
SOUDANESE SENTRY	182
HAPPY NIGGERS, PLENTY TO EAT	183
MPANGA RIVER	188

LIST OF ILLUSTRATIONS. xxiii

	PAGE
BRICK-MAKING, TORO	192
POLES FOR BUILDING PURPOSES	193
MISSIONARIES' MUD-HOUSE, TORO	194
THATCHING	196
GARDENING IN TORO	198
FRENCH MISSION, TORO	203
CRATER OF EXTINCT VOLCANO, TORO	208
CRATER OF EXTINCT VOLCANO, TORO	209
SWAMPY GROUND	212
MWENGE	213
OFF TO SEE PRINCE MATU. (REFRESHMENT BY THE WAY)	215
BAMBA	222
HOT SPRINGS	223
NATIVES WASHING IN HOT SPRINGS	224
BAMBA WARRIORS AT THE HOT SPRINGS	225
TABALO, CHIEF OF MBOGA	227
CHURCH AT MBOGA, WITH TWO WAGANDA TEACHERS	228
MWANGA, EX-KING OF UGANDA	231
DAUDI CHWA, PRESENT KING OF UGANDA	234
SOUDANESE TROOPS	235
KATIKIRO OF UGANDA, WITH HIS SON	239
A FAITHFUL UGANDA CHIEF	241
MY PERSONAL ESCORT DURING SOUDANESE REBELLION	243
MIKA, MY FAITHFUL GUN-BEARER	244
HARD AT IT	247
A WILD COUNTRY	271
EARTHQUAKE CAMP	280
RWIMI RIVER	282
WAKONJO VILLAGE	286
SALT LAKE	288
THE ANGLO-BELGIAN FRONTIER	291
KARIMI	293
THE FERRY	295
FORT MBENI	297
FIRST CAMP IN FOREST	300
INTERIOR OF ANT HILL	301
MY CARAVAN CROSSING RIVER IN PYGMY FOREST	303
MY CARAVAN IN FOREST	305
CROSSING A RIVER IN THE FOREST	307
A VISIT FROM THE DWARFS	311

xxiv LIST OF ILLUSTRATIONS.

	PAGE
BISHOP TUCKER AND PYGMY LADY	323
PYGMY TEMPLES	325
A ROGUE ELEPHANT SCATTERS THE CARAVAN	327
A RIVER PEEP IN THE FOREST	331
BELGIAN OFFICER, AVAKUBI	339
HOUSES, AVAKUBI	340
BUYING IVORY FROM THE CANNIBALS	341
CANOEING ON ARUWIMI	343
PASSING THROUGH CANNIBAL LAND	344
A BANGWA VILLAGE	347
BANGWA WARRIOR CHIEFS	349
CANNIBALS	351
CANNIBAL FISHERMEN	354
FLEET OF CANOES	355
CANNIBAL POTTERY	357
THE BICYCLE AND THE CANNIBALS	359
YAMBUYA	362
BASOKO	363
BARUMBU	366
CANNIBAL HOUSES ON THE UPPER CONGO	367
ARRIVAL OF THE STEAMER	368
UPOTO	369
FUEL STATION, UPPER CONGO	370
NATIVE TYPES, UPPER CONGO	371
DOVER CLIFFS, STANLEY POOL	372
TYPE OF MEN USED AS BOATMEN ON STATE STEAMERS	373
LEOPOLDVILLE	375
OLD CARAVAN ROUTE TO COAST FROM LEOPOLDVILLE	376
THE NEW WAY	377
VILLAGE ON CONGO	378
RAPIDS ON LOWER CONGO	379
STOPPING FOR WATER	380
RAILWAY SHEDS	381

MAPS.

CENTRAL AFRICA. (SHOWING ROUTE TAKEN BY A. B. LLOYD)	21
TORO CONFEDERACY . . . *Insert between pages* 158 *and* 159	
TORO AND ARUWIMI DISTRICTS. (SHOWING ROUTE OF A. B. LLOYD) *Insert between pages* 274 *and* 275	

IN DWARF LAND

PART I

ENGLAND TO UGANDA

CHAPTER I

ENGLAND TO ZANZIBAR

The *Gaul* Passengers—The Doctor as an entertainer—Musical talent, &c.—Lisbon—The Portuguese—Teneriffe—Sunday on board—Cape Town—We meet with friends—Algoa Bay—Durban—The Kaffirs—Delagoa Bay—Beira—Mozambique—Zanzibar—Hotel d'Angleterre—Change of plans—We secure porters, boys, &c.—"Mission boy"—We select donkeys—Universities' Mission—Ramazan—Tippu-Tib—Ready to start.

IT was on July 14, 1894, that the ss. *Gaul* steamed out of Southampton Docks, having on board a mixed cargo and a large number of passengers. Of the former I shall say nothing, of the latter but little.

We were bound for Zanzibar by way of the Cape. But the good ship *Gaul* first claims a share of our attention. To myself—an inexperienced voyager, who up to that day had been upon no larger craft than the Fleetwood to Dublin boats—it seemed like fairyland; and as I wandered up and down its gangways, in and out of its saloons, I decided in my own mind that no better ship was ever afloat.

I was one of a party of four missionaries of the Church Missionary Society, bound for Uganda. We travelled second class; but even the second-class cabins of the *Gaul* seemed luxurious, in spite of the fact that the one in which I was to live was occupied by three others.

Being a twin-screw, flat-bottomed boat, the rolling which I had experienced on a fishing smack on the North Sea some few weeks before was almost unknown, and I was able to enjoy to the full a stroll on deck, without the inconvenience of being obliged to hold on to everything that came within one's reach.

The passengers were a mixed company. There was the first-class section, consisting of the South African millionaire, the fashionable Colonial girl, the wealthy trader, and the wild young English gentleman going out to the pleasure fields of Africa, seeking to pass away a few years of his life with a little adventure and excitement.

Of the second-class passengers but little can be said. The missionary element was strong, for, besides the party to which I belonged—which consisted of the Revs. A. J. Pike, G. R. Blackledge, and Mr. H. B. Lewin—there were two other clergymen bound as missionaries for South Africa.

I don't know why it should be, but still it is a fact, that missionaries on board an ocean liner seem to be looked upon as a class of individuals who are to be carefully avoided, and to be given a wide berth on all occasions, and on this particular voyage such a state of affairs seemed to threaten. We determined that it should not be our fault if it were so. If we are missionaries, we are *men*, and if, instead of giving up our lives to the seeking of earthly riches in the shape of gold dust and diamonds, we have deliberately given them up to what we deem a worthier cause, namely, that of seeking to raise the degraded heathen from a state of ignorance, darkness, and sin to righteousness and to God, surely " a man's a man for a' that," and it should not mean that we are to be looked upon as those who are not worthy of the notice which is paid to any ordinary being.

However, on this particular voyage nothing could have been more pleasant; from our good captain to the humblest person on board the missionaries received the greatest kindness and goodwill—in fact, missionary and gold-digger, cleric and millionaire, all conversed and joked together during this memorable voyage.

The leading spirit on the boat was undoubtedly the doctor. As the weather was good and the sea calm, there were not many who were afflicted with that most troublesome of all complaints, *mal-de-mer*, the doctor therefore had all his energies directed in another and more pleasant channel, that of entertaining, and we were all far more glad to take his jokes than to take his pills. Almost every evening some kind of concert or entertainment was arranged by him, beside the ordinary games that are played on an ocean liner, such as cricket, quoits, bucket quoits, skittles, &c.

We had a considerable amount of musical talent amongst some of the passengers. A lady pianist, whose brilliant playing always attracted great attention, was most long-suffering, and always ready to do her best to entertain the company. The violinist called forth even louder praise from his enraptured listeners. Out on the open sea, with no other sound than the gentle splashing of the waves against the mighty sides of the ship, the melody rose and fell in glorious cadence, sometimes like an angel's whisper, and then suddenly changing to the weird cry of a soul in bitter agony and distress.

The vocalists, too, were by no means deficient in talent, and what with the rollicking sea-song, the pathetic and sentimental love-song, we had great variety and endless amusement. Another entertainer hailed from the third-class quarters, evidently an old hand on ocean steamers. His entertainment consisted of a phonograph, for which he had a very large number of cylinders, and at all hours of the day this machine was called upon to issue forth its strange reproductions of music-hall songs, &c., which it did with wonderful distinctness. All these different sources of amusement tended to make the journey to the Cape very enjoyable, bearing in mind the fact that the weather was delightful and the sea calm as a mill-pond.

Our first stopping-place was Lisbon, and as we made our way up the river and approached the town, we were much struck with its beauty; but upon landing, our eyes were opened to some of the disappointing sights. The houses, which in the distance looked spotlessly white, seemed now to be dirty, plastered buildings.

It was at Lisbon that I was first introduced to the Portuguese, and I cannot say that I formed a very high opinion of them. Very dirty in mind and person seems to me a brief summary of the ordinary Portuguese.

The population appeared to consist, for the most part, of fat, well-favoured priests, who drove about in carriages, and gaudily dressed women. We visited several of the churches, and on account of the large number concluded that the Portuguese must be a very religious people; and, indeed, they are to a certain extent, if ceremonial and church-going count for anything. The churches, from the outside, appear to be well built, and one expects the inside to be in keeping, but again comes disappointment—tinsel and gold-painted walls; images, which at a little distance appear to be fine pieces of sculpture, are nothing, upon close inspection, but plaster and wood.

As tradespeople the Portuguese amused us very much. We went into a shop to buy a hat; the good man produced a great number, and one at a time tried them on his own head, all shiny with grease, and then handed them to the purchaser. Deciding upon one of these hats, we asked the price; 600 reis was asked ; we immediately said 500, and, without a word, the shopkeeper assented. We gave him the equivalent in English money and walked out, he, taking off his hat and bowing most politely, and we, returning the compliment, retired, hardly controlling our amusement.

After twelve hours' stay in Lisbon, the *Gaul* proceeded on her way, and another three days brought us to Teneriffe. We dropped anchor at 8 p.m., a most glorious night, full moon, and a gentle breeze blowing from the land, where the gay Spaniards seemed to be enjoying the cool air, promenading up and down the sea front, listening to the bands of music which were adding an additional charm to that of the quiet evening stroll. As we stood on deck admiring the beautiful mountain peak of Teyde, some 12,180 feet high, the moon casting her silvery light over the scene, making it one of exceptional beauty, the strains of music came to us borne upon the soft night air, mingled with the hum of voices from the shore, while the water rippled at our feet, and our thoughts were lifted up to Him the Maker of all things, in whom we live and move and have our being, and holy desires filled our hearts as we thought of the work before us amongst the heathen who know not God.

Our stay at Teneriffe was a short one, and before midnight we were again under weigh.

Sunday on board an ocean liner has been described as a "slow day." This at any rate could not be applied to the Sundays on board the *Gaul*. In addition to the ordinary services held in the first-class saloon by the chaplain on board, the captain very kindly allowed a service to be conducted on the after deck, and it was found that this move met with a most hearty reception from all the passengers. The stewards brought up a large number of chairs for the occasion, and bright singing and speaking were characteristic of the services. Each Sunday evening sacred songs were sung by various passengers, and so the days passed by.

On August 5th we arrived at Cape Town, and here the majority of the passengers left the boat.

We were delighted with the very hearty reception we received from our friends in Cape Town. As soon as ever we arrived at the harbour side, a letter was put into our hands from a warm C.M.S. supporter, inviting us to spend the day with him; and we were afterwards met by Mr. Wilmot and taken off to Mowbray, to the north of the great Table Mountain, a most lovely place, nestling at the foot of this great mountain, and here we were welcomed by numerous warm-hearted colonists.

Meetings were immediately arranged, and the day after we arrived we were called upon to address three distinct gatherings. They were all of a large and enthusiastic character, and when one realised that all the advertising was done in the course of a few hours, it was a great wonder that in so short a time a meeting could be convened.

The fact was that the more enthusiastic among the promoters went round to their friends with their carriages, and brought them in these to the meeting. It was a delightful break in a long voyage, and we all look back upon those three days with the greatest pleasure.

After calling for two hours at Mossel Bay, we proceeded to Algoa Bay. The view of the seaport town, Port Elizabeth, from the ship, was very fine; and going ashore we were at once struck with the imposing appearance of some of the buildings, such as the Customs House, Post Office, Free Library, Market House, Museum, and others. Bullock waggons are largely used, we noticed some teams of from sixteen to eighteen. The bullocks are fastened to the waggon in pairs, by a long chain from the yoke on their necks. Tram-cars and phaetons of the latest improved kind are seen everywhere. In one of the former we drove out to the park about a mile from the town; the gardens were beautifully decked with all kinds of flowers, such as one is accustomed to see only in conser-

PORT ELIZABETH MARKET HALL.

vatories. One of the greatest charms of Port Elizabeth is the abundance of the eucalyptus and all kinds of gums, which grow in great numbers even along the streets of the town, filling the air with their sweet fragrance. India-rubber and castor oil plants grow as large as oak trees at home, and plumbago is seen in the hedges. Our next stopping place was in East London, but we only remained a few hours, steaming along quite close to the coast, near enough to enable us with the aid of our glasses to see very distinctly the houses and people on shore.

On the 16th, we passed the mouth of the River St. John, which divides Cape Colony from Pondoland. The coast is very pretty, and the hills which rise from the water's edge are well covered with trees.

The same day we reached Durban. We were particularly charmed with this place; it seemed quite Oriental in character. There were coolies wearing white costumes and turbans, such as one associates with India, and numbers of Ayahs too, who seemed to be more of the Hindu than African type. Probably in the early days

DURBAN BREAKWATER. (SHOWING CHAIN GANG.)

of colonisation, these coolies were brought from India to work in the sugar plantations, but now have become settlers in the country, and take all kinds of employment. Some are waiters in the restaurants, others are employed as nurses to the little children of white colonists.

The Kaffirs are of course quite different; very fine fellows physically, and thoroughly good-natured. Their clothing is curious, being a mixture of all kinds of left-off European apparel, and on one occasion I saw a great fellow dressed up in a pair of lady's corsets. Their ears are pierced, and in the hole they carry numerous trinkets, lead pencils, safety pins, beads, &c. When at work, these coolies are conspicuous for their want of costume; a little piece of sacking worn round the waist is all they think necessary.

On the breakwater, we noticed a gang of convicts at work in chains; they seemed quite satisfied with their lot, laughing and joking together as they performed the task assigned to them.

At Durban fruit is very cheap; even before the real

DURBAN TOWN HALL.

fruit season, bananas were sold, twenty for 3d., pine-apples 2d. each, tomatoes 3d. per pound. In the fruit season pineapples can be bought for a halfpenny each, and the other fruits proportionately cheap. We finished up a very pleasant day in Durban by a " rickshaw " race down to the quay. The men were all Zulus, and started off with us at a good hard trot; my man was particularly strong, and ran the whole way, some two miles, to the quay side, thus winning the race, for which he received an extra sixpence.

From Durban to Delagoa Bay, it is a twenty-four hours' run. There is nothing very striking about the bay, apart from the fact of its being a magnificent natural harbour; if it were not so very shallow, I suppose it would be one of the best harbours in any part of Africa. As it is, it is necessary for a large ship to go very slowly, and to take constant soundings. The Portuguese, not being a very enterprising people, appear to do little or nothing towards improving the harbour. The town is called Lorenzo Marquez, and although it is a Portuguese settle-

BEIRA CANTEEN.

ment, English is spoken pretty generally. The whole style of the place is most depressing; it appears to be built in the midst of a desert, for just outside the main streets, sand is everywhere.

We reached Beira on August 23rd. This is a very queer place, houses and stores all built of corrugated iron; streets ankle deep in sand. There are about five hundred white inhabitants, and each seems to keep his own carriage, and instead of horses, they have natives to push them. One that we saw was like a small trolley, with seats for two; others were capable of accommodating between six and eight passengers. There appeared to be no beasts of burden, except the native, for, alas! he seems to have to take their place, but we saw one donkey and one horse.

From Beira we had about three days' run to Mozambique, one of the early Portuguese settlements dating from the year 1500, built upon a small island just off the coast.

At one end of the island still stands the old fort built by the Portuguese when they first took possession, and it is still used as a fort, and also as a prison for unfortunate convicts, and woe betide the poor wretch who once finds himself within those prison walls, for he will be lucky if he gets out again. The town seen from the sea is very picturesque, and the streets, although very narrow, are clean and well kept. Oranges were very plentiful here, six being bought for a penny.

All day long huge sharks were swimming round our boat, seen distinctly in the clear blue water; one, a very large one, kept coming quite to the surface of the water, and would devour any kind of food that was thrown to it.

After one more stoppage, at Ibo—a small place of which we saw nothing, as the water was so shallow the *Gaul* could not approach the town—we finally, on August 30th, cast anchor off the coast of Zanzibar.

It was not long before we made our way to shore; the heat was intense, 95° in the shade. We were met by our agents and conducted to the Hotel d'Angleterre, a very typical Zanzibar hotel; it contained a large open drinking-bar on the ground floor with a small stage at one end, little tables scattered over the room, and a multitude of chairs. The chief occupants of the bar upon our arrival were British and German man-of-war's men, each vainly trying to understand the other, and all in a more or less happy condition. Upstairs we found a spacious dining-room and good bedrooms, altogether a very comfortable place.

Our first desire was to know from our agents what had been done about a caravan for up-country, as we were very unwilling to make a long stay at Zanzibar.

They told us that to proceed along the northern route *via* Mombasa was quite out of the question, on account of a famine caused by a plague of locusts, and that all

ZANZIBAR.

porters on the northern route were wanted by the Government. Our only course, therefore, was to go through German East Africa to the south of Lake Victoria, then across the lake to Uganda. A large number of porters had come to the coast bringing ivory, &c., from the interior for Mr. Stokes, a trader. They were Wanyamwezi and Wasukuma from the districts just south of the Victoria Nyanza. These men, wanting to get back to their own country, were only too ready to be engaged by us as porters. There were close upon five hundred of these fellows, but of course we only required about thirty each; the rest would carry cowrie shells for Mr. Stokes. This was very fortunate, as otherwise we might have had great difficulty in procuring porters.

In Zanzibar we had our work cut out, first, the engaging of servants—boys, as they are called; we were again fairly fortunate. We each had an experienced cook, a personal boy, and a donkey boy. My cook had been several times to Uganda, the last time as cook to Major Williams, and was therefore quite at home as a campaigner. He could speak a kind of English which was understandable after a little acquaintance with him, and had a good stock of information with reference to the country.

Some of our personal boys did not turn out as well as we expected. They came to us saying that they were "mission boys," and we, of course, took this as a recommendation; but, alas! we had not learned that this term is used by all the scamps in Zanzibar in order to procure a place for themselves, no matter whether they have ever been to the mission or not. They know perfectly well that a new-comer to Africa would at once think well of a mission boy, and the Zanzibaris are sharp enough to know it. This has often given rise to a very wrong idea with reference to missionary work at the coast. I have often heard travellers in Africa say: "Oh yes, I had a 'mission' boy and he turned out a young scoundrel, and that's what your missionaries are doing, spoiling the natives."

Apart from the impossibility of Christianity, which, to put it at its lowest estimate, is the highest and purest form of moral teaching, and could not possibly spoil any man, black or white,—the very fact that these boys use the term "mission boy," shows that they themselves recognise that if they can associate themselves with the mission, they will be looked upon as trustworthy boys.

My own personal boy, of whom I shall have to speak later on, was not such a bad fellow after all, and but for the fact that he disgraced himself on one or two occasions, he proved a most invaluable servant to me.

We also had to procure donkeys, by no means an easy task. When we had made our requirements known, great numbers of donkeys were brought to us of various prices, from 200 to 700 rupees each; some of them very much faked up, others, fine sturdy little animals, which needed not to be specially prepared for the sale.

Of course each one had to be tried, as we were to use them for riding purposes, and in this we had various experiences. I had set my mind upon a fine female donkey, and therefore took her out for an afternoon's ride, and I shall not forget it. At first when I mounted her, she would not move, in spite of all my most tender persuasions, and finally she began to back. Now the streets of Zanzibar are very narrow, and coming up behind me was a large bullock waggon, and my sweet-tempered donkey backed herself right on to the horns of the bullocks, and then, it was not a case of making her go, but of trying to make her stop. Away she flew, right along the Naza Moja road, and nothing that I could do would stop her headlong career; in fact I soon got tired of trying, and so let her go, and on she went right in among the cocoa-nut trees, dashing along, regardless of everything, until she came to a steep bank and here she stopped. This showed that she had good sense, and I therefore decided to keep her, and a great boon she was to me in our weary tramp up to the Victoria Lake. Our next business was to arrange our loads. Those wanted on the road were to be marked and given out to the most sturdy men among the porters; everything was carefully

ZANZIBAR AFTER BOMBARDMENT.

weighed, no load being more than 65 lbs. was allowed, but even this we found was too great a weight to be carried by one man day after day for three months.

One man, however, who carried my bed and blankets was a veritable giant in strength, his load weighing over 70 lbs., and he wished to carry it alone, and did so the whole way and never once was late into camp, nearly

A PORTER. (WITH HIS LOAD.)

always being at the head of the caravan. The Wanyamwezi carry the loads on the shoulders, not on the head as do the Swahili porters, but although not so strong as the Swahili, they go along much quicker, indeed three miles an hour is what our men usually did when the roads were good.

Before starting up-country, we visited our friends of

the Universities' Mission at Kiangani, and although on account of the short time at our disposal we saw but little of the work done by these devoted men and women, still what we did see impressed us as being of great value. Their Church in Zanzibar, however, could not please a Protestant Churchman — high mass, altar lights, the confessional, incense, Mary altars, all abounded, and it would be difficult to find any difference between this and an ordinary Roman Catholic Chapel. Perhaps no difference was intended.

We also witnessed, during our stay in Zanzibar, the great festival of the Mohammedans on the occasion of the Ramazan. It took place in front of the Sultan's Palace, the Sultan himself taking part upon the verandah of his palace; thousands of devout Mohammedans flock to this place for prayer with the great idea in their minds of fulfilling a religious duty. The festival is kept on the first day on which a certain new moon is actually seen, and as there is always some little variation as regards the day on which the moon is visible to the naked eye, no man is ever quite certain that it is the day of the festival. After a brief reading of the Koran, during which all stand by their kneeling mats with bare feet and covered heads, the whole congregation bows low in deep reverence, and then sways backwards and forwards chanting some prayer to Allah. The whole scene is most impressive and every one seems in dead earnest.

During the first day of the feast (which lasts a whole month), no food or drink is supposed to be taken by the devout Mohammedan until night fall; and when the month is over and another new moon begins, all meet in the morning in the most public manner possible to perform their devotions. Any one who has at all studied the Mohammedan religion cannot but be impressed by the fact that, at any rate, during prayer time, the Mohammedan is most devout, but, alas! this great religious system falls short. Where woman is looked upon as a thing to be bought and sold, and to exist only to satisfy the lowest passion of the man, and where she is told that as a dog she must die, and have no hope hereafter, from thence can come no good, and through all heathendom no places are more dark and need so much the "Living Words of God" as the Mohammedan lands.

The same day as the Ramazan festival, I had the

WASUKUMA PORTERS.

pleasure of making the acquaintance of the notorious Tippu-Tib, meeting him one day in the street. He is quite an old man now with long grey beard, but his eyes were keen and sharp as ever, and as he walked along in great state under a small escort of Zanzibar police, one could not but think, what a history such a man has! I afterwards had great cause to be thankful that ever I met Tippu-Tib. The reader will remember him in connection with Mr. H. M. Stanley when on the Emin Pasha relief expedition. For many years he was a great slave trader with a very large following of Arabs, flourishing in the district which lies between Stanley Falls, on the Congo, and Lake Tanganika. He was employed by Mr. Stanley to convey to Stanley Falls about seventy-five tons of ivory which was in the possession of Dr. Emin, and was stored on the Lake Albert shores; and he was also made governor of Stanley Falls, at a regular salary from the Congo Free State, to stop all persons from raiding the natives for the purpose of obtaining slaves, and to stop the practice himself. It was therefore just a case of "setting a thief to catch a thief." He did not keep faith with Mr. Stanley, and all his promises were broken, and very serious trouble arose from the fact of allowing this notoriously bad fellow to retain any kind of power in Central Africa.

At last, after exactly one month's stay in Zanzibar, all was ready for the start up country. Porters, boys and donkeys, all eager to cross to the mainland at Saadani. There, in Messrs. Boustead and Ridley's yard, were all our goods, everything ready packed. There were the "chop boxes" for the road, and the "chop boxes" for up-country; the cook's box and the cooking pots, clothes boxes for the road, and clothes boxes for up-country, tents and beds, camp tables and chairs, all in apple-pie order. As we looked at these our possessions, we could not help wondering how many of them would ever reach Uganda. We were told the way was all clear up to the Lake, that there was no famine, as on the northern route, that the tribes were all absolutely friendly, and that we should find plenty of food and water all the way. We were further assured that our porters were the finest set of men that ever formed a caravan, and that our head-man (a big Wanyamwezi chief) was the best head-man that ever led a caravan. Thus our hopes were naturally high in prospect of a very successful journey. How far we realised this anticipated success will be seen in the next few chapters.

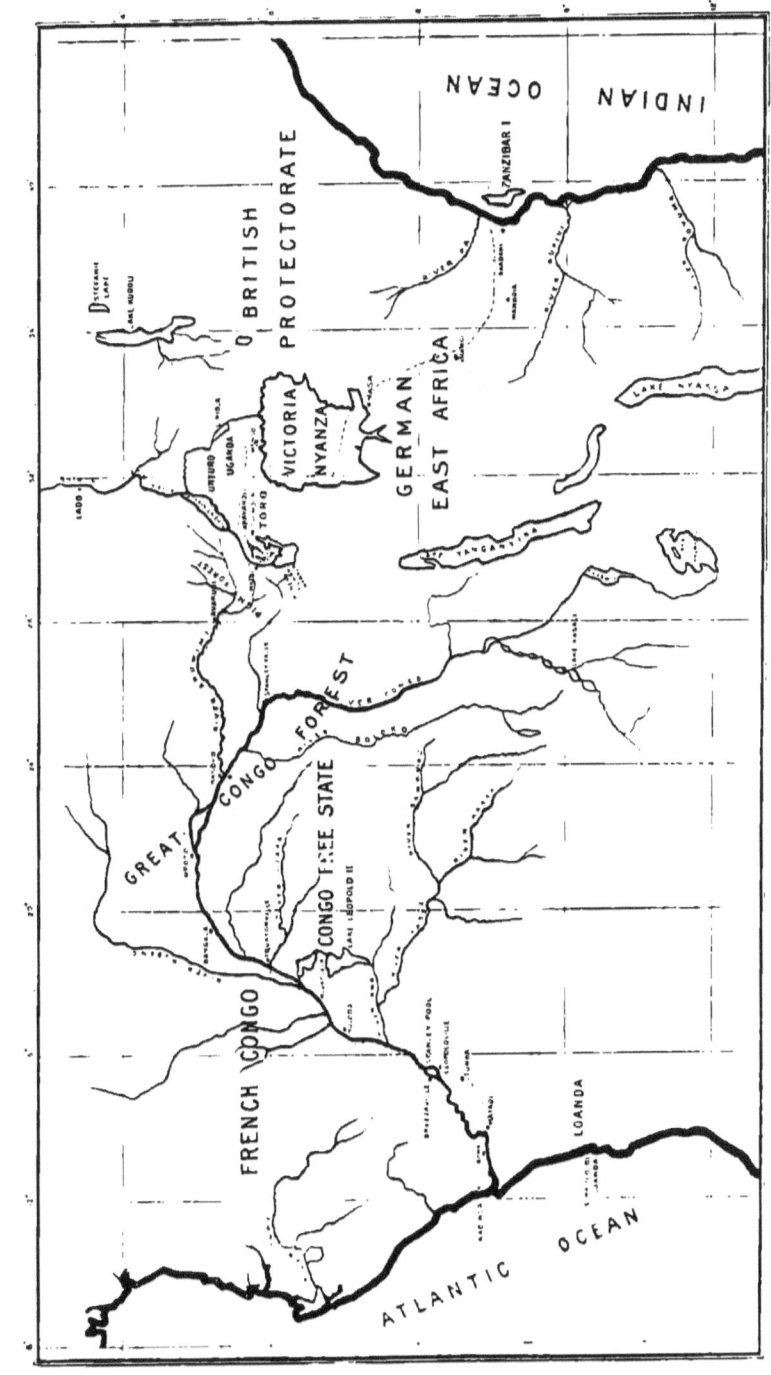

CHAPTER II

THE START

Eleven hours in an Arab dhow—Waiting and whistling for the wind — Ashore at last—First night in Africa—A restless night—Final preparations—K'shimba—Reviewing our porters—Our first camp—Great oration by K'shimba—The lion's roar—Discomforts of camp life—Famine ahead—We send for fresh supplies—Dr. Baxter—A ministry of love—A pot of porridge—And what came of it—The power of an Englishman—Letters from home—Scarcity of water—The horrors of human porterage—Leopard in the tree—Lost in the forest.

FROM Zanzibar to the mainland is a distance of about thirty miles; it was necessary for us to cross in a boat of some description which would be capable of accommodating ourselves, our boys, and our bag and baggage. A passage was therefore arranged for us on an Arab dhow, and on Monday, October 1, 1894, we got on board, bound for Saadani.

It was a terrible experience, and we shall not soon forget it. To begin with the heat was intense, and even with pith helmets and umbrellas with extra covers the sun seemed to have such power that it was as if we sat by a furnace. There was, of course, no cabin, and we had to sit on the little after-deck, all huddled up together with our luggage. The sea was a little choppy and this stirred up the filthy water at the bottom of the boat, and the odour was like that from a stagnant pool. The whole boat was in an abominable condition. Every one expects to "rough it" when he goes to Africa, but I confess we thought this a little premature, and fervently prayed that we might soon get to shore.

The journey across under favourable circumstances takes about two hours, but we were cooped up on this horrible craft for eleven long, weary hours, for about half way across, the wind dropped and there was a dead calm. We tried to look cheerful, but we certainly did not feel so. Flop, flop, flop, went the sail against the mast, whilst the burning sun blazed down upon us as we sat in this cramped position, waiting for the wind. Foolishly, we had taken no food with us, and about 3 p.m. we began to feel very hungry.

Our skipper was an old Arab of very quiet demeanour; he had not much to say to us, hardly answering our questions. By and by he began to whistle a low, plaintive tune, looking up wistfully at the loosely-hanging sail as he did so. We wondered what this meant, and asked him; he replied that he was whistling for the wind, so we let him whistle and fervently hoped that it might be of some avail. However, it was not until about 5 p.m. that the breeze got up again, and we were even then within sight of Zanzibar.

The dhow proved to be a fast sailer with the wind, and in about two hours and a half we arrived at Saadani. It was quite dark, and no moon, and the only way we knew that we had arrived was a terrific bang into the sandy bottom.

The next business was to get ashore; we could not tell how far we were from dry land; a few lights were burning in what seemed to us to be the far distance. At last our skipper, by dint of continued shouting, was able to apprise some one on shore of our arrival, and a native put out to us in a small boat. When this came alongside we discovered that there was about a foot of dirty water at the bottom of it. However, we got in, and sitting almost up to our knees in water, waited whilst our goods were handed into the boat to us. There was no lantern on board, and only a limited supply of matches, so it took some time for our boys to find our things and put them into the boat. Add to the discomfort of sitting in pitch darkness with dirty and offensive water half way up one's legs, the rolling and tossing about of the little craft in which we sat—and it will be easily understood that our tempers were not of the sweetest.

At last all was ready and we pushed off from the dhow, only to get stuck fast in a sandbank a few yards away. By this time we had had quite enough, so we got our boys to carry us ashore, which was still some one hundred yards away.

Our agent now met us and conducted us to his house, which consisted of one large, barn-like room, unfurnished. Here we fixed up our camp beds all among the numerous rats and lizards which did not seem to object at all to our presence; indeed, they were most demonstrative in their reception, mounting up on to our beds, and examining our boxes like well-trained custom-house officers.

Our first anxiety was to procure some food, and so we ordered our cooks to get some fowls, light a fire, and prepare a meal. All this they did in a surprisingly short space of time. It is indeed astonishing what a Zanzibari cook can do; given a chicken and a box of matches, he can, in a most remarkable manner, produce all kinds of luxuries, and often under the most trying circumstances our cooks got most tempting meals for us out of a mere nothing.

We then retired for the night and hoped to get to sleep. Personally, I was too hot and it was not until past midnight that I finally dozed off. How long I had been asleep I cannot say, when I was suddenly startled by hearing a strange sound like the sniffing of some animal just outside the house. The door was open on account of the heat and naturally I thought at once of the lions, which we had been told abound round about Saadani. I got up very quietly and put my eye to the hole which answered for a window. I could see nothing, all was thick darkness. I crept back to bed, but still the noise continued. I was afraid to go outside, having no gun at hand, so I just lay still upon my bed, listening, listening. I should think for two hours, when, suddenly, I was plunged into a cold perspiration by hearing a terrible noise. What could it be? Not a lion I was certain, for the sound was a familiar one. I sprang up, and made for the door, when, to my intense relief, I found out that it proceeded from no more dangerous an animal than—a donkey! This was the creature that had caused me so many sleepless hours.

The following day we spent at Saadani making final preparations for the start. We found plenty to do; many things to be arranged with our agents; "posho" (food money) to be given to the porters, and after that a final review of the whole caravan. Our head-man, who was a Wanyamwezi chief, was a great character; a very powerfully built man, magnificently shaped arms and legs, with a broad, well-developed chest. His eyes were bright and piercing to a degree, aquiline nose, and thick, protruding lips. His name was K'shimba, which means "a lion," and in many ways he deserved his name. He was brave and fearless, but had an unfortunate habit of losing his temper; at such times it was most difficult to get on with him. His power over his porters was decidedly autocratic, and it was a bad look-out for any poor, unfortunate fellow who displeased K'shimba. However, his power seemed to show itself as a caravan leader more than in any other way. He was one of Mr. Stokes' most trusted head-men, and had many times been backwards and forwards between the lake and the coast, and had never lost a caravan. He was delighted with the idea of a review, and called all his men together for that purpose; and they arranged themselves in horseshoe shape, four or five deep, K'shimba standing with his two servants in the foreground. It was an imposing sight and I think a finer set of men never started off up-country.

WANYAMWEZI PORTERS.

It is said that at one time these Wanyamwezi were absolute cannibals and great enemies to Europeans, but now their enmity, at any rate, has long ceased, and as to their cannibalism, that too is almost unknown.

Our first march was accomplished on October 3rd. We packed up all our bedding, &c., and got everything square, and about 2 p.m. left Saadani.

K'shimba headed the caravan on this occasion; then the four Europeans, closely followed by the four donkeys; then the boys, &c., and the five hundred porters in single file. It was an imposing caravan, and every one seemed in good spirits. The first tramp was a short, uninteresting one of about ten miles; the country was very rugged and sandy, and almost devoid of green vegetation. All the stunted trees were dried up, and what was once green grass was now dried stubble. The heat was intense, and the reflected rays from the sand added greatly to it.

Then came our first night in camp. Our tents were put side by side, and then, all around us, the porters made their frail huts, or pitched their little tents, each man making a big fire in front of his dwelling. Around these fires they sat in little groups of five or six, with the pot or " sufariya " on the fire, in which they boil their rice or millet. It was a strange sight that met our gaze as we looked out of our tent doors that first evening in camp: between seventy and eighty fires burning all around us, and these little groups of men, some talking and laughing, others looking very seriously at the pot of food, no doubt longing to see it boil. As we looked on this strange, weird sight a sudden hush falls upon the men, and silence reigns as K'shimba mounts on a little rising in the middle of the camp, and, stretching out his hands, begins to deliver a great oration. His eloquence is wonderful, judging from his gesture and rapid flow of language. We, of course, could not understand his words, as he spoke in the Wanyamwezi lingo; but our cooks told us that he was exhorting his men to be faithful to him as chief, and to the Europeans as " great white masters; " bidding them neither to steal their loads, nor raid any of the villages through which they might pass. After he had continued some time in this strain, he changed his tone a little, and to a kind of chant he said, " Will you obey K'shimba," and then all the men replied in the same tone, "We obey you, K'shimba." This was repeated over and over again, and then suddenly K'shimba stepped down from his elevated position, and walked with great state into his tent. The hum of voices is again heard, and then one by one the tired porters roll themselves up in their blankets, and silence reigns, save for the incessant noise made by the frogs and crickets.

The second night was much more disturbed than the first, for at about eleven o'clock a lion began to roar, and by his noise seemed to be quite close to the camp. The porters, however, kept up the fires, and no harm happened to any one, excepting, perhaps, to us poor Europeans, who, of course, could not sleep with a lion roaring a few hundred yards away, not knowing when it might think it worth its while to pay us a visit in our tents. It is a very different thing to stand in the Zoo and watch these magnificent creatures through iron bars, from lying shaking in a small canvas tent, and nothing stronger than this between it and yourself. I know this first time I heard the lion roaring, apparently very near to the tent, I sat on my bed nearly the whole night, with a loaded rifle across my knee.*

We soon began to experience some of the discomforts of camp life. The insects, for instance, gave great shocks to our systems from time to time. Occasionally, during peaceful slumber, one would suddenly be aroused by some strange creature leisurely making its way across one's face, and during its progress, causing a sensation as of in-

* "Familiarity breeds contempt," and I well remember the last time I heard a leopard -an equally dangerous beast trying to get in at the window of my little house in Toro. I was very tired, but it woke me up, and I was annoyed at being thus disturbed, so I picked up my heavy boot which was by my bedside, and threw it at the window, rolled over, and went to sleep again. Of course the creature would know from this that I was awake, and not daring to enter the house when observed, simply made off about its business.

numerable pins being driven into the skin; it finally turns out to be a centipede. These abound everywhere in Africa. A centipede is an insect which varies from one to eight inches in length, and is very much like a giant caterpillar, only that its body is covered with a hard scaly skin, and it has any number of legs, as its name implies. These horrible things are continually in our tents, and seem never so well satisfied as when they can settle themselves just by one's nose while in bed. But centipedes are nothing to the red, biting ants, and every traveller in Africa will have an encounter with these little pests sooner or later. During one of our long tiring marches, we happened to sit down by the roadside, without particularly noticing where; but in an instant we were literally smothered with these "siafu," as they are described by the Swahili. Shake yourself as you will, they will not drop off, and one has to literally pull them off, and even then they hold on with such tenacity that you sever the head from the body. Fortunately the bite is not poisonous, so that no irritation remains when the insect is removed. Cockroaches large and cockroaches small are *everywhere;* in all your boxes, boots, and jam-pots, in blankets, pockets, writing-cases, everywhere are they to be found. A second-class cabin on a British India boat is a perfect paradise in the matter of cock-roaches. Mosquitoes I need hardly mention; *of course* they are a nuisance, and seem to be met with particularly in low-lying marshy districts. Fleas we consider very clean as compared with those slower and far more disgusting creatures, lice; but both are met with everywhere, and abound. Snakes, too, caused us sometimes a little uneasiness. Once under my bed I discovered one of these reptiles quietly sleeping, and often as we marched we came across them. These are some of the discomforts that the traveller meets with in Africa; he has to get used to them sooner or later, and the sooner the better, or they will be a constant source of trouble to him.

Other things are equally trying during the first few weeks of camp life. To have your boy come into your tent at about four o'clock a.m. when all is dark, and shout at the top of his voice, "B'wana" (master), and then to have to pack everything into boxes and bags and tramp off to the next camp, is trying, to say the least. Then if you happen to see your boy, as I once did, cleaning your plate by licking his hand and smearing it over,

CAMP LIFE.

and finally drying it with his dirty loin cloth; or, if you see your cook patting down the rice pudding into a dish with his hands, or basting your chicken with the same tools, or washing out the saucepan with the water in which one has bathed (no doubt on account of the scarcity of that fluid), I say that these are things that are constantly occurring, and every day some new kind of horror presents itself, and the novelty of the "picnic" soon wears off.

After we had proceeded about a week's journey on our way to the lake, a very serious difficulty presented itself, namely, famine. We had been told that we should not be troubled with this, the greatest of all horrors, and when we therefore found that it was actually raging in the district through which we now had to pass, we were very much disturbed in mind.

A huge caravan like ours required much food to be provided, so that all might have enough, and although we were only really responsible for the men who carried our own loads, yet the claims of a common humanity made it our duty to do what we could for the others. We accordingly sent back to Saadani for fresh supplies of rice to be despatched without delay by special porters, and this was done; but how was it possible for us to keep five hundred men from starving! with nothing but the slender purse of a missionary from which to draw.

With this prospect before us, K'shimba arranged for another great oration to his men, and this time the burden of his cry was: "Although famine is raging before us, let us not blame any man, neither let us steal the scanty victuals from the villages close at hand; let us go bravely forward, and, if you steal, both I and the Europeans will leave you. Stealing is wrong," he said, "and we must not do it." To this they all agreed, as usual, and replied, "We obey you, K'shimba."

Just about this time we had the very great pleasure of welcoming amongst us the veteran missionary, Dr. Baxter, also of the Church Missionary Society.

We had camped for the day, being Sunday, to have a real day of rest, when, towards the close of the day, to our great satisfaction, the Doctor came strolling into camp. He accompanied us for the next few days, and right glad we were to have the benefit of his well-nigh twenty years' experience in Africa. Being a medical man he was able to help several of our poor porters who already were suffering from the effects of unsuitable food, and the whole time he was with us, his bright Christian character made itself felt. Our porters were delighted to have him amongst the party, as some of them knew him, and all very soon learned to love him for his true, gentle, and loving spirit. He, at any rate, does not think that a black man is so far beneath him that he merits not the ordinary kindness that is shown to the white man, but by his unselfish ministrations to those poor black fellows, he exhibited the spirit of the Master whom he serves. The idea is prevalent amongst many who visit Africa that the African is little better than a dog, and should never be treated in any other way than that in which a beast is treated. Such men are not worthy to be associated with humanity themselves: for although the black man is ignorant and degraded it is not his fault, and perhaps if Christian England had done her duty to Africa, there would not be the darkness that there is.

Dr. Baxter, by his ministry of love, soon won the affection of the porters, when in the evening he would sit with them, read to them, and talk to them about the God and Father of us all: Who, loving us, sent His Son to redeem us. One could see how the acts of kindness had attracted them to listen to the words of love.

But even Wanyamwezi porters are human, and when suffering from the stress of hunger one can almost forgive them anything. One of our porters suffering in this way was passing through a cultivated field when he espied in a corner of the field a pot of porridge all ready cooked, and no doubt very savoury. Not seeing any one about, and being sorely tempted, he grasped the prize and was making good his escape, when almost at the same moment some one grasped *him*, and this proved to be the owner of the mess. The injured party dragged the captive before our head-man, but K'shimba, like Gallio of old, "cared for none of these things," and ordered both parties out of his presence, laughing at the man for leaving his porridge about, and sneering at the other for not being sharp enough to evade capture. The plaintiff then brought the case to us Europeans, apparently in a towering rage with K'shimba, and bent upon making a row. It would have been a most difficult matter for us to settle had it not been for Dr. Baxter. He called K'shimba, and had the accused brought up. It was K'shimba's turn now to lose his temper, and when he came to us he was in a great passion, and forthwith abused the accuser and his people (who had by this time gathered round). He shouted out to them that he was K'shimba (the lion), and that they had better take care how they played with him, and that if they wished, he and his men would go down into the valley and meet them there and have a game with guns. At this Dr. Baxter angrily stopped him, and showed in a moment what a power an Englishman has in Africa, for immediately K'shimba was cowed, and although a big, powerful chief he came and sat at our feet as quiet as a lamb, and the whole matter was settled by giving the offended party a little present and sending him away. We heard no more. If, however, we had not been present in camp at the time that this case was brought up, there would most certainly have been serious trouble, probably a fight between the porters and the villagers, which would have brought the whole country side down upon us.

Thus it will be easily understood that a European going up-country is very much at the mercy of his porters, and a constant watch has to be kept over them.

On October 14th there was great excitement caused by the arrival in our camp of a party of mail men, bringing to us letters from home. Although we had been about twelve days on the journey from the coast these men had accomplished it in five days. They are chosen for their

A MINISTER OF 1907.

strength and endurance, and some of them will walk thirty-five and forty miles a day, carrying their mail bags as well as their sleeping mats and food.

I do not wish to enlarge here upon the pleasure of receiving letters and papers from home, but I must say Solomon of old was not far wrong when he said, "As cold waters to a thirsty soul, so is good news from a far country." The old country never loses its charm, no matter how many and long are the years that we spend away from it, we always look with eager eyes for any news con-

EAST AFRICAN MAIL CARRIERS.

cerning it. I know of nothing so trying in Africa as to be obliged to be content for months together with nothing but a few old newspapers to read; even these become precious, and many a time I have read over and over again leading articles and scraps of news long out of date, and have even gone so far as to read through the advertisements.

For the first week on the journey, the only water we could get was from holes dug in the clay, and in which the rain had collected; it was therefore very thick with mud and sometimes very offensive, with a slight saline taste. We had to both boil and filter it, and even then we could not get rid of the unpleasant flavour.

The porters also caused us a great deal of trouble with reference to the water. Immediately upon reaching camp some of them would run down to the water-holes and stir up all the mud in their anxiety to get a good drink; some would even stand in the water itself and drink, and often we would find them washing their bodies quite close to the water-holes. It was most trying, after having given strict orders to have the water guarded, to find the guards themselves doing such things as these. However the heat was so great, and we ourselves were so terribly thirsty with the mere exertion of walking, that we could almost forgive the clumsy eagerness of these poor porters to get to the water after four or five hours' march under the burning rays of the sun, with a 60 lb. weight to carry.

Would to God this fearful practice of human porterage were not necessary; it is barbarous work, and sometimes when I saw a poor thin fellow, suffering the awful pangs of hunger, and perhaps with a terrible ulcer on each leg, with his heavy load on his poor blistered shoulder, I almost wished I had no loads at all; and when I saw as alas! I did sometimes, one of these poor fellow creatures fall down from sheer exhaustion, and see A.B.L. printed on the box he was carrying, it made my heart bleed with pity and I felt half guilty. But we could do nothing; the loads must go, and there was no other way than this. Of course a large number of the men seemed to think nothing of their loads and were perfectly happy with them, fine, strong fellows, apparently hardly feeling the burden at all.

During the first week there was little or no shooting to be had: very occasionally we saw species of antelope in the distance, but they were always too wild for us to approach within range; partridges, quails, pigeons, &c., were sometimes seen. As I have said, lions were in the district, but at present we were far too new at the hunt to attempt such dangerous game.

At this time I had rather a disagreeable experience. I had gone off alone with only my shot gun, with No. 6 shot for pigeons, and had got into a very wild sort of jungle.

EAST AFRICAN HUT, WITH STOCKADE AND DEVIL HUT.

It was well on towards evening, and so after wandering about for some time and seeing nothing, I began to retrace my steps. This, I soon found out, was not an easy matter, and after pushing first in one direction and then in another, I began to give up hope of getting back to camp that night. It was just about a quarter of an hour before sunset, forcing my way along a narrow track which

I believed would eventually take me to the main road, when, suddenly a huge leopard sprang from a tree just in front of me. I levelled my gun, but feared to pull the trigger, thinking that the result of putting a hundred or so No. 6 shot into him would only aggravate the beast; so, with my gun to my shoulder, and my eye fixed upon the leopard, which had alighted on the ground only about ten yards in front of me, I gradually drew back. The creature just crouched upon the ground like a huge cat lashing its tail backwards and forwards, snarling horribly, showing all its fangs. And thus I left it. It now began to get dark, and I was much alarmed at the prospect of being kept out all night in so weird and dangerous a quarter, therefore I commenced to blow with all my might the whistle which I always carried in my belt. I don't know why I did not think of it before. After blowing away for some time I heard a call and making off in that direction suddenly found myself entering a village. The natives, when they saw me, fled in all directions, and I could not get near enough to make my request for help known to them. I wandered about in the village for a little while and then blew my whistle again; this time with better success, for from out of the thicket emerged my cook, who, missing me in camp and expecting that I had got lost, had set off to find me, and hearing the whistle was led to me by that. I found that we were a long distance from camp, and I did not arrive until quite dark. Very thankful I was at last to get into my little canvas tent, and I had learned a lesson, which has stood me in good stead during all my travels in Africa —viz., never to wander off alone in a country that you do not know, particularly in a forest-covered district.

CHAPTER III

GLIMPSES OF CAMP LIFE

Under the tamarind tree—Refreshment for the cows—Hope deferred at Mbuzini river—The Wami—First real wash in Africa—Famine stares us in the face—Fever—Crossing river on African bridge—Tent left behind—The cook's story—Overtaken by Bishop Tucker—The wild ass—The Bishop to the front—Long solitary march—Kindly reception—Lions in the path—Mamboya—Hospitality in Central Africa—The "Mission boy" again—Practical Christianity—We split our caravan—The porters rebel—How we squashed the rebels—Peace making—Mpwapwa—Kisokwe—Famine and its horrors.

ON the 11th of October, we pitched our camp at a place called Pongwi, the chief of which was called Kolwa, a regular old scoundrel, who did his very best to fleece us. The usual custom of a chief upon receiving a visitor into his country, is to bring to him some kind of present, for which he expects the traveller to give a present in return equal in value. This old gentleman Kolwa, evidently saw that we had not travelled in Africa before, and therefore he wanted to make the best of his opportunities. He first brought us a sheep with a fat tail, and for this we gave him a suitable present, although we could have done well enough without the sheep. He went away, to return with a few eggs; for these he again expected a return present, which he did not get, however. He then asked for some soap and went first to one European and then to another, bothering each for a piece of soap. He was very dirty, and needed it badly, so, as I had with me some good strong carbolic dog soap, I gave him a piece and with this he seemed delighted, especially with the scent. After this he went away chuckling, and showing his followers what he had received, and I think he was thoroughly satisfied.

With a temperature of 96° in the shade, we pitched our camp under a tamarind tree, and right glad we were to gather the ripe beans which hung from the branches. Their acid flavour seemed in some way to allay the pangs of thirst which could not be satisfied with the horrible salty water, which was the only kind procurable in this place (Pongwi). A very good drink can be made from the tamarind bean, which is broken up, and boiling water poured over it with sugar to taste, and then left to cool. So scarce was the water that we had hardly enough to wash in, and our cows (we had two with us) had to be content with the water that we had used for our wash, which, however, they swallowed with the greatest satisfaction.

We were glad enough to leave this droughty place early the following morning. Our guide told us that about four hours' journey further on we should come to the beautiful river called the Mbuzini; our porters were therefore most anxious that we should push on as fast as possible, for already the terrible thirst was beginning to tell upon them. Occasionally we would come upon some of them trying hard to extract a little moisture from some root; others would dig holes in the hollows, hoping to find the precious fluid they so much needed.

We left camp at Pongwi before it was light and walked for five hours with scarcely a stop, and then, when we were beginning to feel the heat of the day most oppressive, and were simply dried up for want of water, the guide suddenly pointed out to us in the distance a long stretch of trees, and these he said were growing on the banks of the Mbuzini river. We pushed forward with greater energy than ever with the prospect of at last having plenty of water, for by this time we were almost suffocated by the thirst and ready to give in.

Presently we entered the wooded country and almost ran to the banks of the river. But no sound of rushing waters greeted our ears, not even the ripple of a tiny

CAMP AT MBUZINI.

stream. Oh, bitter disappointment! the river had dried up, and only a few muddy puddles told us of its previous existence. Our hearts sank within us. With swollen lips and parched tongues, we stooped down to drink, and never did water seem so sweet to us, as did that from the muddy pools of the Mbuzini river bed.

Our guide, who was quite as disappointed as we were—

for he said that only a month or so before he had passed that way, and found the river full—went off up the river bed for some long distance, and by indefatigable effort, at last found a tiny spring of good water, and with care, this was sufficient for the whole caravan.

To give some little idea of the oppressiveness of the heat that day, I may mention that even a little terrier dog that was in the party, was so much fatigued by the heat, that it lay down under every bush and tree we passed, and when we went on, it howled most piteously, and then ran on to the next. A large mastiff, which was also with us, literally fainted after reaching camp. It can be imagined, therefore, how much we Europeans suffered if these creatures were affected by it in the way I have described. Some of our porters never reached camp, and one of our tents was left behind.

The following day, our hopes, which were deferred at the Mbuzini river, were abundantly realised at the Wami, a broad rushing river, plenty of water. It was quite impossible, after being so long with such a limited supply, to keep out of it and so we had a most delightful bath. We were warned against crocodiles so had to choose a very shallow part, but to have water all over one's body, after hardly having sufficient to moisten one's tongue was indescribably delightful. Having finished our first real wash in Africa, we looked out all our soiled clothes and sent our boys to the river to wash them, and in the afternoon the neighbourhood of our tents looked like the drying ground of a large laundry.

Again we had the awful fact brought before us of the scarcity of food. K'shimba came to us and said that a number of our porters had deserted on account of the shortness of food, leaving their loads by the roadside, and that he anticipated others doing the same. The loads were brought on by the head-men, but it was clear that if

USAGARA LANDSCAPE.

famine continued and many more men deserted, it would be impossible to proceed. Our own extra loads of food were gradually becoming less, as each morning we gave out a cup full of rice to the needy ones. But this could not go on for any length of time.

We next reached Matungu, but still no food to be found. The natives were unwilling to sell what little they had, and we greatly feared lest our porters, driven to desperation, would try to raid the villagers.

To make matters worse many of the men were getting

FAMINE-STRICKEN DISTRICT.

ill from other causes; some were beginning to display huge ulcers, sore shoulders and backs, caused by carrying the loads; dysentery, and even small-pox.

At Matungu we were told that we should find antelope, and thus we hoped to be able to provide some food for the porters. I started off when I got into camp, and I soon saw some antelope in the distance, but the heat was so intense that I was far too exhausted to stalk them, and I turned homeward. Before I could reach camp, I knew that fever had got hold of me.

Fortunately the good Doctor was still with us and he did everything possible for me. All night the fever was raging and the patient Doctor sat by my bedside tending me with almost motherly care. The caravan left next morning but the Doctor and Mr. Pike remained till evening with me, when I was able to proceed on my donkey. We caught up the others at 11 p.m., had a few hours' rest, and then we all continued our journey as still there was a great scarcity of food, and famine with all its horrors seemed to stare us in the face.

Ngulu was reached on October 18th, and again we pitched our camp, near the beautiful river Wami. The water was very pure, and it was quite delightful to have plenty, after the muddy fluid we had been obliged to drink.

Our tents were pitched at the foot of a low range of mountains, the whole surrounding country being covered with scrub and sycamore. The natives were very friendly and were able to sell us a little food. Maize grew in great abundance, also a kind of pumpkin or vegetable marrow, which is very palatable. We remained a few days, to allow our porters to do their best to procure what little food was available, and then we proceeded.

We had to cross the Wami river; the porters waded through the water which at its deepest was not more than four feet, while we Europeans crossed by a native bridge, a very rickety affair, made by the natives of the districts. It consisted of a few forked stakes driven into the ground at the bank, and corresponding stakes in midstream and on the opposite bank; then from stake to stake there were stretched strong timbers, and upon these were laid a quantity of thinner branches. We had to cross very carefully as nothing was secure, and some of the stakes had been washed away by the current. Soon after leaving the bridge we missed the way, but were not sorry as the path we took led through some very pretty places. At times palms and bananas, and other large-leaved plants completely over-arched us, and bigger trees were growing over our head. Wild pepper shrubs also, in great abundance; the natives seem to use these in some way as food. Later on we passed through plantations of maize and what is called " mtama," a kind of millet seed, which makes a very good porridge, and we frequently used it in this way. It grows in a kind of reed some 12 feet to 14 feet high, and is very prolific, but is always the first thing attacked by locusts, and in this part these insects had been very busy. They go about in huge clouds and sometimes quite block the sunlight, and when they settle, all green things disappear. Guinea fowl were plentiful, and seemed very tame. Sometimes we would walk quite close up to them before they took flight, and constantly we were able to supply the larder with these most acceptable birds.

Although we missed the way on this particular occasion, yet we got into camp ahead of everybody else. The porters were very tired, having had a long, roundabout march in the heat. One of the tents, to our great consternation was missing; we therefore sent back the cooks at once to look for the porter who carried it and to bring it into camp. However, night came on before the tent arrived and we were obliged to make one tent do for two. In the very early morning the cooks came back bringing with them the porter and the tent. This is the cook's story:—They got right back to our former camp, and there they found the tent all rolled up, but no porter to carry it. They waited until nine o'clock, when the runaway turned up. The rest must be told in the cook's own language. "At nine o'clock we see him come, we say, 'Come on'; he say, 'I must stop and sleep.' We then sit down and think till ten, then we get up and beat him with a stick, then he come." They were walking all night, reaching us about 5 a.m., and started off with us at 5.30, getting into camp again at 11 a.m. When I asked the cook how he was after his long walk he said, "My feet very large, master; I rest here," and well they deserved their rest.

One of our party now fell sick, Mr. Blackledge, fever being, of course, the complaint. We therefore rested a few days in a most lovely camping ground among the

USAGARA WOMEN AT HOME.

Mpamwani Hills, with a clear rushing stream quite close to us.

During this time of rest we had the great pleasure of welcoming into our midst good Bishop Tucker. He was on his way to Mamboya, and having only a small caravan he was able to push along quickly although he left the coast nearly a week after we had done so. Our party now numbered six Europeans, and about five hundred and twenty porters.

About mid-day, after the Bishop's arrival, a wild ass got into camp and commenced fighting with our donkeys, and made such a noise and disturbance that we called up the whole camp to catch it. It was a very shapely little animal and had most extraordinary powers of dodging those who tried to secure it, of kicking and braying also. With the combined energies of five Europeans and a whole host of Wanyamwezi porters we felt sure it would be caught. The Bishop was very much to the front in this hunt, and made several good attempts to lasso the little creature, but still it evaded us. At last, however, while the ass stood for a rest at a good distance from its hunters, one of the men leapt from the grass where he was completely hidden, almost under its nose, and swinging his arms right round its neck, clung on, in spite of all its plunging. We then gathered round, and soon were able to secure the now frightened ass. I found to my great satisfaction that it was my own boy who had thus captured the animal. He told me that he was a great hunter, and seemed very pleased to display his power of concealing himself, which I admit was most extraordinary (especially was this the case if I happened to want anything in a hurry). We tied up the wild ass to a tree and left it with the natives, who were most delighted to have it.

From this camp to the next was a distance of about eighteen miles. There was supposed to be a large river at the camp, but when we got there we found only a dry river bed, all covered with deep cracks; apparently no water had been there for months. We searched about and found some pools of muddy water, and by the side of these we camped. It was fairly good when boiled and filtered, and only tasted a little like dish-water, but we were about used to that, so thought nothing of it.

At 3 a.m. next morning we were off again, a long, solitary march through the most wild country we had yet passed.

The start was a most difficult one. Our way led right

over a high range of hills, and the path was narrow and very stony, and terribly steep in places. It was sometimes literally a climb in the dark, for although there was a moon nearly at its full, its light was almost entirely lost to us by the thick trees overhanging our path. My boy and I went on ahead to secure a good camp, and for six hours we marched with only one stop of five minutes. When we arrived at the village we were making for, Magubika, the chief came out to greet me. He was a fine-looking young fellow, rather above middle height, well-proportioned, and with a searching eye. He shook hands with me, and then called to one of his numerous attendants to bring a stool for me. This was soon given to me, and I sat to exchange with him the few Swahili compliments that I could think of. He was dressed in a bright red cloth, with a leathern girdle round his waist and a white turban on his head; he had a great crowd of attendants and slaves, and gave one the impression of being a very important man. He brought me a big cup of curds, which was very refreshing; and then he produced a large prepared cowskin, and upon this I curled myself, and in the midst of a crowd of staring natives I was soon fast asleep. My little dog "Sally" that I bought at Zanzibar, stood guard over me, growling angrily if she thought any native approached too near. I slept for two hours, and then was suddenly aroused by hearing the report of a revolver. I started up, fearing something was wrong, but found out that it was Mr. Lewin who was signalling to a party of porters who had missed their way. We pitched our tents under the shade of some bananas, and the caravan gradually filed into camp, all being very tired.

The Bishop informed us that he intended pushing on in the afternoon to Mamboya, to prepare the missionaries there for our arrival. Accordingly he set off at about two o'clock, to be followed in an hour's time by a man carrying one of his boxes. After the latter had been gone about two hours, he came running back into camp saying that he had met two men who had just escaped a lion, and were fleeing from it, so he joined them and came back into camp with the Bishop's box.

The next day's march was to be a short one, so we

SALLY.

did not have to start before 6 a.m. I must say that long before this I had grown very weary of the early morning starts; I think this is the greatest of all camp life trials. One is roused sometimes at 4 a.m., *always* before light, and while the heavy dew is on the ground one has to pack up everything into boxes and bags, and turn out of a warm bed into the cold and damp night air, while the boys and porters pull down one's tent and roll it up, and cram everything into the boxes. No one ever feels ready for a breakfast at that unearthly hour, and yet if breakfast is neglected one gets faint and weary long before the end of the march.

It only took us two hours to walk from Magubika to Mamboya; we camped at the foot of the Mambira Hills, about half an hour's walk from the Mission Station of the Church Missionary Society, which is beautifully situated among the hills, in a most healthy position. There were six missionaries, viz., Rev. and Mrs. Wood, Mr. and Mrs. Deekes, the Misses Waite and Colsey; there were also two babies, the Deekes' having a boy of two years, and the Woods' a girl of three months.

There is no doubt Mamboya is one of the prettiest C.M.S. stations in Africa. The houses are nicely built, and when we arrived there it was just like getting home once more after a few weeks of rough camp life. We were most heartily welcomed by Mr. Deekes, who came down the hill to our camp in the valley, and escorted us up to the Mission. Here we found the Bishop, who had arrived the day before, and seemed none the worse for his long march, and he had seen nothing of the lion.

It was a great treat once more to sit down before a nicely spread board, but what seemed to take our fancy most was the delicious home-made bread, which of course we had not partaken of since we left Zanzibar, and this is one of the things one misses most in tramping through Africa; the tasteless " chupati " or the roast sweet potato, has to take the place of bread on the march. Milk, too, and fresh butter, and a whole leg of mutton, instead of condensed milk, tinned butter, and scraps of fried meat.

We spent five days at Mamboya, and thoroughly enjoyed the rest, and the kindness which we received from the missionaries was very great; they insisted upon our

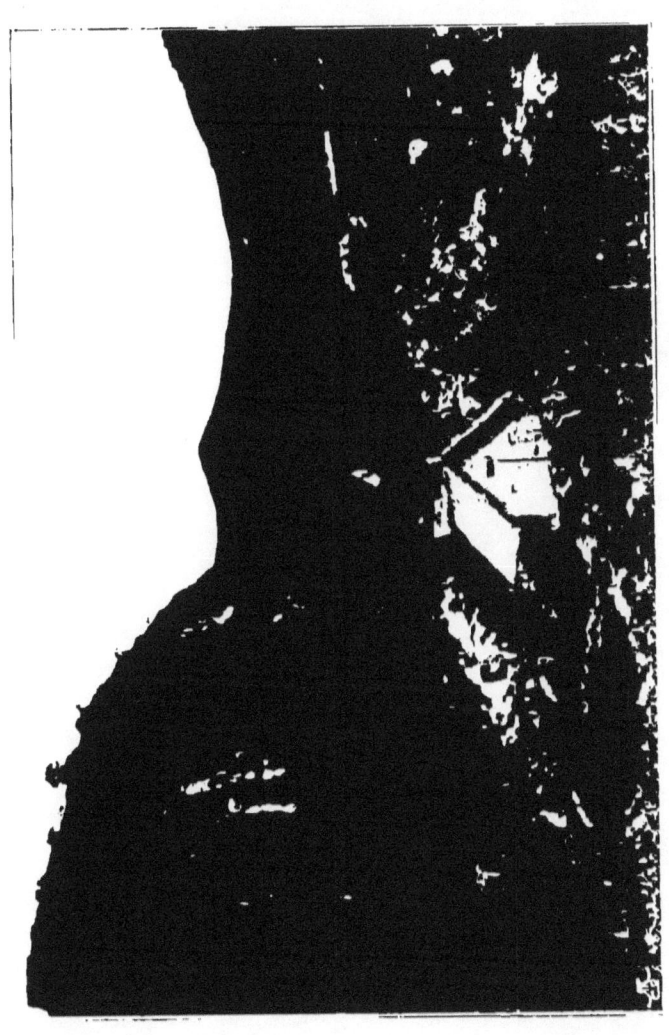

taking all our meals up at the Mission, and we used to go up the hill at 8 a.m. not returning to camp until late in the evening.

Soon after we arrived here some of the Europeans' boys declared that they wished to leave, and they brought their parents to us, who lived at Mamboya, who said that they would not allow their sons to proceed with us any further. It will be remembered that when they came to us they declared themselves to be "mission boys," and upon that recommendation we engaged them, and we

CHIEF OF MAMBOYA, WITH HIS SON AND WITCH DOCTOR.

now found that they were not mission boys, and that their reason for engaging themselves to us was merely to get back to their home at Mamboya. We had paid them for two months in advance, and so insisted that the money for one month should be returned to us if the boys remained behind. After some hesitation it was brought to us in the shape of sheep and goats. Fortunately for me my boy had no relations and was quite willing to proceed to Uganda with me, and as he had pleased me so far, I was very glad to retain his services.

The population of Usagara is large and scattered, but the people are generally very poor, largely as a result of their laziness, and also on account of the constant famines. They rely upon their crops of mtama and maize almost entirely, and if locusts come and eat these up there is nothing left for them. Their flocks and herds are not large, but each chief seems to possess a few. Woman, as almost everywhere in uncivilised Africa, is the slave and drudge of the family, bought and sold by the man, and ill-treated at his pleasure.

Missionary work amongst such a tribe is necessarily difficult, and must be of a very practical kind, and undoubtedly this is a very marked feature of the Mamboya mission. The real self-denying character of its missionaries, and especially of the two young ladies, who, living in this wild place, are seeking to help their dark sisters into a better life, is a *sine qua non* for the success of the work.

During the famine time, hundreds of pounds of rice are distributed to the needy ones, and thousands flock to the Mission premises to receive the precious gifts of food. This is what appeals to the savage, for in it he can see *love*, an attribute which is little known among them. At this station Dr. Baxter has his headquarters, and every day has a great number of patients come to him for treatment, and during our short stay he had several important operations, which he performed with his usual skill.

We left Mamboya October 29th, and can look back upon our stay there as one of the very pleasant incidents in our life in Africa. Such kind and hearty, not to say generous, hospitality received right away there in Central Africa, was better than all we could have hoped for, and as we bade our friends goodbye, it was with mingled feelings. The road that lay before us was very dark, famine hovered about us like some beast of prey, and at Mamboya we were to leave behind our good and trusted friend Dr. Baxter, whose help had been so readily given in managing our great caravan during the short time he had been with us. We now split our caravan into two parts. Selecting the loads, &c., that would be required by us on the journey up to the Lake, we gave them to a party of the strongest and best men, and with these we were to push forward, leaving K'shimba to follow on with the main body of the caravan. He, of course, would be obliged to go much slower than it was necessary for us, and we felt that the sooner we could get to the Lake the better; our health was already beginning to suffer from the exposure and roughness of camp life, although we hardly knew it.

Four hours' march from Mamboya is a lovely little glen, through which runs a clear bubbling stream, and by the side of this we had our tents pitched. Mr. Pike and I then went off into the thicket to try and shoot guinea-chicks, but failed, and when coming back to camp after sunset, walking in the faint light of the moon, a huge snake suddenly reared itself just a yard in front of me. I darted back not a moment too soon, and it then glided away with its head reared and its eyes fixed upon me; it was a narrow escape, another step would have taken me to certain death, for I saw that it was a black and yellow-breasted adder, one of the most deadly snakes in Africa.

At Rabayo, two days from Mamboya, we had a little excitement. It was the first sign of a rebellion amongst our porters. They had had but little food, and water too was scarce, and feeling that their head-man, K'shimba, was far enough away to be harmless, they organised a raid upon one of the villages near to the camping-ground. I had just selected a suitable site for my tent and was looking about for the porters and boys to put it up, but the camp seemed deserted, when to my utter astonishment I saw all the porters, armed with their knob-kerries, sticks, spears, &c., making their way rapidly up the hill, upon the summit of which was the village. At once I guessed their design to be that of theft, and this would of course mean disaster to our caravan in a thickly populated district, as this was. There was not a moment to spare, and so, picking up a stick, I ran at full speed up the hill, caught the first man up, and then turned round upon them all, and in the best Swahili I could command ordered them back again, telling them that I knew what they were after. There were about seventy of them all told, and at first they seemed to ignore me, and some attempted to force their way past me, looking threateningly first at me and then at the weapons they carried. When I saw this, I knew that they had made up their minds to carry out their purpose in spite of the resistance offered by the European, so I dashed at the man who was leading them, seized him round the waist and gave him the "throw," at the same time bringing my stick down across his bare shoulders with considerable force. Although he was a man half as big again as myself, and carrying a gun, he was thoroughly cowed, and picking himself up stared at me in blank astonishment. I immediately followed up the impression I had made by a sudden rush at the whole gang, and they all, with about ten exceptions, ran away as fast as their legs would carry them, and I chased them, flourishing the stick above my head. Mr. Pike then joined me, having discovered the trouble, and he entered into the chase with great enthusiasm. What a sight it was, to see about seventy great stalwart fellows, all armed—any one of whom, if he possessed pluck enough, would have been a match for either of us so far as strength is concerned—racing headlong down the hill, chased by two Englishmen armed with nothing but sticks! In this manner we drove the main body of the porters back to camp; but further trouble was ahead of us.

We walked back up the hill to the village to try and make friends with the villagers, but we found that while we had been driving back to camp the greater number of the men like a flock of sheep, the rest had crept past us in the long grass and had entered the village, driven out all the startled inhabitants, and were freely helping themselves to the little food there was. The villages of this district are built either in a square or triangular form. There are two main entrances to the village, and the houses are all joined together and form a wall around it, with an open square in the middle. There are no windows in the rooms, but small holes about two inches in diameter, are apparently used for spy-holes by the inhabitants. Of course, as soon as we entered the village there was not a soul to be seen, but we knew that ten or a dozen of our men were somewhere in the houses hiding themselves. Without any hesitation (although, as we thought of it afterwards, it was rather risky) we rushed into the nearest house. All was pitch dark, and not a hand's length could we see before us. We felt our way about from house to house as best we could, and every now and then we could hear some one glide past us in the darkness, and if we made a dash at this invisible person, we were sure to come violently in contact with either the wall or the doorpost. It seemed hopeless for us to try and catch these fellows, besides being somewhat dangerous, as I suppose none of them would have been particular about using their spears if they had been caught. We therefore stationed ourselves one at each entrance to the village on the outside, so as to pounce upon them as they came out. We waited and waited, but not a man stirred. They were too sharp for us, and presently on looking down the hill we saw a number of them stealing back to camp; they had climbed over the houses, and thus evaded us. However, we recognised several of them as they crept in the grass with stolen food, fowls, &c., in their hands, and when we got back to camp pounced upon them, and they were punished by the head-man with a few smart lashes. In the evening of the day we had a great oration. Mr. Pike spoke to them by interpretation, telling them why we had stopped them from stealing, and pointing out the great danger in which they placed the caravan by indulging in such raids upon the villages. We then went up to the village again, to call back the people if possible. At first no one could be found, but after a little time I saw a man whom I believed to be the chief, at some distance, trying to hide himself behind a tree. I called him to me, but he refused to come, and so, throwing down my umbrella and the small stick with which I had been belabouring the rebel porters, I walked towards him with outstretched hands. He then saw that I meant peace, and came to meet me. I explained as best I could that we were Englishmen and wished to be his friends; and that we had been trying to prevent our porters from stealing his property. He then embraced me most affectionately, and we walked hand in hand back to the village. He next called his people together, and we had a great peace-making, and they all showed themselves most grateful for the deliverance we had wrought on their behalf. But there is a very serious side to the whole matter. We heard afterwards that immediately our porters commenced to raid the village, the chief sent off messengers through all the district calling the native warriors to fight against the caravan. When we found this out we asked the chief to send other messengers to assure the people that all was peaceful; but it will be seen what great trouble might have arisen from such an act.

As I have said, the European is largely at the mercy of his porters. Sometimes these unscrupulous fellows would actually tell the village people that the Europeans had sent them for so many bags of corn, or so many sheep or goats, and that if they did not send them to him, he would come himself and fight them, and the village folk, being greatly afraid of the European's guns, would rather give away all they possessed than make an enemy of him, and having done so look for an opportunity of attacking his caravan when least expected, and so take their revenge.

GERMAN ROAD, EAST AFRICA.

We next had to cross an immense Masai plain, called Mlala, over which these well-known warriors of Eastern Africa wander in bands with their cattle; being entirely nomadic in their habits of life, they never settle in one place for long, and of course never cultivate the ground. The plain was full of game of all descriptions. We saw quantities of antelope and zebra, but were unable to leave our caravan to hunt, lest our porters, being left for a time, should again try to raid the villages *en route*. As we marched we were able to get a shot now and then;

bustards, guinea fowl, partridges, quails and pigeons were in abundance, and made useful additions to our larder.

On Friday, November 2nd, we reached the second inland station of the C.M.S., called Mpwapwa. The missionaries here were the Rev. J. H. Price and Mr. Doulton. They received us very kindly and put us up in the mission houses. They could not speak of any very marked results of their work, as the people were very dull and thoroughly indolent. Still there were the few who had been raised into a better life, and who shall

GERMAN FORT, MPWAPWA.

say that Missions are a failure if it be but the few that are raised and made better?

At Mpwapwa the Germans have a large fort and two or three officers live there. Their rule is very strict and decidedly military in character, the natives being very much afraid of them. It would be difficult to find what real benefit the natives themselves derive from this military occupation, and I think it must be a minus quantity, for apart from the fine houses built for the Europeans and a broad road leading up to the fort, there seemed to be no attempt at improvement in the country. The native builds the houses and makes the road. The former are no use to him, and the latter, in his opinion, is quite unnecessary; he can do equally well with a footpath a few inches wide.

From Mpwapwa to Kisokwe is only two hours' walk, and here again we met with friends, missionaries of the C.M.S., Rev. and Mrs. Cole, Rev. and Mrs. Beverley, and Mr. Briggs. We remained a few days at Kisokwe to allow K'shimba with the main portion of our caravan to

KISOKWE.

overtake us, as we heard that he was not far behind. Several of the porters that we had agreed to take on with us had deserted, and it was necessary for us to procure from K'shimba a few more trustworthy men, that we might proceed without delay to Nasa.

We were told by our friends at the Mission that famine was still raging in the district, and that we might expect it all the way to Nasa. How important it was to hurry along will therefore readily be seen. While waiting at Kisokwe for K'shimba we amused ourselves by going out hunting. There are numbers of antelope living on the Kisokwe Hills, and we had several very good hunts. There are also numerous leopards in the district, and one of Mr. Cole's goats was killed by one of these animals. The herdsman, however, drove the leopard off before it had time to devour its prey, and poison was put upon the carcase, with the result that a fine big leopard was found dead by the side of it the following morning. One of our donkeys died suddenly at this place, and hyenas spent the whole night hovering about the carcase, making most objectionable noises. All had disappeared by daybreak, donkey included.

After leaving Kisokwe some of the awful horrors of famine came under our notice. The porters could buy no food; they must get it somehow or else die. They were in a terrible state and ready to do anything. One day they came upon the corpse of a man who had been dead some days and was quite decomposed, and yet so famished were the poor fellows that they actually took the corpse and devoured it, and this was repeated the next day when some natives were seen carrying the body of a man, who had just died, into the bush—they seized it and consumed it. Some of them were like living skeletons, and the majority were so very improvident that even if they did procure a little food they never thought of making it last for more than one meal, and the consequence was that they did not derive proper benefit from it.

But we still hoped for better things. Sometimes we were told that in three days we should be in a district where there was plenty of food, and at others we were informed that the famine reached even to the Lake shores. We could only keep moving, trusting God to help us and provide for our poor half-starving porters that which we in our helplessness were unable to procure.

CHAPTER IV

CAMP LIFE (*continued*)

Wagogo thieves—K'shimba in distress—Trouble in the forest—The Martini rifle—Our hunting expeditions—When the boots wear out—Burungi, the land of plenty—Rains are upon us—Buying food—The Warungi—The warriors and my dog Sally—How troubles come—Irangi—A courteous reception—We tend the sick—The Governor as a patient—An African's gratitude—K'shimba turns up—He relates his troubles—Bwana Kitangi to the rescue.

WE were now entering the country of Ugogo, the people of which are very much given to stealing, and it was necessary for us to keep a sharp look-out for these notorious robbers. Although the country seemed very little populated, so far as we could tell by the number of villages, still large bands of the Wagogo were constantly met with, and we never knew when they were in our neighbourhood. Any straggling porter was liable to be murdered by them and his load stolen. We therefore split up the Europeans into two sections; two of us went at the head of the caravan to prevent any going on too fast, and two of us remained with the head-man at the rear to stop any from loitering behind. In camp also we all kept close together with the loads stacked up in the midst. But even with all our efforts to protect the porters their own utter stupidity frequently led them into trouble, and as we marched the two Europeans in the rear had the greatest difficulty to keep the men together.

We knew that in every thick part of the forest through which our way led there were enemies waiting for the stragglers, whom they would at once spear, and then steal the loads; and although the porters knew this perfectly well they did not seem to mind at all, and for the sake of a little rest were willing to risk their lives.

I remember one day when I was behind the others, suddenly coming upon a number of Wagogo thieves, armed with their spears and bows and arrows. They were in the act of creeping up to a few of our porters, who were foolishly sitting down by the roadside smoking. When they saw me they entered the bush and I hurried the porters on to join the caravan. We had not gone many days' journey from Kisokwe, however, before we received news from our head-man, K'shimba, who it will be remembered was in charge of the main caravan, and was a few days' journey behind us, that he had lost a number of his porters in this way. Staying behind, they had been murdered and their goods stolen. He sent on to ask us to allow forty of our men to return to him to help bring on the loads. We of course could not do this until we had reached Irangi, which was still some days ahead of us. We therefore sent back to K'shimba telling him to follow us on as best he could, and that when we reached Irangi we would send him help if possible.

Between us and Irangi there was a thick forest to go through. Hour after hour we toiled along in the terrible heat—there seemed to be no air to breathe—now pushing our way through the tangled undergrowth, now stooping almost double under some bending trunk of a tree, then climbing over another only a few yards distant. Add to all this the sickening want of water and proper nourishment, not to mention the weary work of urging on the porters, and it will be seen that these few marches through the forest were very hard indeed. And if it were so hard for us who had nothing to carry but ourselves, and if *we* felt to such a degree the burning thirst, what must be said of the poor creatures who carried our loads! Amongst them death had become quite common; some through want of food, others from various causes had to give in and simply lay themselves down to die. Pike and I were walking together at one time when we came upon a poor fellow sitting, or rather reclining, by the roadside. We went up to him and tried

UGOGO VILLAGE.

to urge him to come on, but he simply shook his head. We raised him to his feet, but he could not even stand upright. What were we to do? There were no villages for miles and miles around. I felt his pulse; it seemed to have stopped, and his heart scarcely beat at all, and we knew that all would soon be over. As a last act of kindness we carried him to a more comfortable spot, gave him all the food we had with us and the bottle of cocoa that I carried on my back, and with sad and aching hearts we left him there to die.

It seems inhuman thus to leave a dying man, but as men who might be speedily overtaken by the same fate, we felt it our duty to go forward. Before the last man of the caravan had passed that spot this poor dark heathen soul had *gone.* Gone! but can we doubt for him a Father's care? No! I cannot bring myself to believe that such as he will be left and forgotten, without the watchful, pitying eye of the loving Father. Africa is full of the most heartrending scenes, and hearts must be made of adamant that will not melt with compassion. What, therefore, can be the feelings of the sympathising Christ for these dark, ignorant souls that go down into the valley of the shadow of death with no glimmer of hope?

We were now getting near to the land of plenty, at least so we were told by those we met on the road, and our porters began to gain courage. Moving out of camp one morning, only about five hundred yards away from the outskirts of our camping-ground, I came upon the body of a man who had been dead only a few hours; a little way from him were his broken cooking-pot and mat, and an *empty* water-bottle. In his hand he still grasped a little iron hoe, and a few yards away was a deep hole that he had evidently been digging in order if possible to procure water, but, overcome with thirst, he had probably fainted, and the pangs of death laid hold upon him—so near to our camp that he might almost have heard our voices, and had he pushed on but a few hundred yards he would have received from us the precious liquid he so sorely needed. When at last we emerged from the forest we found ourselves upon a huge plain, well watered and abounding in game of all sorts—buffalo, zebra, rhinoceros, and all kinds of antelope both large and small. Each day upon getting into camp we would go off hunting, trying to provide ourselves and our porters with food. Sometimes we were successful, at others we came back empty-handed. I found that the Martini sporting rifle was by far the best for antelope and smaller game. Some antelope, however, are most difficult to get. They will run off with a bullet in the shoulder as if nothing were wrong, and suddenly disappear in the thicket. The hunter is apt to think that they have made good their escape, but by a careful search along the trail the wounded animal will be found reclining, only to race off again if a second shot is not soon forthcoming. A

GAME DISTRICT.

rifle with smaller calibre seldom drops an antelope, unless hit right through the heart, and even then I have known them run fifty yards before falling. For elephants, buffalo, hippo and rhino, there is nothing like a ·303 calibre, but the sportsman must have a steady hand and a strong nerve, as a ·303 bullet will not stop a charging elephant unless it penetrates the brain, which is not an easy shot.

To give some idea of the vitality of the antelope, I fired at two hundred yards with my Martini at a large

Kob; the bullet entered the hind quarters and broke the thigh, it then ran quite a quarter of a mile; I stalked it, and again fired at about the same distance, and this time the bullet expanded and literally turned the poor beast inside out, but even then it made off at a headlong gallop. Just as it was entering a thicket I fired the third shot, and this time the bullet pierced the heart. A few herds of the larger Koodoo roamed about on the plains, also Jacksonii, Spring-buck, Reed-buck, &c.

My next personal trouble was the wearing out of the only pair of boots I had with me. I had hoped that they would last until we reached Irangi, where we were to wait for K'shimba, but they came to an end before I expected, and so I had to tramp along the rough roads with large holes in the soles of both boots. Blisters were the result, and I bid fair to become a cripple. It may be wondered why I did not ride my donkey; the fact was, the donkey was now in constant use as a pack animal, and each day carried a large load of things, as many of the porters had either died or deserted us, and it was the same with the other two donkeys that remained. So I had to walk, and many a weary hour I spent in this painful way.

Friday, November 16th, found us in the country known as Burungi, very beautiful, and in reality like an immense plain surrounded by hills on every side, covered with villages, and plenty of food. We waited here a day or two so that our tired porters might buy food and recuperate a little after the very tiring time they had passed through. We anticipated difficulty in getting them to start again from such a place where there were so many allurements for the weary traveller. There was, however, still so much ground to be covered, and the rainy season was coming on so fast, that we felt it wrong to stay more than two days.

We therefore got up in good time on the third morning after our arrival, pulled down our tents, and packed up our camp furniture, but our "darling" porters sat still around their fires unwilling to budge an inch. We urged them with kind words, but they only laughed and looked pleased. We urged them with angry words, then they seemed quite sorry for us, but stuck manfully by the flames. At last we got really angry, shivering as we were with cold in the early dawn, and with no tents to shelter us. We finally rushed upon them and began to scatter their fires about and to drive our now startled "Wanyams" out of camp.

When we thought all had gone and were striding out of camp ourselves, we discovered about a dozen of the lazy fellows hiding from us in one of the huts, eating away as hard as they could. It was now time to make an example of one of them, so I seized hold of one great fellow, and with a thin cane that I carried I gave him a pretty smart thrashing. He then shouldered his load and walked merrily out of camp along with the others, and he did not appear again until I arrived at the next camp, when he came up to me as pleased as possible to show himself. Of course, as with children, so with Wanyamwezi porters, we have to make our anger short-lived, and so, when this stalwart old fellow came into camp, I praised him for getting in so soon, gave him a biscuit, and generally made a fuss with him, and, it is a fact, I never had any more trouble with that man.

About the middle of November the rains began in real earnest, and we were brought face to face with another serious difficulty, this time not scarcity of water, but too much of it. If there is one thing an African dislikes more than another it is rain, and our Wanyamwezi porters were no exception to the rule. As soon as ever a shower came on, down went the loads, and away went the porters into huts, under trees, *anywhere*, out of the rain. Of course the loads didn't matter, they could be left on the roadside! and beautifully wet our things got. So much so that by the time we got to Nasa many of our clothes were simply rotten and utterly spoilt. Day after day this would happen, and we began to wonder whether we should ever be able to get along. It is true that these poor fellows die like rats if they are exposed much to the rain, and they would sit crouching in the tiny huts of the natives or in bushes by the roadside, and, all wet as they

RAINS UPON US.

were, they soon got ague and fever, and the best thing we could do was to urge them on. As we entered one house and drove them out they would enter another, and hide on the shady side, hoping not to be detected. Then perhaps the rain would stop, and we would set them going once more, and for an hour or so all would go well, but when the rain comes down again, away they all run, and we give up in despair, and, soaking wet ourselves, creep into one of the filthy huts, full of smoke, which nearly choked us, rats and other vermin abounding.

Thus, huddled up together with our naked porters, we "wait till the clouds roll by."

The Burungi natives are a very fine race of men. They are warlike and bold, and tolerably industrious, for although all around famine was raging, they had plenty of food stored away, and they were very good in selling to our porters. Every morning they would come into our camp bringing all kinds of produce, also sheep, goats, fowls, and eggs, and it was pleasant to stand by and watch the sale proceed. Our porters had but a few trade goods left, having paid exorbitant prices for little bits of food through the famine-stricken district, and therefore they did their best to cut down the price asked by the Burungi warriors; but they were not to be had in this way, and they stood upon their dignity, asking a fair price and expecting to get it, and when offered a few inferior beads for a full-grown cockerel the way they would toss their heads and stride away in their dignified manner was most delightful to see.

Sometimes a large number of the Warungi would come to our tents and ask to see our various belongings. I think what astonished them most was my Berkefeld filter, to see dirty water transformed into a beautiful clear liquid simply did for them, and was more than they could understand. The camera also was a great wonder in their eyes, and to look through the view finders and see their companions all sitting round was to them most remarkable. My field-glasses also were a source of great amusement, and they never tired of looking at them.

They are great hunters, using dogs and nets for the smaller game, and digging pits for the larger animals. Their own weapons consist of spears, bows and arrows of a very primitive kind, and they certainly do not excel as iron workers.

Another incident occurred which greatly amused me.

I was some long distance in front of our caravan, accompanied only by my boy and my faithful little dog Sally, when, as we came to the top of the hill, we suddenly saw a large body of the Burungi warriors in full war-paint racing towards us. I immediately thought that they intended to attack us, and as I stood still I called my little dog to my side and spoke a few words to her, something about "going for them," when she started barking, and charged down upon the warriors, tail in the air. It was a grand sight and worth going to Africa for, to see these *warlike* men run for their lives, with Sally at their heels. Upon inquiry, I found that the warriors were conducting a supposed witch back to her hut. She had been charged with the evil eye, and brought before the medicine man, who had made medicine and found her not guilty. They therefore took her and covered her with a kind of white paint from head to foot and were in the act of taking her back to her hut chanting strange warlike hymns, when their course was slightly altered by reason of meeting with my little dog Sally. But to show the contrast of this little joke when a small army was put to flight by a little dog. These same people, after we left, attacked our head-man K'shimba, and his caravan of about 300 men, killing 20 (so report said) and wounding many others. Not without cause was this attack made, for the usual misconduct of the porters stealing from the villagers had brought it about.

I often used to say that I and my little dog Sally might walk across Africa alone in perfect safety, and undoubtedly where trouble with the natives does happen to a caravan with Europeans in it, it is usually occasioned either by ill feeling between the tribe to which the porters belong and the people through whose country they pass, or else it is caused by the porters making petty robberies from the villages. I have known of exceptions, however, when

the European himself has been headstrong and hard with
the natives, treating the people with utter indifference and
making demands upon them for food, &c. It is then not
to be wondered at if the natives do attack the caravan,
and if the European lose his life. If the African is trusted
and generally treated as a human being, and not as a
lower animal, it is perfectly easy to get on with him, but

TREE FERNS.

suspicion or high-handed treatment on the part of the
European will always bring disaster in the long run.

On Monday, November 19th, we reached Irangi, a large
settlement consisting of well-built houses and beautiful
gardens, with an Arab (Bwana Kitangi) as its chief. We
were received by the Arab and his followers in great style.
He and about thirty others, dressed in their beautiful
flowing robes, walked down to the river-side just outside
the town to meet us. Such splendour would hardly be

thought possible right away there in Central Africa. We shook hands all round, and were conducted by the Governor into his house, while our tents were pitched near his enclosure. In front of his house was a long flagstaff, and the German flag was flying, Bwana Kitangi being in German employ, and placed here at Irangi by the Germans. He took us to the verandah of his house, and regretted that we had not sent him word of our coming, as he would have met us more suitably. In every way he was most polite.

After a few moments' rest, we went to see to our tents, and then about an hour or more afterwards, while resting, Bwana Kitangi sent to us two trays with a large pot of tea on each, a roast fowl with curry and eggs, and two different kinds of pastry, also some bananas. In the afternoon we all went to see him and to thank him, and as we sat under the verandah of his house he ordered coffee for us, which was served in tiny little bowls holding about half a wineglassful. These were filled several times, and we very much enjoyed it, the coffee being extremely good.

After we had returned to our tents, he sent us two fat sheep, a lot of sweet potatoes, a bag of native flour, ten sticks of sugar-cane, and a quantity of yams. Each morning we went up to the Governor's house to "told" him "good morning," as our good cook put it, and then he "told" us "good afternoon." Quite a little bit of society life in this wild land.

Presents followed one upon the other—fruit, consisting of bananas, guavas, &c., and each day a present of pastry. We began to feel as if we were running up a big bill, as our friend would expect a large present from us before we left.

Our tired porters were faring no less sumptuously than we were. Great loads of food were carried into camp every day, and alas! "Pombi" also found its way amongst them. This is a fermented drink made either from the millet seed, or else from the banana. It is a mild intoxicant, but of course the black man has no idea of moderation, they therefore suffered very considerably from intoxication. Especially was this the case with the head-man, who had more money to spend than had the ordinary porter.

During the few days that we spent at Irangi we had our work cut out to attend to the various sick folk; not only did many of our porters need treatment, but the people of Irangi also came in large numbers. I had told the Governor that as he had been so kind to us, we should be very pleased to give medicine to any of his people who needed it. He was very delighted, and to my surprise and consternation he put himself into my hands, complaining of pains in the shoulders and limbs. From what I could make out (my medical knowledge being very limited) he was suffering from chronic rheumatism, and as he was an elderly man it was of course a difficult case. However, I did my best for him, I need not say here what treatment I used; suffice it to say, in a few days he declared himself quite well, and seemed most grateful. In consequence of this wonderful cure he sent to me all kinds and conditions of men, women, and little children. Once a chief came, bringing one of his wives suffering from a very bad internal abscess. It was rather a difficult undertaking for me, but I got through in a most professional manner, and the poor woman was very thankful to be free from pain. This kind of thing was kept up all through the daytime and at night; one was very tired and yet thankful to have been some little use in alleviating some very few of the sufferers of this great land.

Some of the cures were rather remarkable considering the ingorance of the physician. One case in particular called forth the admiration of the people. A poor fellow who for weeks had been suffering from dysentery in its advanced stage was brought to me in a very terrible condition, simply a living skeleton and utterly powerless. Naturally I felt very unable to do anything for him, but I did what I could. Day after day he was brought to my tent during our stay at Irangi, and before we left he was so changed that one would hardly know him. The last

USAGARA QUEEN.

day he came to me I asked him if he had come for more medicine. "Oh, no," he said, "I have come to thank you very much, I am quite well." He then produced a large fowl that he had brought to me as a thank-offering for having recovered from that terrible sickness.

Some people seem to think that the black man has no gratitude in his nature. I can only say that my own experience leads me absolutely to deny such an idea.

There are of course exceptions, but even these can be accounted for according to the custom of the people, but the majority of Africans are most truly grateful for any real kindness shown to them, not in a merely patronising way, but acts of kindness prompted by love always call forth true gratitude from them.

K'shimba arrived at Irangi on Thursday the 23rd, and immediately entered most joyfully into the delight of having plenty to eat and, best of all, plenty to drink. The first evening he got into camp he was very drunk. Pike and I found him in the village rolling about and making a great noise. So we took him, one on each side, to his own tent. He went quite willingly, and each time we spoke to him he said, in a drunken voice, "Yesh," which means "Yes," being the only English word he knew. We were more amused with our experience of taking home a drunken nigger than we ought to have been. When we got to his tent he immediately called for his wives to come and entertain us, and he ordered hot water to be brought for tea, and food to be prepared, and was evidently most hospitably inclined, but we excused ourselves, saying we were tired, and came away and left him to sleep off the effects of the intoxicant.

The following morning he gave us the true story of his experiences in the forest with the natives of Burungi. He stated that his loss of men amounted to twenty-two killed and ten wounded; of these thirteen were killed by the people of a village to which they went on the 14th presumably to buy corn, probably to rob, and who seem to have been mistaken by the villagers for other natives with whom they were at war. Of the remainder, three were loitering at the end of the caravan with their loads next day, and were attacked by the Warungi warriors and speared, but one man managed to overtake the caravan before he died of a ghastly wound between the shoulders, and men were sent back by K'shimba, who rescued the loads before much damage was done, after a short, sharp struggle with the robbers. The remaining six died from want of food and water in the forest, the result, probably, of their own improvidence, for when these people have food they eat away for hours together, although they know perfectly well that they may be unable to procure more food for days to come.

Before leaving Irangi we had another review of our porters, and all the loads were counted. To our great surprise we found that none of our personal belongings were missing; K'shimba had done his best, he said, to preserve our private loads, and if a porter deserted or died who had been carrying our things, he had given the load to some other man, preferring to leave behind some of Mr. Stokes' cowrie shells rather than call forth denunciations from us. We highly complimented him upon his skill as a head-man, and promised him big presents if we got to Nasa all safe and well. He was very proud and glad to receive our compliments, and especially our promises. The porters themselves were greatly improved by the few days' rest and abundance of food. Some were looking quite fat again, and all seemed eager to press forward.

"Posho" (food-money) was given out in the shape of cloth to all, and a clear day allowed them in which to buy food for the next few days' journey. K'shimba asked that now, as we had much difficult country to pass through, he might accompany us, and that there should be no splitting up of the caravan. He assured us that where-ever *we* were there was safety, and it was only when they were alone that the danger was great. We readily agreed, and decided that however much longer it might take to reach our journey's end, it was only right that we should remain as protection to our poor black porters who were carrying our loads.

We were told by K'shimba that two ways were now open before us, and it was for us to decide by which we should proceed; one way would take us five days to the border of the Wanyamwezi country, and another month or so to Nasa, but the five days' journey would be through a country the people of which were wild and hostile to Europeans. The other way was much longer, taking a circuitous route of fifteen days through the forest to escape the hostile natives.

We referred the matter to Bwana Kitangi, the Arab Governor of Irangi, and he told us that he knew yet another road, taking only ten days to Wanyamwezi country, with plenty of food and water all the way, and friendly natives.

We therefore chose most readily this new road. But our many experiences must be related in another chapter.

CHAPTER V

THE LAST STAGES

Farewell to Bwana Kitangi—Rains—Washed out Floods—Swampy ground—The porter's slave—Sandawi—More troubles—Considered himself a dead man—A hostile people—Turu—Poisonous roots—Christmas Day—The Wanyamwezi country—Sickness—We reach Nera—Meeting with Messrs. Gordon and Nickisson—Carried in a hammock—Arrival at Nasa—Rest at last—Native cloth—Embarkation on Lake—Our canoes—Hippopotami—Ukerewe—Mr. Stokes—A narrow escape—The German Station—The stormy winds do blow—The Wasese—Crocodiles—The last day.

THE rest which was so welcomed by us at Irangi, came to an end on the 27th of November. We felt very grateful for all the kindness shown to us by the old Arab governor, Bwana Kitangi, and as a mark of our appreciation, we gave him a watch and a quantity of coloured clothes, with both of which he was highly delighted. He was up very early in the morning to see us off, and expressed a wish that we could have stayed longer with him, thanked us for the presents we had given him, and finally bade us farewell.

Our path led along a dry river bed for some distance, and in the evening of the first day from Irangi we camped on the river bank. Rain came down upon us in the middle of the night with truly frightful force, it seemed as if our little tents would be utterly washed away. This continued till daybreak, and then when we got up and looked towards the river we were amazed beyond measure, for the whole of the immense river bed was full of raging, roaring water, which dashed along in great waves like the sea, carrying away trees and vegetation of every description. As our path lay on the opposite bank of the river, we had to wait until the water had gone down a little.

At this camp a large number of our porters deserted us, and we were consequently delayed, re-arranging our loads. Fortunately we had been able to procure a reserve of men from Bwana Kitangi, and the delay therefore was only a short one.

On again we went, into a thick forest, in which there was an abundance of game of all kinds—elephants, zebra, giraffes, buffalo, and antelope. We were able to supply our larder with many good things.

The rains troubled us very much the last few weeks, and nearly every day there was a downpour, our clothes never seemed dry, and it gave one a creepy sensation to be obliged to put on cold, wet clothing in the early dawn. At about eleven o'clock one night I awoke, to find the rain pouring down upon us in sheets. I called to my boys, who were sleeping under a tree, and told them to come into my tent to lie down on the floor on which was my ground sheet, and go to sleep, which I also tried to do; and in spite of the lightning, which kept my tent ablaze with light, just as if the whole forest were on fire, and the thunder, which was like incessant artillery close to my ears, I dozed off quite calmly. Not for long, however, for presently I heard the boys talking wildly together, and when I was fully awake I found that the ground on which we were camped was all flooded to the depth of several inches, and the bottom of my tent was like a rushing stream. The two boys were standing in one corner of the tent, shivering, and on my bed was my poor little dog Sally, and a monkey that had been given to me at Irangi, both curled up against my legs, their little backs quite wet. We endeavoured to pack everything that would be likely to spoil on to the table and chair, and finally, I did what I had never done before, namely, shared my bed with a black man. That is, I allowed my two black boys to curl themselves up at the bottom of my bed, taking up as little room as possible, and then, with my knees up to my chin, I also curled up like a mouse and went to sleep.

At daybreak I awoke and looked round and could not help laughing heartily. There were my two boys so much doubled up together that I did not know to which one a prominent leg or arm belonged—sound asleep. There also was my little dog cuddled up with the monkey, both asleep; and last, but not least, was the rushing stream of water—by no means asleep. Everything, including blankets and clothes, was wet, and, shivering from head to foot, I slipped into my marching " toggery " and we set off. The other Europeans had suffered in much the same way as I had, but fortunately none of us were any the worse for it.

And now every day we had to battle with fresh difficulties occasioned by the rain. Huge districts flooded with water through which we had to wade, or else a tramp of five or six miles through a thick swamp of black plastic mud with a few inches of water on the top.

Soon after we had left camp, a few days past Irangi, we came to a great river which had to be crossed. I was preparing to wade, the water being only up to one's waist, when one of the head-men came and offered to carry me across. About half-way he tripped against a hidden tree stump and rolled backwards, putting me under. I struggled to shore like a drowned rat. After the river came a great plain which was really a bog of thick, black mud, and extended for a mile or so. I shall not easily forget it.

WHERE ARE'S SUNNY FOUNTAINS.

The first difficulty in this bog was—the donkey got stuck fast and it was only by literally carrying the poor beast, that we could get it to dry ground at all. It was an awful experience, standing up to our knees in most offensive mud; the rain pouring down upon us with relentless fury; and a poor donkey hopelessly stuck fast. I too got fixed, and then I could more truly sympathise with the donkey. I sank in the mud up to my thighs and could not stir; Pike and several of the porters finally dragged me out, but my joints seemed dislocated by the strain. Then, far worse than this, lying in the swamp was a poor fellow, quite dead, with just a green bough of a tree put over his body by a companion. The poor man had apparently struggled on till he dropped. As we looked upon that corpse by the roadside with the green bough over it, I think I never before realised what a solemn thing Death is. Alone, that soul had passed through the dark valley, so truly dark to him. Alone! passed from this world of sorrow: and as I looked at the newly budding branch, one could only pray that this might be a bright simile of what it was with him, a birth into a better life. The winter of his darkness over, the springtime come. As we passed the body a large black adder glided from beside it and disappeared into the bush.

We next came upon a poor boy, a porter's slave, who carried a small load of cooking pots for his master, lying in the mud in a dying state. We gave him what food we had and tried to urge him on, but it was useless. Finally we took his load and carried it ourselves and I think I never fully sympathised with our porters until I had that small load of cooking pots on my shoulder; but the boy could not even walk then, so we gave the load to one of our boys and then took it in turns to carry the poor little slave.

At last we got through the swamp and found one of the

donkeys waiting for us, so we put the boy on its back and finally reached camp more dead than alive. We all decided that another day like that would be the end of us.

On December 5th we reached Sandawi, a large populous district, the people of which were friendly and had plenty of food. But alas, alas, our troubles had not ceased; there are more sad stories to tell.

K'shimba came to us in great excitement and said that one of our boys had just come into camp with a great quantity of food that he must have stolen. He had five

SANDAWI NATIVES.

fowls and a great lot of corn, and as he had a very little cloth for bartering purposes, it was plain he had stolen the things. Two others had been out with him and they had returned to camp loaded with all kinds of good things. They readily admitted that they had stolen them. The case of the boy was, of course, the worst. His master had trusted him, and we all liked him, but he had gone about his thefts so deliberately that we found that it was not the first time. He had received permission from his master to go and buy food and he immediately went into one of our tents, took up a gun that he found there, and as we afterwards discovered, he went off to the villages round about and said that the Europeans of the big caravan had sent him to demand food: and in their fear the people gave what they could. He was publicly punished very severely, and also the two porters who had accompanied him. His master also reduced his position to that of donkey boy.

Late the same night K'shimba came to us again, this time bringing one of the under head-men, who had been stealing. He was a man we had all liked because of his pleasant though somewhat forward manner. As a headman he should have been an example for good conduct to the rest of the caravan, and have done what he could to prevent stealing: and this was therefore considered a very bad case, and thirty strokes were awarded as a punishment, in full view of the whole caravan. The stolen property was collected and given back to the natives.

About nightfall of the second day at Sandawi a porter came in with a severe spear wound on his head and thigh, saying that he went to a village to buy food and the people took his cloth from him; and when he tried to recover it again they stabbed him with a spear. K'shimba and our whole caravan were highly indignant at this grievous insult and declared that they would go off and fight the people and burn the village down. We restrained them with some difficulty, for we ourselves suspected that the man had been trying to steal, and had been speared in the act, and had only received his rich deserts.

An investigation was made, and the culprit who speared the man was brought to us. He said that he had been out hunting, and upon his return he found his house had been robbed of corn by some of our porters; and when one of them came a little while afterwards asking to buy food, he decided to keep his cloth, and he speared the man to make him give it up. He was afterwards told by the other villagers that there were four Europeans in the caravan, and he was frightened at what he had done and let the man go. He described to us most graphically how he already considered himself a dead man, and how the head-man of the village had sent him to be punished before we should fight them and how the people crowded round him, mourning and bewailing his expected death. "But," said he, "when I go back alive, they will all be angry with me for making trouble." The chief gave five goats to the man who had been wounded and so the matter ended, but our sympathies were quite with the accused.

Again K'shimba had a difficulty; he came to us at night with three of the head-men, all carrying their guns, and said that one of his sons together with four others had gone off to buy food a few days before, and they had not been heard of since; and K'shimba declared that they must have been killed by the natives from whom things had been stolen, so he wished to kill the porters who had been stealing, to revenge the death of his son. We pointed out to him that they had already been punished, and told him not to think any more about it. He certainly did not seem to feel the loss of his son very keenly. When a man has sixty children, as he says he has, one less or more can make but little difference. K'shimba's threat to kill the porters who had been stealing, somehow or other became known to the caravan, and several of the culprits, including the head-man who had been beaten, made off during the night, so we were again reduced in numbers, and more shells belonging to Mr. Stokes had to be left behind, so that the porters might carry on our things, which were of the first importance.

In the middle of the night of December 4th an alarm was given. K'shimba again came running to our tents carrying his gun, and drew our attention to a peculiar cry or shout, apparently about a mile away, which he said came from some of the porters in danger. He called out some command, and at once the various head-men appeared before him armed to the teeth with guns and spears. It was a great surprise to us to see them come so promptly, in answer to their chief's call, for it was raining heavily at the time and was very dark. He next sent these off in fives, in various directions, and in the meantime the cries were getting nearer, and we certainly did not think they proceeded from men in much danger. After a time we heard the head-men coming back, chanting something which sounded rather pretty, and as they approached us, we could see by the light of the camp fire that they were dancing and brandishing their weapons, and the crowd standing around us caught the enthusiasm and began to sing and dance too. At a word from K'shimba they were all quiet. This was their war-song and dance. They had brought back two men who had been making cries, one of them being K'shimba's son who was supposed to have been murdered, and who said that they had been to buy food, and at one village they were captured and tied up as thieves, and threatened with death, but they had escaped. Of course the great K'shimba made a few remarks about going to fight the people who had *dared* to tie up two Wanyamwezi warriors, but soon altered his mind; and I do not think there was much fight in them for all their war dances.

Our march on December 11th was much delayed by a long consultation between K'shimba and ourselves, and the chief of the village we had left the day before. A message had come from the people of the district Turu, which we were to enter the following day, to the effect that they would not let us go that way, but were prepared to fight us if we attempted it. To avoid their country we should have been obliged to go a long way round, adding five days to our journey, and taking us through uninhabited parts; as the men were already short of food, it would have been a serious matter, and in all probability

YOUNG OSTRICH.

we should have lost a number of our men. Finally the chief of the village we had just left, agreed to go and persuade the people of Turu to let us pass. On his return he bade us, in the name of the Turu people, to enter their country without fear, and so we started. We took every precaution to keep the caravan together as the path led through a thick jungle, and we feared treachery.

Presently we emerged from the jungle and at once saw a great extent of country thickly covered with villages, large and small. We made our way towards one of the largest of these, and here we only saw the armed warriors and none of the women. After a little while they grew friendly, and by interpretation we were able to chat with the chief and he was quite pleased, and brought us presents of corn and flour, as a proof of his friendship. They told us we were the first white people they had ever seen and they therefore greatly feared us. The chief informed us that he had received a message from a native a few days before, telling him that four white men were coming to fight him, but that if he would send two tusks of ivory to him he would be able to stop them from coming. This he had done, but the white men had come for all that. We were much struck by the appearance of this race of people, tall, active looking men, with most intelligent faces. Their dress (or undress) was peculiar, and seemed to consist of a few bracelets on their arms. All the women wore large ornaments in the lobe of their ears, and also a few of the men. There was an abundance of food in this district, and all the time we were there the natives were bringing supplies into camp which the porters bought with their "posho" cloth.

We had several hunting expeditions while the porters collected food for themselves, and we were fairly successful.

A number of the porters died at this place from eating a poisonous root that they gathered in the district. We warned them when we saw them eating it, but it was of no avail, and in one day eight men died and several became alarmingly ill. They told us that it was a root that made them strong for work, and better able to march. Alas! it proved too strong for them.

At Mongula, a large town that we reached on December

23rd, we left behind fifty-five loads, so as to be able to proceed more quickly to Nasa.

Christmas Day came and went as any other day, excepting that we devoured a plum pudding, brought out from England by one of our party, but it was a sorry dinner party. We tried to look happy, but it was almost a failure. Our tents were pitched inside a large village which had a rough sort of stockade all round it, and it was well for us that we did pitch them there, for all kinds of wild beasts roamed about at night. Our constant visitors were wild sort of people who sat and gazed upon us with the utmost astonishment. They told us they had never seen white people before. These were our surroundings on Christmas Day. All four of us were a little unwell, and the strain of the journey and the privations which we had so long been suffering, were beginning to tell upon us; and we each had constant attacks of fever, dysentery, &c. Even on Christmas Day we were obliged to march, although it was only for two hours, the constant stoppages seemed to demoralise our porters, the inevitable result being that they would go off to the villages, stealing whatever they could lay their hands upon.

We had to cross several huge plains after leaving Mongula, and upon these roamed game of various kinds. It was upon one of these plains that I saw a great many rhinoceros; ostriches also in large numbers; buffalo and antelope; but the spirit was getting knocked out of us, and we no longer cared to go off hunting after a long weary march during the heat of the day. Walking before the caravan we often came close up with zebra and antelope, and then a shot or two was fired, but it usually meant that we did not leave the path to follow up the wounded game; and unless the animals were shot in a vital part to cause instant death, nothing resulted.

On one of the plains of which I have spoken there was a quantity of water, and for several hours we were wading through this: sometimes up to our knees, and in the middle, right up to our waists. The water seemed to be the result of a flood, for it was very muddy and did not rise above the top of the long spear-grass, and the bottom was very soft and slippery, which made walking very difficult, and many a struggle we had to keep our perpendicular.

For our porters, of course, it was far more trying, for they had been in the habit of resting every half-hour or oftener, and now to have to walk on and on for close upon four hours through water without any rest was more than we expected them to be able to accomplish. Our greatest fear was lest they should slip and let our precious loads into the water, but with one exception all came through without a soaking.

As soon as we were on dry land again we called a halt and rested for half an hour, and then proceeded to camp, another two hours further on. There was no village, and we pitched our tents on the open plain.

The New Year was ushered in by a great thunderstorm, which seemed to burst upon us in fury. Such a deluge of rain I had never seen: the whole surrounding country was soon under water, and the small streams became rushing rivers. Two of us were down with fever, and we still had a long way to go, and to cross the now swollen rivers was by no means an easy task. Sometimes balancing ourselves upon a tree that had fallen across the stream, at others holding on to some kind nigger who tried to help us, and yet again wading breast-high into the swollen tide—none of these things tended to improve our state of health, and it became very serious.

We reached Kakora on the 3rd of January, and here more of our men deserted. We were then on the outskirts of the Wanyamwezi country, and this accounted for it. The district was thickly populated, and K'shimba did his best to secure fresh men to take their places.

But at this place I began to lose interest in everything; life seemed a burden, fever burning the spirit out of me. I was too feeble to walk. Fortunately my donkey was still in the land of the living, and he carried me along many a weary mile. My companions too were in a

CHIEF OF NERA AND WIVES.

similar condition to myself, and we did all we could to help each other.

On January 9th letters came to us from Messrs. Nickisson and Gordon, C.M.S. missionaries, stationed at Nasa, at the south of the Victoria Lake, saying that they were coming to meet us, and we expected to see them the next day.

When we got to Nera, which turned out to be K'shimba's native place, great crowds of gaudily dressed women came rushing to meet our head-man and the few surviving porters. There was great rejoicing. Alas! we could not enter into it, and heartily wished that the yelling crowds would disperse and leave us in peace. K'shimba brought us his wives to gaze upon, a comely set of women, about ten in all, but far too noisy for our shattered nerves that day. The chief of Nera and all his attendants also came to visit us and presented us with various gifts of good things. He did not impress us as being a very intelligent specimen of humanity, nor did his wives, who accompanied him; but perhaps it was through ignorance of native character that we failed to see their good qualities.

It was January 10th at noonday that once more we looked an Englishman in the face. It was a great treat again to see white faces and to feel that our journey was now nearly over. Messrs. Gordon and Nickisson, according to their promise, met us at Nera, and at once attended to those of us who were sick, and continually contrived some new scheme for our comfort.

I was put into a hammock and carried the rest of the way; the others either rode donkeys or were likewise carried. It was only four days' march from Nera to Nasa, but it seemed to us the longest part of the journey. Every movement or jolt of the hammock in which I lay caused me frightful pain as with parched lips and throbbing head I was trotted along on the backs of two stalwart Wanyamwezi porters. Once they dropped me, but it seemed delightful to again reach solid earth, and I rolled over in my hammock and went to sleep, only to be aroused by the constant bump of the hammock as the carriers changed the pole, on which it was slung, from shoulder to shoulder.

But rest came at last, thank God! No one ever needed it more than we did. We were sick and tired of camp life, our provisions were running very short, and the constant worry with the porters had driven all the pluck out of us. I was told by K'shimba that out of the five hundred porters who started from Zanzibar with us, not more than twenty-five arrived at Nasa. Many had deserted, and many, alas! had died, and the greatest wonder was that ever we reached Nasa at all.

C.M.S. MISSION STATION, NASA.

But get there we did, and I shall not soon forget the feeling of real rest when I was lifted from my hammock, and gently laid upon a comfortable bed in a nice clean house in the Mission compound at Nasa, and at first I almost wept with delight at the strange sensation of comfort. But I was soon fast asleep, absolutely content to sleep on.

The Mission premises at Nasa are stationed about a

mile from the lake shore, and command a most extensive and magnificent view of the lake, and surrounding country. There are three European houses, a church, kitchens, and outhouses, all substantially built of "wattle and daub." A beautiful garden in front of the buildings supplied the occupants of the station with fresh vegetables and fruit. At the back was a large cow kraal, and there were plenty of cows. Oh, the luxury of fresh milk to us who for three and a half months had been living upon tinned milk of a very inferior quality!

KAPONGO, CHIEF OF NASA.

I am afraid that while we were at Nasa we caused our good friends, Messrs. Gordon, Nickisson, and Hubbard,[*] much trouble in nursing us. The leader of our caravan, Rev. A. J. Pike, after suffering from fever and other slight but none the less trying complaints, had a very severe attack of rheumatism, which rendered him quite helpless. Rev. G. R. Blackledge and Mr. Lewin had considerably recovered from their indisposition upon their arrival at Nasa, and a few days' rest put them all right.

[*] Nickisson died June 28, 1896; Hubbard died March 9, 1897.

Personally I suffered a great deal, for even when I had got rid of the fever and dysentery, pleurisy again laid me low.

Yet in spite of all the worry we must have caused our brethren by our constant need of attention, with true Christian brotherly kindness they did everything in their power to help us, and never once complained. On February 1st two of our number were able to proceed

NATIVE LOOM, USUKUMA.

across the lake by canoe to Uganda—Rev. A. J. Pike and Mr. Lewin. I was still too unwell to be moved, and Mr. Blackledge kindly offered to wait until I was sufficiently recovered to make the journey across.

During my stay at Nasa I had an opportunity of examining some of the cloth made by the natives with their own loom. I was surprised to find of what comparatively good quality it was, and, considering the rough instruments that had been used, it was difficult to understand how it was possible to get such good results. The whole process is done by hand, and requires immense patience, but as a rule an African is not deficient in that quality; time is nothing to him; to-morrow or next year are as good as to-day, and if you worry him he will often reply, "The whole of my life is before me."

On February 19th I was well enough to start, and although I had to be carried down to the boat on

READY TO EMBARK ON VICTORIA NYANZA.

account of excessive weakness, I soon regained strength while on that magnificent inland sea, the Victoria Nyanza. Five canoes were procured for us. They were of very different construction from what one expected. Instead of the ordinary African dug-out canoe, which hitherto we had seen, there was a large, well-shaped craft varying from 15 to 50 feet in length by 3 to 5 feet beam—long planks neatly sewn together with a tough creeper that grows on the lake shores. The keel is composed of a solid piece of wood carved into shape, and protruding some 6 feet in the bow of the boat. Upon this are fixed the horns of some antelope, and a quantity of plaited grass to give an ornamental appearance to the whole. They were painted red, and were decidedly fine-looking boats. They were propelled by a number of boatmen with small paddles with leaf-shaped blades; some of the boats contained twenty or even thirty boatmen; and we were much surprised at the great speed that could be attained.

Into the stern of the boat were placed our hammock chairs, and with an umbrella to shade us from the sun, nothing could have been more pleasant to us who had been toiling along over hill and dale for three and a half weary months. Being the rainy season, we had constant storms: and they always came on so suddenly that we had to be most careful not to get too far from land, for although in calm water the canoes are seaworthy enough, when the waves begin to dash with violence against them, they are most unsafe; it is not at all an uncommon thing for these canoes to break to pieces. It will easily be seen that the fibre which holds the planks of the canoe together, must get rotten in time, and if it gives way, the whole thing tumbles to pieces at once.

The boatmen were Wasese, and live on the islands to the north of the lake; they were most kind and attentive to us, and did all they could for our comfort, especially for me during my weakness. There is a kind heart beats under the dark skin of many an African, low and degraded as he may be in his habits of life, his manhood will come out, and will easily be seen by those who look for it. I have been both surprised and delighted to find this true. There was a time when I did not believe an African capable of any kind of goodness; I was sadly mistaken, and I am glad I have lived to find out my mistake. He is not appealed to by rough blows and hard words, these only make him the more a savage, but he is softened and moved by kindness and his own heart reciprocates it; and happy is the traveller in Africa who learns this lesson, before he has steeled himself against it.

The boxes of provisions needed for the voyage were taken with us in our canoes, while the rest were left to follow later on in other boats. Each day we started about 6 a.m. and pitched our tents on some island of the lake about 3 p.m. in the afternoon. The scenery was magnificent, some of the islands being thick with tropical vegetation, while others were wild and rocky and desolate looking, but each had a grandeur of its own.

There were great numbers of water fowl on the lake, and we lived almost entirely upon them. Spur-winged geese, Egyptian geese, and small black and white ducks abounded, and we were fortunate enough to shoot sufficient for our need. Black and white " divers " went about in clouds; we also saw pelicans, egrets, cranes, and numerous species of water hens. Crocodiles basking on the rocks in the sun, and huge hippopotami floundering about in the water, frequently putting their great ugly snouts out of the water to gaze at us as we passed. The boatmen are afraid of them, and they told us that there was great danger of a hippopotamus charging down upon the boat with open mouth; and they had been known to bite the canoe in two.

Our first camp was at Nafa, a small island near the mouth of Speke gulf. The people were not particularly friendly, but did not trouble us, as we left in the early morning for Ukerewe. It was at this place that Mr. Stokes, the English trader, had his headquarters. A splendid house built of burnt bricks facing the lake, the grounds beautifully laid out with European vegetables.

The caretaker kindly allowed us to spend the night in the house, and I was shown into Mr. Stokes' own room and slept upon his bed. It was a strange coincidence that just about that time Mr. Stokes, away there in the Congo Free State, met with his death at the hands of inhuman men, for, to put the matter in as mild a form as possible, his execution by the Belgians was an act of

UKEREWE, CHIEF'S ENCLOSURE.

inhuman cruelty. For a solitary Englishman to be murdered by another European, right away in the very heart of Africa, with no proper trial, and but a mock investigation into the charges made against him, appears to me to be one of the most dastardly deeds that could be perpetrated by a civilised being. I believe Mr. Stokes was an honest trader, legitimately procuring the ivory from the country, he was thoroughly respected by the

BOA CONSTRICTOR KILLED ON ISLAND OF TMEREWE.

natives wherever he went, and one never heard him spoken unkindly of by any one. The fact is, in that part of the country there were two opposite forces at work; both were traders; the one procured his ivory by fair and honourable means, the other simply got it at any cost whatever to the poor sable son of Africa, and one cannot but suggest that jealousy was at the bottom of that atrocious act, which stirred up so much indignation in England and elsewhere.

It is well known that the Belgian officer on the Congo is simply a commission agent, who, for every pound of ivory and every pound of rubber, gets a percentage, and there are many unscrupulous fellows who are sent out as officers of the State who will not let anything stand in their way of procuring these things. Hence, if an honest trader comes upon the scene, the natives gladly bring to him their ivory, &c., knowing that they will get a fair equivalent for it, and thus jealousy is caused.

On the island of Ukerewe are great numbers of snakes. While there I saw several, and one very large one was killed a few weeks before which took four men to carry. It was a large boa constrictor, and, although its bite is not poisonous, its strength is so great as to crush the life out of the strongest.

We had one rather narrow escape after we left Ukerewe. The water was a little rough, and a strong wind was blowing. Our boatmen begged us not to proceed that day, but we insisted upon doing so. We had to cross a large expanse of water to get again to the mainland, and when about half way a regular hurricane came on. The boatmen lost heart and threw down their paddles, and cried, "Oh, we're dead; we're dead!" The water was beginning to rush into the boat, and it seemed as if the tremendous force of the waves dashing against the canoe would soon break it to pieces. It was only by picking up the paddles, and putting them to rather different purposes than those for which they were originally intended, that I was able at last to make the men realise that there was still a chance. After receiving from me a smart whack or two, they seized their own paddles once more and pulled for all they were worth, making for the shore, which was but a few miles distant, although it was only

STORM ON VICTORIA NYANZA.

occasionally that we got a glimpse of it on account of the blinding rain. When at last we got to shore our boat was nearly half full of water.

On the 24th of February we camped on an island called Nswaswa, a most lovely spot. It receives its name from the water lizard, and the whole island seemed alive with these creatures. They are quite harmless, and are much appreciated by the Wasese as a luxurious dainty. The island was absolutely uninhabited, and only about a mile in diameter, but is one of the prettiest of them all.

From Nswaswa we had four days' row to the German station on the west of the lake, called Bukoba. The houses of the Europeans were by far the most substantial and the best built of any that we had seen in Africa. All were built of bricks and were very lofty, well-ventilated places. They were enclosed by a high brick wall with loopholes and windows, at the four corners of which were bastions for seven pounders and Maxims, making it an almost impregnable position. We were kindly received by the officer in charge, Lieut. R——, and by Dr. M——, the medical officer of the station. The soldiers employed were drawn from many nationalities—Soudanese, Manyema, Wasukuma, Wanyamwezi, and a few Swahili. They were a fine set of men, well drilled and nicely equipped with brown kaki uniforms and leather accoutrements.

The officer in charge asked us to put up in one of the houses in the fort, but as we wished to start early in the morning we declined to do so. However, we dined with the officers, and a right jovial meal we had together. Before dinner Lieut. R—— gave us an exhibition of pistol shooting which impressed us very much. At forty yards he hit a 6-in. bull three times out of four, and repeated the feat several times. He also showed us his various trophies of the chase, including a fine collection of rhinoceros' and antelopes' horns. There were also some parrots, a chained eagle, and a few species of wild fowl in the fort. And of course the inevitable monkey and the scavenger dog.

Very early the following morning we were all aroused by a terrific gale. Our tents were pitched by the lake shore and the pegs were driven into the sand, and when the stormy winds began to blow with all their fury our tents swayed about in such a manner as to make us expect to be blown away. I jumped out of bed and clung to my tent-pole, with all the strength I could command; peg after peg gave way, and disaster seemed inevitable. I never experienced anything like the violence of this storm. My companion's tent could not withstand it, and down it came, exposing the poor sleepy occupant to the rain and wind.

VIEW ON SESE ISLANDS.

The boys very readily helped to hold up my tent and re-build Blackledge's. After about half an hour the storm abated. Never shall I forget that day: thunder and lightning such as I had never before thought possible; wind and rain such as one had never dreamed of.

March 2nd brought us to the first of the Sese Islands, and we then found how thoroughly kind-hearted the Wasese are. They brought us all sorts of presents, and did not even wait to receive anything in return. One man, chief of a small island, gave me a large goat and a great quantity of food. I asked him how it was he could afford such a big present. He simply said: "You are one of the great white masters and you will need the food." To all strangers it is the same with the Wasese; they are not wealthy and only exist by their fishing, but for all that they are most kind and hospitable to visitors.

On one of the Sese Islands I had rather a startling

WASESE FISHERMEN.

adventure. I was walking by the shore gathering some very pretty flowers, when my eye was arrested by some movement in one of the bushes about fifty yards from the water. I went up to the bush and peeped in, thinking it might be a water lizard or some kind of bird. I pressed forward right into the bush, when suddenly there rushed out upon me a huge crocodile with mouth wide open. I jumped on one side only just in time, and then it made off down to the water. These horrible reptiles do constant damage amongst the inhabitants of the island; at one place I visited a man was taken from the bank and never heard of or seen again, and the next day a cow also was dragged down into the water by a crocodile and lost.

On March 6th we arrived at Ntebe, which was then the headquarters of the military forces of Uganda; from this place to Mengo is twenty-three miles by road, and would take about two days by boat. We made up our minds to proceed by boat, starting at about 12.30, midnight, to arrive in Mengo the next day at noon. We got up

DEAD HIPPOPOTAMUS.

and had breakfast, pulled our tents down and packed up, and then began to hunt up the boatmen. To our astonishment we found they had disappeared. We searched about in the cold, looking everywhere, and were beginning to give up all hope of starting before dawn when my head boatman came to me and, in a most miserable tone, told me we should all die in the night. I laughed at him and ordered him to fetch the men, and then bundled into the boat. It was then an hour before dawn, and was very dark and a sky like ink, and on the horizon before us was a cloud which told of a severe storm coming up. We had not gone far when it burst in all its fury upon us. The boat in which I was had been very shaky during the voyage and so we immediately put into a small uninhabited island. I jumped out on to land, having a lantern with me, and discovered a little cave where we could shelter from the rain. I crept in and was about to sit down upon what appeared to me to be a large boulder, when I saw the boulder move, and up jumped a hippopotamus. It nearly knocked me over in its headlong flight to the water, into which it disappeared.

The storm passed over and we passed on, and by twelve o'clock noon we were at Munyonyo, the port for Mengo.

PART II

UGANDA. THE SOUDANESE WAR

CHAPTER VI

UGANDA

Our entrance into Mengo—The four hills of Mengo—Kampala—The British Government of Uganda—Troubles from without—Missionary occupations—Native customs—The Waganda—Woman's position—Missionary efforts—Loyalty of the native Christians—Medical work—The chief dresser—Native industries—Iron-working—Wood-working—Pottery—Basket work—The bark cloth—The native market—Efforts to catch zebra.

MENGO, the capital of Uganda is about seven miles from the lake shore, and this would have been rather a stiff walk for one who had so lately recovered from fever and pleurisy. Fortunately our requirements had been anticipated, and a pony, belonging to the notorious king Mwanga, was brought to me with his permission. I was delighted to have this assistance into Mengo. As we approached the capital we were much impressed by its imposing position and by the good style of the native houses. Those we had seen on our journey up-country had been of such a very inferior type, but these were fine lofty dwellings, with beautiful fences built all round them, enclosing the gardens. They were constructed with the reeds from the tiger grass which grows in great abundance in the country, and thatched with the coarse spear grass called "senki." The roads were wide and well kept, with a fence on either side.

The capital is built upon four distinct hills, called respectively Mengo, Rubaga, Namirembe, and Kampala. Mengo being the hill upon which the king's house is built, the capital takes its name from that. Rubaga is the hill on which stands the Roman Catholic

MENGO.

Mission; Namirembe, the Protestant Mission; and Kampala, the Government fort.

The king's house, or perhaps we should say palace, is a large two-storied building, made entirely of reeds, and thatched with grass. At the back are the houses of his wives, and in a separate enclosure those of his pages and other dependants.

The whole crest of the hill is surrounded by a huge reed fence, some 15 feet high, forming a complete circle. This fence is perhaps two and a half miles in length, and it contains various entrances to the king's enclosure, or

Lubiri as it is called, each one being guarded by a couple of men who act as sentries, and whose little huts are built just outside the large fence.

Rubaga used to be the hill occupied by the King of Uganda, but when he left, and built on Mengo hill, the French Roman Catholic priests took up their abode there, and they have erected a very beautiful station; a high brick wall or fort, surrounds the whole.

On Namirembe, which is the highest of the four hills, the Church Missionary Society in Uganda has its head-

INTERIOR OF MENGO CATHEDRAL.

quarters, consisting of a large imposing church or cathedral built on the summit, and a number of reed houses scattered about the hill, which are occupied by the missionaries.

The Cathedral from the outside has the appearance of a large barn, and inside that of a pine forest, there being about three hundred poles supporting the roof. It is by no means an elaborate building, but answers its purpose, providing room for about three thousand five hundred people, and the natives of Uganda are not slow in availing themselves of the privilege of attending the services, the building is generally quite full on Sunday mornings, and during the week a good average attendance is maintained.

Around the Cathedral are built several smaller churches or schools, each one large enough to hold five hundred people, and in these the classes are held. In 1894 the large church was blown down during a great storm that swept over the country; but a new one was at once started, and ultimately completed by the Katikiro, or prime minister of the country, he being a native of

MISSIONARIES' HOUSE, NAMIREMBE.

the finest type and a man of great power as a statesman or chief, and above all as a *Christian*.

The missionaries' houses, although plain and unostentatious, are nevertheless comfortable; each man has his own house and small garden. A large two-storied house was in the course of construction upon our arrival, and when we inquired its purpose we were told it was for a party of English ladies who were expected to arrive towards the end of the year, and indeed they did so on October 4th, a noble band of women, who ever since have been working most devotedly amongst their dark sisters.

Kampala hill is the smallest of the four, but for all that is of the greatest importance, and at the top is the fort which has now become almost historic. At the time of our arrival there was no fort at all, nothing but a rough stockade enclosing the houses of the Commissioner and the officers in charge.

INTERIOR OF MISSIONARIES' HOUSE.

On the eastern slopes of the hill were the Soudanese quarters; on the north, the encampments of the traders, &c.; and on the west was the large drill ground, where each morning would be seen about three hundred stalwart Soudanese soldiers, performing their drill.

Kampala is the busiest of all places in Mengo—caravans coming and going every day; a labour bureau in full working order, where hundreds of natives flock to seek employment. Here one also sees the Swahili and Arab traders bartering their goods for the ivory brought in by the Waganda, and all is bustle and stir. Just inside the stockade was a large house called the Baraza; there every week the king with his parliament met the British Commissioner to talk over and arrange the affairs of the state.

The British Government of Uganda is undoubtedly on the right lines; it is distinctly a civil government, and the "powers that be" already in the country are not ignored, but controlled and used. The consequence is

KAMPALA.

that each chief has become a man of much more importance since the occupation by the British than he ever was before. He is respected by the British officers, and trusted to do his duty, and until he proves himself incapable of controlling the district allotted to him by the king he retains his chieftainship.

The native government of Uganda forms an excellent base upon which the British can work. The king is controlled by twelve big chiefs, called Masaza, and he can do nothing without their agreement. Therefore the

Government, working in conjunction with this assembly of chiefs, by tact and good management can rule the whole country, and it is well to bear in mind that the troubles which have disturbed Uganda of late years have been brought about largely by outsiders, for the big chiefs, or Masaza, have nearly all remained loyal to the Government.

In the case of the rebellion caused by the flight of Mwanga, the fault no doubt was with the Soudanese, who

THE FORT, KAMPALA.

revolted shortly afterwards and joined forces with him, for although the news of the Soudanese war came suddenly and unexpectedly to the ears of the Foreign Office; there was no doubt whatever that it was brewing for months before the actual outbreak, and many signs were given of its coming; but more of this later on.

Soon after our arrival in Uganda we were sent off to various districts where our missionary work was to be done; and although it is not my purpose in this record to give many details of missionary work, still a short sketch

IN DWARF LAND.

of a missionary's life in Uganda would be of general interest.

Let me commence by saying that his occupations are varied, and by no means is his life that of a Sunday-school teacher every day of the week. He *is* a teacher, but he must also be a builder, for houses, cattle-pens, stores, and outhouses have to be constructed by the

MWANGA AND HIS PARLIAMENT.

missionary. He must also be a doctor of medicine and a dentist; he must dose the sick natives, who will trust him implicitly to cure them of even leprosy, and he must be able to draw the most solidly rooted molar that ever grew in the skull of a black man. More than this, he must be his own cobbler, and when his boots wear out he must be able to re-sole them with good understandings, and must be content sometimes with nothing but a few

French nails and a piece of cowhide with which to accomplish it. His own socks he must darn, and keep his temper while he does it, or his fingers will come off second best; and it must be done well too, or else he will go for weeks with a blister on his toe. Better for him, if he cannot darn, to cut the foot off the stocking and put his bare foot into the boot. He must be his own carpenter and house decorator, as well as furniture maker; chairs and tables constructed out of old chop boxes are not the easiest things to make with no other tools than a small

HIS OWN COBBLER.

hand-saw and a chisel. But he must also be his own lawyer, accountant, and book-keeper, and when the currency takes the form of cowrie shells, as it does in Uganda (where three hundred tiny cowries make a shilling), it is not easy to keep the accounts right. He must marry and divorce, give judgments and baptize. He must be gardener, cook, and dairymaid, grow his own food, and look after his live stock. In addition to all this he is the parish minister, to help and comfort all who come to him.

During the first few months in the country, when the language is quite unknown, curious mistakes occur, as a result of his ignorance of the customs of the people.

Soon after my arrival a most embarrassing incident happened. A young damsel of very handsome appearance came one day to visit me at my house, bringing a basket of fruit, asking my acceptance. Of course I thanked her as best I could and accepted the gift. The following day she came again bringing another present, and again I gladly received it. But when this went on day after day for nearly a fortnight I began to think that something was wrong. I therefore sent for one of my boys, who explained to me the meaning of these constant visits. It appears that this is one of the native customs. Any young woman seeking a husband, and finding a young man to whom she feels drawn, immediately brings him a present, and if he receives it she is encouraged to renew the gift; each acceptance makes it more certain that she has found favour in the sight of the young man, and at the end of a certain time he is expected to propose to her; and she becomes his wife. Imagine my feelings when I heard the story and thought of the many undeniable proofs I had unconsciously given her that she was an accepted suitor. With great embarrassment, therefore, I had to tell her that my ignorance had caused me to do what otherwise I should not have done, and finished up by telling her that a white man could not possibly marry a black woman. Alas! she did not seem to see the reason why it should be so, and I fear went away with a heavy heart.

The people of Uganda, or the Waganda, as they are called, are really a fine race. Surrounded as they are by naked savages it is a great wonder that they have not degenerated and become like them. Instead of this the ordinary Uganda man is as much above the savage as the

Englishman is above the Arab. There is that in his nature that desires improvement, and anything that really appeals to him as a benefit he will do all he can to possess. Good roads, for instance, strike him as being a decided advantage for the traveller, and the chiefs of the country, therefore, are most anxious that these should be made, and in many parts there are splendid roads, swamps and rivers bridged, and forests cleared. However, the disturbed state of the country during the last three years has greatly hindered this work, and the paths that once were six feet wide and well cleared of vegetation are now overgrown again.

The Waganda are not a tall race, but thoroughly well-built and muscular, and as a fighting force, if properly trained, would undoubtedly compare very favourably with any other native regiment. They are brave as lions, and will rush up to the cannon's mouth without the least sign of fear. But, like all other untrained soldiers, when severely beaten they are soon demoralised, and a heavy loss will dishearten them. The Waganda are certainly very sly and capable of great craftiness, and if they can deceive a European they consider it a very smart thing indeed: but among themselves I believe, generally speaking, they are truthful, and a lie is looked upon by them as a shameful thing, excepting when a European is concerned. One can understand this to a certain extent with an uncivilised race, and the Waganda have not always been treated with the utmost candour by Europeans, and, indeed, frequently have been deceived. This being the case, there is little wonder that they should copy the white man's vices and forget his virtues.

In his own home the native of Uganda shows to his best advantage, and it is there perhaps that a man's character is more clearly understood. He loves his children and enjoys family life, but he is a decided autocrat, and all must be subservient to the master of the house. Generally speaking he does not treat his wife unkindly, and I have known many a man and wife in Uganda as truly united by love as man and wife should be, but his dependants are treated with the utmost severity, and as a rule the female section of the household slaves, has rather a miserable time of it. With the spread of Christianity through the country woman is undoubtedly being raised to a better position. A few years ago it was a thing unknown for a woman to partake of food with her husband, but now in thousands of families this is done. Then, women were bought and sold for a few sheep or goats or a few thousand shells, now, this is no longer the case.

A Christian government has, little by little, introduced laws based upon the Ten Commandments, and now even wife beating is illegal, and a woman thus treated can enter an action against her husband. A slave need no longer remain as such, his freedom is secured to him if he desires it.

But what of the missionary's efforts? It is not for him to interfere with State affairs; it is not for him to attempt to hold any political influence, he is to mould the native character, to instil into the untutored mind the great principles of Christianity. By any and every means at his command the missionary's clear duty is to help the individual, and whether this may be done by reading-classes, by industrial mission work, hospital work, visiting the homes of the natives, preaching in the by-ways or in the great cathedral, it is his duty to see that in every way possible he is fulfilling this mission. This, I feel confident in affirming, has been the sincere desire of the C.M.S. missionaries in Uganda, and to the most disinterested it is plain enough that a great work has been done. I know there are some who will visit a place like Uganda and spend a year or two there, and will come home and declare that missionary work is either a failure, or that it has been greatly exaggerated. Let the loyalty of the Christian Waganda during the late rebellion silence for ever such statements as these. It was during the rebellion that I think the eyes of all were opened to see that the *Christian* native was then the one to be relied upon. Mohammedans and heathen alike joined with the rebels,

THE HOSPITAL, NAMIREMBE.

and it was the Christians who showed their loyalty in standing by the Government from the first to the last day of the campaign. And this at no little discouragement to themselves. Among the killed and wounded were their best, the flower of their nation; the quarrel was not their own, nor anything to do with them, it was the white man's quarrel, but for all this they did their best throughout.

Before leaving Uganda for Toro, which is a large country to the far west of Uganda, I had an opportunity of seeing some of the splendid medical work that was being carried on in Mengo. If there be one side of missionary work that must appeal to all men—no matter what their opinions are with reference to other methods of missionary effort—it is the medical work. As I have already stated, it is a practical Christianity which appeals to the black man, and it is only this kind of Christianity that is worth anything at all. Indeed there is no other.

DR. ALBERT COOK AND STAFF.

To watch the crowds of suffering humanity, gathered together every morning in the waiting-room of the Mengo hospital, and to see how one by one they are carefully and skilfully attended to, their wounds dressed with the best appliances, their disorders treated with European drugs, and to hear their grateful words of thanks as they pass on their way, speaks to one in a way that is difficult to express. There was a time when the missionaries in Mengo, or at any rate as many of them as were able, had to attend each morning to the sick folk that came to them. Many a time have I watched good Archdeacon Walker sitting in the verandah of his house, dispensing medicines to the poor sufferers as they came to him for aid. But the time arrived when a noble young doctor, with all the highest prospects of success before him in England, chose rather to go where he felt he was most needed, and where he might do the most good. And so it came about that early in the year 1897 Dr. Albert Cook arrived in Mengo.

A little hospital was then built to accommodate about twenty in-patients, and a dispensary close at hand for the use of the out-patients. Some thousands of cases have now been treated, and quite a revolution has taken place in Mengo. It has been found that the lame can be made to walk, that the blind have their sight restored, and that those who for years have never left their beds may now be healed.

Every one who can, pays a few shells for the medicine or treatment that he or she receives, but the poor are attended to without payment. In the wards may be seen Roman Catholics, Mohammedans, heathen, and Protestants, all side by side, each one receiving from a common source the help they need, and all alike are taught to recognise the one Great Physician—Christ—as the only Healer of the ills of the soul. Morning and evening prayers are held in each ward, and bright services on the Sunday, and these meet with the most hearty appreciation of all classes alike.

Dr. Cook has been most ably assisted in this work of love by Nurse Timpson, who for some time held a position of very great trust and distinction in one of the large London hospitals. The women's ward is her chief delight, and her presence there is without doubt the greatest pleasure to the patients. Her kind and cheering word, her sweet smile and loving actions call forth the wonder and deep admiration of all the poor dark souls in that hospital. Not only are the small ailments undertaken, but the most difficult operations are performed by Dr. Cook, and often I have stood by and watched the most critical cases attended to in the operating-room, and great has been the success of these efforts, not only from a doctor's point of view, but eminently from a missionary's standpoint. Dr. Cook's chief dresser is a Uganda boy, who, suffering from an internal abscess, first visited the hospital soon after it was opened and asked for medicine; he was most skilfully treated and recovered. He then offered his services to the doctor to do anything he could to help in the efforts put forward to relieve the sufferings of his own people, and without receiving any set wage, in fact nothing at all but his food and clothing. This young fellow has ever since stood by the doctor in all his work, and by his self-denying, self-sacrificing devotion has not only been able to render very valuable assistance as a dresser, but he has constantly proved that the Waganda are not without the capacity of reciprocating love and manifesting their appreciation of kindness shown to them. But space forbids my enlarging upon this and other missionary efforts that are being put forth in Uganda for the enlightenment of the natives.

In speaking of the Waganda there is one subject that one must not omit to mention, viz., their industries. Although naturally lazy, like all Africans, they have their different occupations, and manufacture various things for general use. Their chief industry perhaps is iron-working. The iron is dug from the earth, smelted by the natives, and then used for making knives, spears, axes, and spades, which are the implements of first importance; but articles of far greater intricacy are also made by the native smith. I have seen a complete Snider rifle made by a Uganda blacksmith, and although it was not sufficiently well made to admit of a strong charge of gunpowder, or a regulation Snider cartridge; still the gun was perfect in every other particular.

When one considers the roughness of the tools used by the native workmen, it is a matter of great surprise that they are able to turn out such really good work. A stone is the anvil universally used; a lump of iron with a flat surface on one side constitutes the hammer, which has no shaft. These, with a few rudely made iron sets, are all the tools he has to work with. The forge is of very primitive construction, but does its work exceedingly well. Two large earthenware basins with tubes, leading from the bottom to a common nozzle, and over the top of each of these basins is loosely stretched a prepared goat-skin, and into each goat-skin is fastened a hollow reed, and these reeds are worked up and down; when raised the hole through the reed is left free, but when forced down it is covered with the thumb, and thus drives the air through the earthenware nozzle. The two reeds being worked alternately, a constant blast is kept up. Charcoal is used for the fire, and a very good heat can be procured and sustained by this simple but efficient method.

Wood-working is also quite a native industry in Uganda, and remarkably well performed. The native stool in itself is a good specimen of their work, carved out of the solid trunk of a tree with all kinds of ornamental work. Some are round, others square, but all are very low, and there seems very little desire on the part of the natives to perch themselves on high chairs. The native bedstead is also thoroughly well made, and consists of a wooden framework with carved legs of various designs and a cowhide spring mattress; they are most comfortable and very strong. But the masterpiece of wood-working is found in the planks which are cut out by hand. Sometimes these are 20 feet in length, and 3 feet or 4 feet broad. They are cut from the solid trunk of some forest giant, and take months to finish.

Pottery also, among the Waganda, is quite a fine art. Very near to Mengo there is a whole village of pottery workers; large cooking-pots and water-pitchers, basins and cups of all shapes are made. No wheel is used, and the only tool is the hand. They are very clever in copying European things, such as cups and saucers, teapots, &c; all are cleverly moulded. The pottery is burnt after it is moulded to shape—huge fires of wood are made, a quantity of fine dried grass being mixed with it, and into the hot ash the pots are placed for an hour or two. Smoking, being almost universal in Uganda, pipes are therefore made by the potter; a finer kind of clay is used, and they are coloured black, with a glazed shiny surface. Some of the pipes are very curious; I have seen them made in the shape of the English brier, and others made to represent a gun. The common Uganda pipe consists of a very large bowl, holding about half an ounce of tobacco, but this amount is seldom put into it, as room must be left for the burning ash at the top.

Basket and mat-making are both industries practised by the people of Uganda, and some very beautiful work is produced, especially in the basket line; so closely are these plaited that some are almost watertight, and indeed are used in which to brew the native beer, which is made from the banana and called "mwenge."

Bark-cloth making is also quite an art; a species of fig-tree produces a particular kind of bark suitable for the purpose. A grooved mallet is made of wood, and the bark being cut into strips is beaten out gradually upon a wooden block. The bark thus treated spreads out, and from a strip of bark a foot in width a piece of cloth will be made, at least three times the width of the original. This cloth is worn by most of the poorer classes, and by all the women, whatever rank they hold. When finished it is dark terra-cotta colour, and very durable.

The women wear the bark cloth loosely thrown round the body, secured at the waist by a band of some other cloth and held in position by the arms, the shoulders being left bare. The men, however, merely tie together the two opposite corners of the cloth, which is thrown over the shoulders, the knot being worn on either the right or left side, the cloth falling carelessly round the figure.

There is a very large native market in the capital, and the people flock to this with their wares, and a great deal of business is transacted; meat and other foods, such as bananas, maize, sweet potatoes, and yams, can be bought or sold here as well as the manufactured articles of the country. Cloth is also on sale in the market, and is brought into the country chiefly by Swahili traders, and is worn by the better-class men in place of the bark cloth.

In Uganda the women do all the cultivating and the cooking, and the men do the sewing that is necessary and the housebuilding. It has been said that one woman in Uganda, by her cultivating, can easily supply food enough to support nine men, and therefore when a man possesses five or six wives it will be seen that the woman's work is not excessively laborious. She goes into the garden at daybreak, remaining there till about 11 a.m. Again in the afternoon from about three to five. The rest of the day she has to herself, for looking after the children or visiting her neighbours.

The chiefs all possess cattle, and the poorer classes have instead, sheep and goats and fowls. The little boys attend to the former and the little girls to the latter.

IN DWARF LAND.

After I had settled down in the country some little time I conceived the idea of capturing a number of zebra to train for transport work; so utterly disgusted had I been during my journey up-country from the coast with the horrible practice of human porterage, that I was prepared to do what I possibly could to substitute for it some other method, at any rate so far as I personally was concerned. I first offered a big price in cloth to any chief or common man who would catch for me a young zebra. To the north-west of Mengo there are great quantities of these animals roaming about, and the wonder to me was that they had never been utilised for this purpose. Whether the chiefs doubted the sincerity of my offer or not I cannot say, but certain it is no effort was made to trap the zebra. I next visited a place not far from the station where I was living, where I knew there was a large herd of zebra. Arriving there in the evening, I called together about twenty men, and got them to promise to help me the following morning in my enterprise.

As soon as day broke I hurriedly dressed, took up my gun and a long coil of rope, called the men together and set off to the plain. We had not started more than an hour when we came upon the herd. It consisted of close upon thirty full-grown animals, with three or four young foals. My first idea was to shoot the mare and then proceed to catch the little one, which I felt sure would not run from its mother's side. We were soon able to decide upon one with a little foal of about three or four months old, and very carefully we crept up in the grass until we were within easy range. I then fired, the mare dropped, and away went the herd, and to our disappointment away went the little one too, leaving its mother dead upon the plain. The meat, however, was not wasted, and right glad were we to partake of zebra steak. It was impossible to get up to the herd again that day, and so we went back to the village and waited, and the next day we tried different tactics.

I collected about one hundred men to go with me, and when we came to the zebra I sent them in single file right round the whole herd, so as to shut them in on every side and then at a given signal to advance slowly, allow the full-grown animals to escape, and catch the young one whose mother we had killed the day before. All went well until we had got the ring round the herd complete, and then a great disturbance took place: a large male zebra, evidently the most important of the herd, came rushing towards me, and the men who were near, with wide-open mouth. All the men fled for their lives, or dodged behind trees and bushes, to get out of the way of the infuriated animal. I had no idea that a zebra would thus attack a man when hardly pressed, but the natives assured me that it was quite a common occurrence, especially with a wounded zebra. Of course the result of this mad rush was that the whole herd again got away.

I next decided to make a huge drive, formed of stakes driven into the earth, culminating in a strong stockade, then to chase the herd into this drive, and finally pick out those required and allow the rest to escape. But as I had already spent two days without any result I thought I would return to my station for a week or so and then renew my efforts. In the meantime I offered an even greater present to the man who would bring me a live zebra, and this time, having seen my earnestness to catch one myself, the natives believed that I really meant what I said. About four days after my return to the station a great company of men set off by themselves to try and catch a zebra for me. They adopted the tactics we had used on the second occasion, that of surrounding the herd and closing in upon it. They were successful, and one fine strong fellow captured a young zebra about four months old, and in spite of all its kicking and biting managed to fasten a rope to one of its legs. They were so highly delighted with their success that they gave the captured zebra into the hands of one of the young fellows, and the rest set off after the herd to try and secure a second. Alas! for

EFFORTS TO CATCH ZEBRA.

them; the young man left in charge was an untrustworthy fellow, and when the little zebra began to kick and prance about he actually loosened the rope and let it go; and when the men came back in the evening, tired and unsuccessful in their second attempt, they found to their great annoyance that the zebra had been liberated, and they all completely lost heart and returned home.

The man who had caught it, however, came to me asking for the present; and when I said, "Oh, but you have not brought the zebra;" he said, "Yes, but I caught it, and you ought to reward me." I gave him a smaller present to encourage him to try again, but it was hopeless; and the next time I went to carry out my scheme of a "drive" I could not get half a dozen men to accompany me. It was also about this time that I was moved from Uganda and sent on to Toro, so that my efforts to catch zebra have been fruitless up to the present.

CHAPTER VII

UGANDA TO TORO

Experiences gained—Toro Ruwenzori—A lay missionary's work—Valedictory feasts—Obtaining porters—The boys—Mika's conversion—A leopard scare—The Mayanja—Mosquitoes—Mitiana—Crossing the Mpamujugu—Elephant country—Antelope steak—Forest glades—Elan—Sally, a distinguished guest—Unfriendly Papists—I nurse a black baby—Cow stealing—Fishing for breakfast—Mwenge—Byakweyamba—The banquet—An embarrassing welcome to Toro.

MY journey was not continued westward until after I had spent fifteen months in Uganda, carrying on there the work of a missionary. They were months full of pleasurable service, and afforded me ample opportunity of learning the native language of Uganda, and also of studying the native character. One trusts that during that time some good may have resulted from the efforts put forth; at any rate the experience I gained during that period has been invaluable to me ever since.

It would be impossible to give full details of my work during those fifteen months. Upon my arrival in the country I was sent to Gayaza, a large district with about ten thousand inhabitants, about twelve miles from Mengo, where I remained for the first six months; taking classes and services for the people; visiting through the district from house to house; making friends of many by distributing medicines to the sick and suffering; and in every way possible, though very imperfectly, doing what I could to make known to all the gospel of the Lord Jesus. I was afterwards sent to open a new station at Nakanyonyi, some thirty miles to the north-east of Mengo. Here I was able to build a station suitable for the residence of a European, and a church accommodating about a thousand people; visiting also Bulondaganyi, the district lying on the left bank of the Victoria Nile, and many other places, endeavouring to open up the country for the reception of Christianity.

In 1895 Christianity was introduced into Toro by native missionaries of Uganda. Toro is a large district to the extreme west of the Uganda Protectorate, having a separate king, and being in no way allied to Uganda, excepting that it receives the protection of the British Government. It lies between the two lakes, the Albert Edward and the Albert, being bordered by the Mountains of the Moon. Kasagama, the King of Toro, had years ago been driven from his country by Kabarega, the King of Unyoro, but was reinstated by Captain Lugard at the beginning of the year 1894. The king became a Christian, and invited European teachers to his country. Bishop Tucker, accompanied by Mr. A. B. Fisher, made a notable journey in the spring of 1896 to the capital of Toro, and the Bishop thus depicts his first impressions :—

" Ruwenzori is indeed a mighty mass towering into the clouds, which give to much of it a mystery and beauty hard to describe. The people differ considerably from the Waganda, but are not so vigorous and robust. The distinguishing bark cloth is not made in Toro, the dress of the people consists therefore more largely of skins."

When the Bishop returned to Mengo after this journey, he decided to send to Toro another European missionary to join Mr. Fisher, whom he had left there, and I was the one chosen to go. My desire had always been to be in the forefront, and wherever pioneer work was necessary I was anxious to go. This was a very natural desire of mine. From a boy I had loved adventure, and sought it upon every possible occasion, and our exploits as schoolboys in the "bricky pits," as we called them, which will ever live in my memory, were good preparations for an adventurous life in Central Africa.

Not only was there the natural love of adventure, however, but the fact of my being a layman left me more at liberty for opening new stations.

Nothing, therefore, could have been more to my taste than this journey to Toro, for although I did not like leaving so much interesting work in Uganda, and I was sorry to say goodbye to so many good friends that I had made among the Waganda during my stay there, still I did not anticipate any difficulty in finding fresh sources of interest and in forming new friendships among the people of Toro.

The last ten days in Uganda I spent in bidding farewell to my native friends, and I was surprised to find how difficult it really was to bid these warm-hearted people goodbye. Several of them had feasts in my honour, inviting me to attend the festive board, but I could not possibly accept all the pressing invitations given to me, and, after all, a native feast is not particularly attractive. Very strange dishes sometimes make their appearance, and to keep in health it is not wise to indulge too freely in these luxuries. One thing, however, at a native feast one can always be tolerably sure of, and that is the plantains or bananas. Cooked as a vegetable while green they are a most nourishing food, and one of which even the European is seldom tired.

To obtain porters for carrying goods or household furniture (not more than twenty loads of 60 lbs. each), I had to go to the big chief of the country, or Prime

Minister, the Katikiro, and arrange with him. He immediately called five of his under chiefs, and ordered each one to provide six men, and after a great deal of delay some of these porters came, and I decided to start at once, leaving the others to follow on.

At 2 p.m. on June 25th, after a hurried lunch, I started with about fifteen men. A very rough set they seemed to be, and I had my fears about getting to my journey's end without trouble; they were all Waganda, however, and that was in my favour, as I could speak their language fairly well. We only walked for about six miles, and then camped on the side of the road near to a large banana grove. The porters never like a long march for a start, and as I wanted to gain their confidence as soon as possible, I allowed them to camp after having walked for two and a half hours. The greater part of the distance I was accompanied by a large crowd of my native friends who had come to see me on my way, and one boy actually carried with him all the way from Mengo a large calabash of sweet banana wine that I might have something to slake my thirst when I arrived in camp.

It must here be explained that, in addition to the porters who carried my loads, I had with me eight boys who accompanied me, not in the capacity of servants, for they received no wage whatever from me, but as my personal friends. Willingly they undertook any work for me, and two of them became most expert cooks after a little tuition. They came to me soon after I arrived in Uganda, and remained with me till the time I left Africa. I taught them all kinds of arts besides that of cooking. Each boy could read well, most of them could write intelligibly; one became quite an able carpenter, another a builder, another a brickmaker, and one I taught to nurse, and when I have been ill and far away from any other European—as I shall show by and by—this boy watched over me with the tenderest care by night and by day; he was always at my bedside, doing all in his power to restore me, and I believe I owed my life to him upon more than one occasion.

The oldest among them (Mika), although he was always called by me my boy, was a full-grown man in middle life, and was a character worth speaking about.

ON THE ROAD TO TORO.

Very tall, and an exceptionally strongly built man, badly pitted with small-pox, and by no means of prepossessing countenance, and yet with a heart as tender as a child's. My first introduction to this fellow took place in a banana grove soon after I got to Uganda. It was while I was speaking to a large number of natives, when on the outskirts of the crowd I saw a strange fellow standing. He was tall, with very long hair, quite contrary to the ordinary Uganda man, who keeps his hair very short by constantly shaving his head, and he was almost nude. In his hand he held a most deadly-looking weapon, a huge spear, such as I had never seen before, with a blade $2\frac{1}{2}$ feet in length and 5 inches wide in the centre, the shaft was half as thick as one's wrist, and at the end a sharp iron ferrule was attached.

When the people who stood near caught sight of him, they all moved away as if from fear. Full well they knew him; the whole district was conversant with his notorious life, his bloody deeds were spoken of by old and young alike; a wild man who had his abode in the jungle, never visiting the haunts of man except for rapine and murder. By the roadside he was wont to lie in wait for harmless and unsuspecting travellers, spear them, and rob them of all that they had. Time after time attempts had been made to capture him, but so strong and active was he that he had evaded every effort. Long years ago he had been one of King Mwanga's famous wrestlers, and once had been sent by his master to take a letter to the gallant Mackay, who was then at Kagei, at the south of the Victoria Nyanza.

As soon as I had finished speaking he disappeared, and I did not see him again until a fortnight afterwards. I had returned to my station, when one afternoon this fellow came to me, just in exactly the same state as he was when I first saw him in the banana grove, and he still carried his huge spear. I greeted him heartily, and he proceeded to tell me that he wished to learn to read, and to hear more of the " beautiful words," as he described them. I conducted him into the church, where reading classes were going on, and, beckoning a little boy, instructed him to teach my new friend to read. Day after day he came, and diligently sat grinding away at the reading sheet with the little boy by his side. He finally succeeded, and became quite a changed man from that time. His old life was entirely given up: the horrible weapon which he had used for the purpose of murdering his fellow-men he gave to me. It was wonderful to notice the change in this poor fellow. One would almost have supposed it to be impossible for such as he, so deeply sunk in sin and wickedness, to become a true-hearted follower of the Lord Jesus, but nevertheless such was the case, and to-day that man is as true and loyal and earnest in his simple faith as he was when he first decided to give up all his evil practices and become a Christian. Surely this is yet another proof of the glorious truth, " the gospel of Christ *is* the power of God unto salvation to every one that believeth."

It was therefore a great pleasure to me to have such a companion as this in my journey to Toro, and in every possible way he extended to me his valuable assistance. The country was known to him most perfectly; he was familiar with every bypath, and many a short cut he was able to take us.

At our very first camp we had a scare with a leopard. It was just about 5 a.m., and beginning to show signs of morning, when the boys, who were sleeping in a small hut close to my tent, were suddenly and forcibly made aware of the presence of a huge leopard in their hut. It had knocked down the reed door, and was in the act of choosing a victim, when one of my boys awoke, and seeing it dimly in the faint light of dawn shouted aloud, and roused the others. The leopard with a snarl of disappointment bounded from the hut, and just rushed past my tent door as I came out rifle in hand, ready for a shot. Its movements were too quick, and the light was not sufficiently good, so I did not fire, and we heard no more of it. The second day we camped in a village close to the great Mayanja swamp, which is about two hundred yards wide, and usually the water and mud are very deep. The chief of the village, poor old fellow, was unfortunately very drunk, but was very kind, and soon had fifteen baskets of food ready for us, which consisted of plantains all ready cooked, wrapped up in the leaves, and neatly put into baskets. He also gave me a fowl for my own personal requirements.

Quite close to the village was a small wood in which

PAPYRUS SWAMP.

I saw many very beautifully marked monkeys, notably one with long dark chestnut-coloured hair, and long tail tipped with bright red; there were also a great number of squirrels. As evening came on we all suffered for our indiscretion in camping so near to the swamp. Clouds of mosquitoes came and literally besieged us, not the great lanky fellow that is so easy to detect coming, but those dreadful little black pests whose bite seems far more irritating. It was simply terrible, myriads of these little creatures buzzing so loudly that it sounded like a swarm of bees close to one's ears. They attacked my face so unmercifully that in a very short time it was all swollen, my hands also were most viciously set upon by these horrors. We tried by great fires to drive them away, but it was hopeless, and the end of it was that I had to go to bed early, so as to get under my mosquito net. But even here it was not much better, for somehow or other they found their way in, and a rare night I spent of it. In the early morning they seemed worse than ever, no doubt being anxious to get a final meal before being driven away by the rising sun.

A march of four hours brought us to Mitiana, one of the C.M.S. out-stations, where the Rev. H. R. Sugden was in charge. A fine healthy station, built upon the hill, with a magnificent view all round, the Lake Wamala lying to the west.

The next day being Sunday, we rested at the mission station, and enjoyed quiet services at the church.

Close to the lake is a Government station called Fort Raymond—a very small place, and the fort wall is built of stakes driven into the earth, with a mud-bank on the inside; but it is always an inspiration to the Briton in Africa when he sees the old flag waving in the breeze. There was no European in charge there at that time, but a Soudanese officer, and a small squad of men.

Soon after leaving Mitiana on the following day, we arrived at the great swamp, which is really an arm of the lake Wamala, and called by the natives Mpamujugu. My faithful old follower (whom I shall in future call Mika, this being the name he took at his baptism) immediately came to my assistance. This swamp is too wide and too deep to bridge, so has to be crossed by stepping from root to root of the papyrus which floats on the top of the mud and water. Mika carried me on his shoulders the whole way, and it took us more than an hour to cross; he never once slipped his footing, and seemed as fresh at the end of the business as he was at the commencement, in spite of having eleven stone on his shoulders for more than an hour. In all, we crossed no less than seventy-two swamps on the way to Toro, and I did not once wet my boots, for Mika carried me over them all.

We next had a huge district to cross, with no

UGANDA LANDSCAPE.

inhabitants but wild animals, particularly elephants. We saw one track made through the long grass by these colossal beasts no less than thirty yards wide. It was like a great turnpike road, cutting right through the country, and must have been made by some dozens of elephants.

One morning, soon after our start, I killed a fine large antelope, which we immediately cooked, as we were very hungry, having been without meat for some days. Fires were made, and each cut a lump of flesh from the carcase, stuck it on to a stick, and held it over the flames until it was nicely grilled, and we enjoyed it immensely.

About seven days' journey from Mengo the whole character of the country is altered, and becomes much more beautiful. Short, wavy grass covered the earth in place of the ugly reed grass of Uganda. The trees were finer, and the landscapes much more rugged. Frequently we passed through lovely forest glades, with every kind of tropical vegetation growing in profusion. Monkeys of varied hues chattered among the branches,

ROAD-MAKING, UGANDA.

and butterflies of most exquisite tints flitted before us as we walked. Some were so large that we could scarcely believe they were butterflies. Parrots and hornbills screamed overhead, and kingfishers sat silently by the brook sides, and all seemed quite indifferent to our presence. In some of these glades it was difficult to force our way through, on account of the thick undergrowth. On the other hand, we often met small gangs of Waganda workmen, with an under-chief at their head, road-making and clearing. Some of the swamps too had been well bridged, and whenever we came up with these gangs we always praised the workmen for the improvements they had made, and this seemed greatly to cheer them. Just the one word "Webale" (lit. "praise yourself"), spoken heartily as we passed, did not cost us much, and it did a great deal no doubt to encourage the workers.

While strolling along one day at the front of the caravan, I suddenly came up with three huge animals,

ROAD THROUGH UGANDA FOREST.

which I thought at first sight were buffalo, but which proved to be elan. These magnificent animals are dying out very rapidly in Eastern Equatorial Africa. The cattle plague of a few years ago caused great destruction amongst them, and it is quite a rare thing to-day to see an elan, at any rate in Uganda. These, consisted of a very large bull, with a fine pair of horns, and two cows. I did not fire at them, and they soon disappeared in the thicket as we came into view. We next came to a small village inhabited by a few Waganda and Wanyuro. They were extremely kind, giving my porters most gladly plenty of food, and providing me with fowls and potatoes directly I arrived amongst them.

And now my little dog Sally came much into prominence. I have already stated that she was a poodle, and as I had not troubled to shave her, she had very long black curly hair, almost down to the ground. When the natives of this village saw her they took a great fright, and declared that a "little devil" had come with the white man. When I heard that this report had spread amongst them I called the chief, and explained to him that it was a dog from Europe, and then a large crowd came round to see Sally perform. First I made her stand upright, like a soldier, with a stick for a gun, then beg, and next hold a stick in her mouth, being dressed up in a cap and a small coat, then smoke a pipe. This last quite overcame them, and they immediately looked upon Sally as an individual of great distinction, and the women went away to collect presents for the strange visitor. All kinds of food were brought to the fortunate Sally, who seemed most thoroughly to realise her importance. One old woman went so far as to actually greet her in Luganda quite solemnly. When Sally curled herself up and went to sleep she looked just like a black ball, and on more than one occasion natives have asked me "which end barks."

As we marched for about six hours each day, we usually rested at noon in some nice shady spot, where we made a fire and boiled water for tea. Packed away in my luncheon basket was always a cold boiled fowl, placed there by my cook, and this, together with a roast sweet potato cooked in the ashes of the fire, comprised my midday meal. The boys and porters also indulged their appetites in a similar way, sometimes with antelope steak, at others with guinea fowl or partridge, which I had been able to shoot for them during the day.

Half way to Toro we came to Lwekula's country, a very big chief, and an avowed Roman Catholic. His under-chiefs also followed his example, and the whole district was nominally Roman Catholic. Whether or no these people had been taught to ignore and be rude to a Protestant missionary I cannot say, but they certainly received me very badly, speaking most rudely to me.

When I asked them to sell us food they absolutely refused to do so. "We are Bafransa" (followers of the French), they said, "and Père —— is our teacher, and when he comes to us we will cook food for him and give him all he needs, but we shall not give or sell you anything." I said, "Very well, we will simply sleep here to-night, eat what little food we have with us, and go on to-morrow." I then asked for a house in which I might spend the night, and they took me to a deserted hut just outside the village, with broken roof, and dirty in the extreme. I will not speak of its inhabitants of the insect tribe, but I only say that I was obliged to sit with my legs on the top of a tin box so as to touch the floor as little as possible.

When I had got the hut into a little better condition, with boxes stacked together in the middle, and my bed made, I went off to visit some of the people. I soon found that I could get on much better with individuals than with crowds. In one house which I visited I saw a little baby boy playing with a kind of rattle made from a hollow gourd with small dried beans inside. I immediately took the little fellow in my arms, and began chatting and playing with him, and it was astonishing what a wonderful effect this had upon the mother, who was heard to exclaim to another woman, "Well, did you ever see such grace as this, a white man nursing a black baby!" I then spoke to the mother and the other people who were in the hut, and they became quite friendly. Presently the woman of the house said to me, "Would you like me to cook you some food?" I thanked her, and she promised to do so, telling me to send my boy round in an hour's time. In this way I earned my dinner, and the dinner of my men also, for after visiting a few more houses and making friends with the people, several large baskets of cooked food were brought to me. The chief finally altered his attitude towards me, and in the early dawn came at the head of quite a little army of boys and girls all carrying baskets of food for the European. As a reward I gave him a little cloth and a New Testament, with both of which he was delighted, especially with the Testament, as he could read, and was very keen to be the proud possessor of a book.

On the tenth morning a little excitement was occasioned among us by discovering that the cows, which I had brought with me from Uganda, had disappeared. I had engaged two men, natives of Ankole, who were recommended to me as being thoroughly trustworthy, but with whom I could not hold much conversation, on account of their dialect, to look after the cows; I soon found out that these fellows had proved false, and had made off with my cows towards their own country, which was only one day's journey away. We at once commenced a search, and after about two hours we found footprints leading in quite a different direction from the one we were taking. My big man, Mika, said not a word, but threw off his bark-cloth, seized a stick, and started off at a full swinging run along the narrow track caused by the passing of the cattle. Two or three of the other boys followed him, but he completely out-distanced them. I stood on a high hill watching him, and for fully three miles Mika kept up the fastest trot I have ever seen, never once stopping to take breath. At last, in the distance, I could just see a tiny speck jogging up and down, and then he disappeared altogether. I was just about to camp for the night, when I heard the bellowing of cows a long way off, and I knew that my faithful friend had got back my lost property. The two cowmen Mika had in safe custody, and when I examined them the only thing they could say was, that they did not intend stealing them, but had taken them to water. I pointed out how absurd it was to talk of taking them for water all that way, when there was plenty of water at hand. It ended by my cutting their pay, and sending them off about their business, and they were glad enough to get off so easily.

We now entered Unyuro, and had several days' journey through this country before we reached the capital of Toro. There were very few villages indeed, and for two days our men were unable to buy food. The second day we should have fared badly had we not again had good fortune. We came to a small pond, and while sitting down there to rest, two wild ducks began to circle round overhead, and these I was able to bring down with my gun. After a little while the porters one by one went into the water, and began catching fish—a large swamp fish very much like that which is called by schoolboys a "miller's thumb," only three times the size. To catch these the porters in a surprisingly short space of time made small nets from the plaited grass, and I was astonished beyond measure to see the great quantity they caught; each man must have possessed himself of at least 2 lbs. weight of this fish. After the catching came the cooking and eating, and we were obliged to pitch our camp quite near to this pond that had so wonderfully befriended us in our need.

On July 10th, we reached the first town of Toro, Mwenge. We had been walking for about two hours that day, when two young men came running to me, and said that the prince had sent them to see me; being a relation of the king's, the chief was called a prince. In a few moments they said, "We are going back," so I told them to see the prince for me, and away they went. They had no sooner gone than two more came running up and saying the same words, and then returned; others came, doing the same thing, and soon there was a steady stream of people running backwards and forwards between the prince and myself; the last few miles quite blocking the road. This is a real old-fashioned custom of the Waganda, when a chief is desirous of giving a visitor a hearty welcome; the more people sent the greater is the estimated joy of the sender. As I afterwards found, this prince had lived some years as a boy in Uganda, and had thus learned this custom from the Waganda.

At last I saw him standing on the top of a hill awaiting me in great state—a tall, fine-looking man, with clean-cut features, dressed in a spotlessly white robe, beautifully worked in Indian fashion, with a large white turban on his head, and surrounded by his attendants. As he greeted me he removed the turban, and made a most graceful bow, and then stepped forward with outstretched hands. I did the same, and we embraced each other very affectionately.

Byakweyamba was his name, a prince of the house of Toro. In his younger days he had been wounded in a battle, and was consequently lame, but a more aristocratic and gentlemanly fellow I never met; he was one of Nature's gentlemen. Somehow or other he had heard of my approach, and had prepared a great feast in my honour. Eight or ten large basketsful of boiled plantains were first distributed amongst the porters and boys, together with two basketsful of cooked meat, for he had killed an ox on purpose. Then three large baskets were brought into the chief's private room, and put on the floor before me, and every one began to leave. I immediately asked the chief and his head boys to remain and eat with me, and to this with some reluctance they agreed. Clean leaves were then strewn about the floor in the centre of the room, and on to these was cast a bright yellow mass of steaming hot plantains; then several small

HEARTY RECEPTION, TORO.

earthenware vessels were given to me, each one containing some kind of vegetable prepared with butter and salt: one like mushrooms, another a kind of vegetable marrow, and yet another much like spinach. The second basket contained meat beautifully cooked; this was divided amongst the guests, and a special pot was brought to me of curried meat. The third basket was full of boiled sweet potatoes. Everything was spotlessly clean, and we had no compunction whatever about falling to, for the state of my appetite forbade much reticence. The prince was delighted with the way I appreciated the food, and offered to make another feast in the evening if I wished. I thanked him, but begged to be excused; once a day is quite sufficient for any man.

Only one more day's journey now before we reached the capital of Toro, but as it was twenty-three miles we left Mwenge very early in the morning. Byakweyamba bade me an affectionate farewell, begging me to come again and see him before long, and this I promised to do.

Monday, July 13th, we reached Kabarole, the capital of Toro. We had a right royal reception, not to say a most embarrassing one. Hundreds of people flocked to meet me, and long before I got within sight of the capital a number of the king's soldiers came running towards me, and the young chief who was in command when he reached me, knelt down and said, "The king has sent me to see you," and when I asked after the health of his Majesty and of all the people he said, "Great joy is going to kill us all." One messenger brought a letter to me; I must give the literal translation :

"To Mr. Lloyd. How do you do, my dear friend? I love you very much indeed. I greet you with great joy. God be praised! He has brought you here . . . and this letter is of very great joy, my friend Goodbye, sir; God be with you.—I am Victoria the Queen Mother."

Then came other letters of similar greeting from chiefs, &c., and no prince could have had a more lordly welcome. As I climbed the hill leading to the king's enclosure all the ladies came to meet me; they were beautifully dressed in many-coloured garments, and the king's wife was in the midst of the crowd.

The road was cleared, the runners standing on either side, and then at a signal from the queen all the ladies walked in great state to meet me. But their excitement seemed to get the better of them, for after a few steps they ran at full speed, and the queen literally threw herself into my arms according to the native custom. They all clung to me, greeting me most warmly, and then turned and escorted me towards the King's Hill. Presently a cry arose, "The king is coming!" and in a moment all fell back, leaving me standing alone in the middle of the road, and I saw at a little distance the king, the queen mother, and my future colleague, Mr. A. B. Fisher, waiting to receive me. All round was the king's bodyguard, Watoro warriors armed with guns, and looking very smart in their white tunics and dark blue putties. Kasagama came forward to meet me, clasping me in his arms and hugging me several times; Fisher and I exchanged greetings and then turned towards the temporary house built for my occupation, the huge crowd of now some hundreds following us to the door, and then, amid great shouting and rejoicing, dispersed.

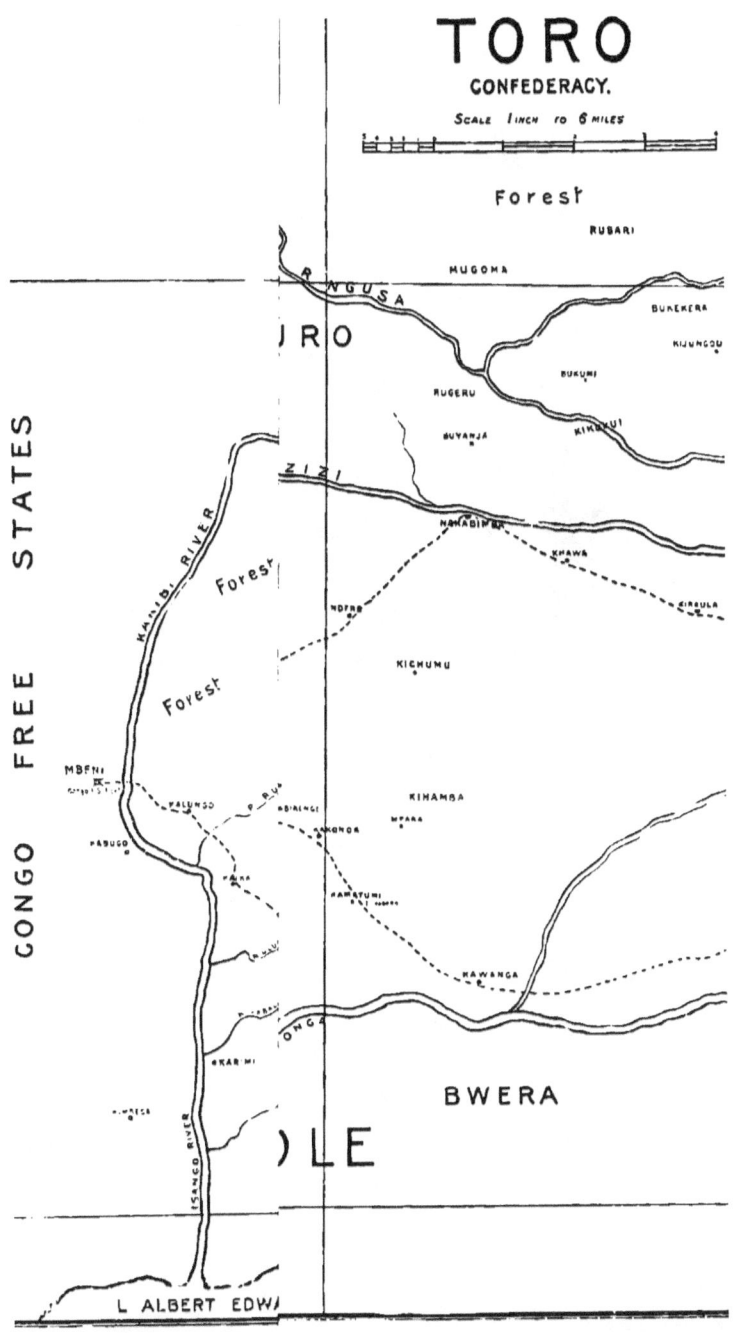

Insert between pages 158 and 159.

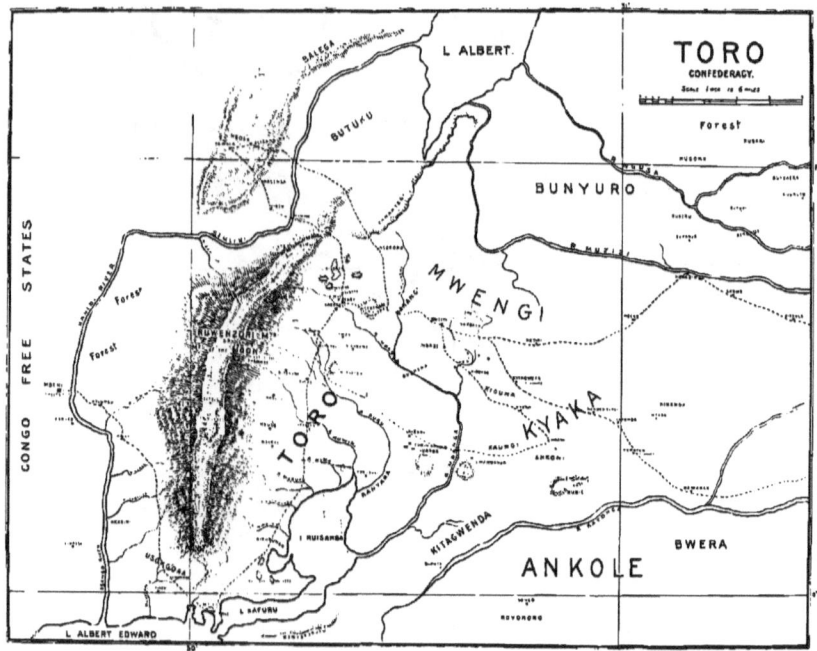

Insert between pages 158 and 159.

CHAPTER VIII

TORO

Brief history of Toro—Kasagama—Developments in Toro—Liberation of slaves—Ruwenzori, Mountains of the Moon—Attending the sick—I build a dispensary—Wanted, a hospital—Leopards of Toro—A midnight scare—Lions—The little hero—The Watoro—Toro customs Teeth-breaking—Burning "Njoka"—Cupping—Drinking parties.

TORO has existed as an independent kingdom for many centuries, and according to tradition has been governed by numerous kings. It is said that the Watoro migrated from Bukedi, the country situated to the north of Uganda, and that the founder of the nation and the first king was Lwanyantoro Lukedi. Disagreement, however, occurred soon after they had settled in the country to the west of Uganda, and Lurega, a man of great influence, rebelled against Lwanyantoro Lukedi, and then a long war was carried on, which finally ended in dividing up the country into two kingdoms; that to the north was called Unyoro, and was governed by Lurega, and that to the south was held by Lwanyantoro Lukedi. After the division of the two countries peace reigned through the land for long years, and no trouble existed, excepting that which came from Uganda, for the King of Uganda always made Toro and Unyoro his own raiding ground, and from thence came all the slaves of the Waganda.

At last a big chief, Kaba Rega by name, was made King of Unyoro. He was a man of remarkable ability as a general, and very soon commenced to look round to see how he might extend the domains of his kingdom. He saw that Toro was governed by a man named Nyeka, a very poor specimen, who was but little esteemed by his people, and so Kaba Rega sent off a very big army to try and capture Toro; at first he failed, but finally succeeded. Kasagama, the son of Nyeka, King of Toro, then quite

KASAGAMA, KING OF TORO.

a boy, fled to Ankole for his life, knowing that Kaba Rega would kill him, being a prince, if he were caught. He was also joined by Byakweyamba, who was a prince of the house of Toro.

For a time the young princes remained in seclusion with a few dependants, and with Kasagama's mother, and finally journeyed to Uganda and were well treated by the King.

IN DWARF LAND.

When Colonel (then Captain) Lugard made his notable journey westward in search of the Soudanese left behind by Emin Pasha, and to mark out the western frontier of the Protectorate, he took with him Kasagama and Byakweyamba, made the former king of Toro and the latter of Mwenge, a large province to the east of Toro, which has since been amalgamated with Toro proper. A number of forts were built throughout Toro, and Soudanese troops left at each to protect the country from the raids that were constantly made by Kaba Rega, for although he was

QUEEN MOTHER OF TORO.

driven from the country by Lugard's column he still remained hostile, and determined if possible to recapture the country, but so well did these Soudanese do their work that he failed upon every attempt. He at last gave up the hope of ever being able to again possess Toro as part of his kingdom.

While in Uganda Kasagama had learned the Uganda language and had also acquired a fair knowledge of the customs, and when he became King of Toro his first desire was to establish there a system of government similar to that which exists in Uganda at the present day, that of dependent chieftainship. When I arrived in Toro it was soon very obvious to me, that his effort to imitate this system of chieftainship had been successful, and that he had by this means a very fair hold upon the country as a whole.

Several months before I reached Toro Kasagama had again visited Uganda, partly to answer some political charges made against him and also to find out for himself more about Christianity, of which he had heard a little from the Uganda teachers sent some twelve months previously. While in Mengo he was baptized and took the name of David, and upon his return he commenced in real earnest to try and act as a Christian king should. In a letter he wrote to "the Elders of the Church in Europe" he says: "God our Father gave me the kingdom of Toro, to reign over for Him, therefore I write to you, my brethren, to beseech you to remember me, and to pray for me every day. ... I praise my Lord very much indeed for the words of the gospel He brought into my country, and you I thank for sending teachers to come here to teach us such beautiful words. I therefore tell you that I want very much, God giving me strength, to arrange all the matters of this country for Him only, that all my people may understand that Christ Jesus, He is the Saviour of all countries, and that He is the King of all kings." Being most thoroughly in earnest to do as he says, "let his people know," he at once upon his return to Toro built a fine church in which they might worship God. He also set about building a house for a European teacher.

When we reached Toro we found the large church well advanced, and the house in which my colleague and I were to live nearly completed, and quite a number of people who could already read the Gospels.

A European officer, Captain Sitwell, was stationed in

Toro when we arrived, whose duty it was to put the country in working order and to help Kasagama in every way possible so that he might exercise his power as king.

Every Monday morning Kasagama's "baraza" was held. This was the great court function of the week, when the King sat in state upon his throne with all his chiefs

A DISTANT VIEW OF MOUNTAINS OF THE MOON.

gathered round him in conference, and when any political cases were to be tried, judgments being given by the King. One interesting announcement was made by the King in "baraza" soon after our arrival in the country, viz., that if there were any slaves in the country who wished to obtain their freedom they were at liberty at once to apply for it. Some fifty Waganda women slaves immediately came forward and were released and returned to Uganda under proper escort. Thus at the commencement of his reign Kasagama proved that he was desirous of establishing Christian rule in his country.

So much has already been written by others about Ruwenzori, or the Mountains of the Moon, situated to the west of Toro, that I need say but little. Its massive grandeur, with glistening peaks, towering for 18,000 feet above the sea-level; the gloriously snowy twin cones and the magnificent Gordon Bennett Mountain with its huge base stretching from south to north some fifty miles, rugged and broken. Once seen the impression made will never be forgotten. Undoubtedly one of the chief sources of the great river Nile, Ruwenzori's melted snows have for centuries past provided Egypt with its sustenance, and the tiny rivulets rushing down the mountain-sides from the eternal snows, broadening out upon the plains into great rivers, and emptying themselves either into the Albert Edward Lake, or into the Semliki river, have ever been the channels of mercy to that thirsty land of the Pharaohs.

As soon as I had settled down in the capital I offered to do what I could to help those who were suffering from any kind of disease. I had with me a small supply of drugs in tablet form, with iodoform, boracic and antiseptic dressings; but I had not bargained for the great rush that was immediately made upon me. The first day fifty sick folk came, and each day this number gradually increased, until at the end of a fortnight no less than two hundred people were coming to me to be attended to. A great majority of the cases, however, were ulcers and wounds of various kinds. My drug store was a very limited one and could not hold out many days with such tremendous claims upon it. Little by little it disappeared, and I had nothing left to give out to the poor sufferers who came to me. An order was sent off to England for a fresh supply, but at least a year must elapse before it could possibly reach us. Still they came, as many as two hundred and fifty in one day, and the great cry was: "We're dead, we're dead, give us medicine, give us medicine!" As a last resource we hunted up all kinds of old newspapers and periodicals, and to every one suffering with ulcers and wounds we distributed little squares of paper. We told them it would not heal them, but it would at least keep the dirt out, and they were delighted beyond measure. Old gentlemen would be seen going away with little bits of the *Times* newspaper sticking to them, in fact quite a new field for

SICK FOLK.

journalism was opened up in Central Africa. Fresh supplies of drugs came before we expected them, however, and we were then able to carry on the healing work, and the real gratitude of the poor creatures that came to us— some suffering most awful agonies—was most touching, and inspired us to do our very best for them. After a little while I built a small dispensary in the Mission compound in which the patients might sit as they waited for treatment. It was astonishing to me to find how much I could help these sufferers with such a limited amount of medical knowledge at my command. Sometimes operations were performed, and then it was that one found out to what an enormous extent the Watoro could bear pain. From one man's leg I removed a piece of bone eight inches long, making an incision of five inches, tying up arteries and veins, and finally stitching up the wound, and all this done without chloroform, or even cocaine, and the poor fellow never flinched the whole time and never uttered a sound. A woman had a cancerous growth under the arm, and this I removed without the use of any

TORO DISPENSARY.

kind of anæsthetic. Both of these were absolute cures. Another man had a bullet deeply imbedded in his chest, and this was extracted successfully; dislocated joints and shattered limbs, snake bites and spear wounds, were all attended to, and great was the rejoicing among the people when a chief of distinction in the country thought to be dying by the native medicine men was brought to life and health once more by the European's drugs.

The number of patients seemed to increase every day, and cases were brought in from long distances.

One poor woman was carried six days' journey on a rough stretcher, to be treated for dysentery, and when such cases as these were brought to us we were at our wits' end to know where to put the patient, for it was impossible for them to return at once. To overcome this difficulty small huts were built close to the Mission compound and allotted to those patients who were unable to return to their homes, and quite a little settlement sprang up on the waste ground close to our houses. Each day after attending to the out-patients I visited these huts to do what I could for the occupants.

But a hospital was sadly needed and a qualified medical man to do the work, for of course many were the cases brought to me for which I was unable to do anything. The king, when approached upon this subject, readily gave a plot of ground for the hospital, but up to the present time nothing has been done towards rearing the building. Each morning, before any drugs are given out, a short service is held in the dispensary, and most encouraging have been the results of this work. Several young men who were successfully treated offered themselves as teachers, and one in particular who I remember went off in this capacity to a tribe of people called the Wakonjo, who live right up the great mountain of Ruwenzori.

We had not resided long in Toro before we became acquainted with the fact of the presence of lions and leopards in the district. Great excitement was caused one day about 6 p.m. by the appearance in the centre of the capital of a huge leopard. The Watoro, who are not noted for their excessive bravery, immediately rushed into their houses and barred the doors, and that night no one ventured outside.

However, in the early morning a great cry arose from the King's Hill, and we hastened out to discover the cause. The story was soon told; the leopard had in some mysterious way managed to get into the king's enclosure; there it had wandered about until it came to an unprotected house where about fifty men and boys were sleeping. It deliberately walked into the house and looked about until it found a young lad who was sleeping between two men, seized him by the throat, and before he could utter a cry strangled him and carried him off without even waking one of the men, and it was not until the early morning that the tragedy was discovered. The leopard

KING'S HILL, KABAROLE.

had actually stepped over the bodies of several men and boys who were sleeping on the floor, as the footprints indicated, without even disturbing them. Fisher and I immediately set off to try and recover the body of the unfortunate boy, and, if possible, kill the leopard. The former we were able to do, although it was terribly mangled, but the latter kept well out of the way.

A few nights afterwards I was quietly sleeping, Fisher being in a room at the opposite end of the house, when I was startled to hear a shout from Fisher calling to me to come to him, declaring that there was a leopard in his room. I sprang out of bed and seized a revolver and proceeded very cautiously in the dark to his room. Bang, bang, bang, went my friend's revolver as I approached, and I began to fear lest I should be hit in the excitement of the moment. Then all was still and I procured a light. There sat my friend in his bed with an empty pistol in his hand, but where was the leopard? When we looked round we found that the door leading from the room into the garden was partly open, having been pushed on one side, and outside there were numerous footprints of the leopard. Whether the beast had been actually in the room or not we could not say; probably it had, and if Fisher had not heard it, that moment would have been his last.

The Toro people are so much afraid of these animals that they seldom hunt them, and when they do, it is only to make a great noise and frighten them away, with no idea of attempting their destruction. The leopards being thus unmolested were very venturesome, and we constantly had them prowling about our premises, and nearly every week we heard of some one being carried off. But I have mentioned the lions also. These are quite as numerous, and far more to be feared than the leopards. They never go about singly, and frequently five or six would be seen together, and even in the middle of the day, in lonely parts, these terrible creatures will seize their prey.

While staying in one of the suburbs of the capital I was one morning called up by the chief to come at once and shoot a lion that was doing great damage in the district and had just killed a poor woman while cultivating her garden. She was stooping down pulling up some weeds when in front of her she heard the awful roar of a lion. Looking up in speechless horror she saw in the grass a few yards away a huge male lion, apparently about to spring upon her, but just at that moment the lioness, which had crept up behind her, sprang out, and with one terrible stroke of the forepaw killed her where she stood, and then carried her off into the thicket. As soon as I heard this story I started off with a couple of my boys to hunt the lion; but although I spent the whole day searching never a lion did I see. The mangled remains of the poor woman we discovered, but the lions avoided us. However, a few days later a party of native hunters, returning from their day's hunt after small antelope, were attacked by the same lions. Walking in single file through the long grass on the narrow path, the man at the end of the line was suddenly seized from behind by the lioness and instantly killed and carried off. The rest of the party made off with all haste, excepting one little boy, the son of the man killed, and he, amazingly plucky little fellow that he is, actually turned back, and, armed with nothing but a small spear, followed the blood-stained track through the thicket. After a little while he came upon the lioness in the act of devouring his father. Without a moment's hesitation this brave little chap rushed at the huge beast, and the lioness, becoming aware of his approach, left the prey and sprang upon the boy. By a merciful Providence the spear which the boy carried entered its breast, and by the animal's own weight was forced right into its body, piercing the heart, and the great creature rolled over stone dead. The boy was utterly unharmed. Rapidly withdrawing his little weapon he went and knelt by the mangled remains of his father, and while bending over him in his sorrow the male lion came roaring through the thicket. The grief-stricken lad sprang up and with almost superhuman courage rushed towards the second lion, waving aloft his bloodstained spear and shouting, "Come on, come on, I'll kill you also!" But the lion was so discomfited by the unexpected approach of the lad that he turned tail and fled, leaving his partner dead by the side of her mangled prey. The boy then went home to his village and called his friends to come and bring the dead lioness to the king, and this was done. The brave little fellow was suitably rewarded

THE LION KILLER WITH HIS SPEAR.

by Kasagama for his wonderful pluck, and he made him his own page.

The people of Toro are by no means above the average African. They are more lazy than the Waganda, and are satisfied with very inferior houses. They wear skins roughly prepared in place of the bark cloth, which they will not take the trouble to make. They are dirty to a degree, and their habits are most degraded. In the country districts many of the women go about in a state of nudity, and the men very little better. As a result of their uncleanly habits they nearly all suffer with scabies and many malignant diseases. And yet there is something good in their composition. They are very warm-hearted and impulsive, and when once enlightened as to better things they are most anxious to improve.

Many of the customs of the Watoro are most barbarous. For instance, they have an extraordinary practice of breaking off all the front teeth on the bottom jaw. This is done when the child is quite young; indeed, as soon as the second teeth show themselves they are broken off or dragged out with the most primitive tools. The chief idea seems to be to improve the looks; and if to look prematurely old is their great aim, it is certainly accomplished by this custom, but it is a thoroughly heathen practice and causes the children terrible suffering. It has also had the effect of making the pronunciation of their language more difficult. Curious lisps are necessary and have to be coped with to make oneself properly understood.

Burning, too, is another of their customs, equally barbarous. For every complaint imaginable this is the one great remedy; whether it be headache, stomach ache, or chest trouble, burning is always resorted to at once. A piece of rough iron is made red hot in the fire, and then pressed upon the bare skin about the spot where the pain exists. I have seen men with burns reaching to the bone, little children whose heads are one mass of horrible scabs as a result of this practice. Chest complaints are very common amongst them, and nearly everybody one meets has old scars covering his chest, where he has been burnt from time to time. I believe the old idea is that all pain is caused by some evil spirit dwelling in the part, and if fire is brought to bear upon that place the evil spirit leaves.

Pains in the chest and stomach are always called "Njoka" (snakes), and the natives firmly believe that it is one of these live creatures moving about within that causes the pain. A man suffering from indigestion once told me that an Njoka resided in his stomach, and from

TYPICAL TORO HUT.

time to time made its way up as far as his throat, and then, just as he hoped to be able to catch hold of it and draw it out, it returned to the lower regions.

Cupping is also largely resorted to when fever is the trouble, and sometimes I have seen at least half a pint of blood drawn from a man's head. The wide end of a cow's horn is pressed upon the part, which has previously been lacerated with a sharp knife, and then through a hole in the side of the horn the air is sucked and the small hole in the side blocked up, so that the suction continues and the blood is thus drawn off in great quantities.

Another very curious old custom, scarcely ever practised at the present day, still not entirely unknown in the country, was in vogue in case of war. If a tribe living near threatened to attack the people of Toro they would send a woman whose breast had been cut, together with two sheep or two cows, to the hostile tribe as a peace-offering.

Great feasts and drinking parties were always organised by the king at the new moons, being held in the king's "lubiri" (enclosure), and all the big chiefs were expected to attend, when drum-beating and blowing of horns and dancing were the order of the day. These drinking parties are the great festivals of the Watoro. The beer is made from the banana juice, fermented with a small millet. About 6 p.m. the drums begin to beat within a chief's enclosure, announcing to all that there is to be a great drinking bout that night. The friends and neighbours of the chief all flock together, young and old alike, men and women. The beer is kept in large gourds, each one containing several gallons. Perhaps ten of these gourds will be provided, or if he be a big chief twenty, or even thirty, are set before the guests. The men sit in groups, and to each group is given a calabash, or gourd of Maruwa, as it is called. Small cups, also made from the gourds, are handed round, and when the chief has taken the first drink all follow suit and the festivities commence. Needless to say, the end of such parties as these is the indulgence in all the evil passions of human nature, fighting and murder, lasciviousness and wanton wickedness. Devil dances of a most disgusting character, witchcraft, and fetishism are all practised upon these occasions, and it is at such times that one sees the utter degradation of heathenism; and yet some people will say, "Oh, leave them alone; they are happy enough in their blindness." If heathenism, immorality, and sin had been left untouched in our own country, where once upon a time it was rampant, the British flag would not

C.M.S. MISSION STATION, TORO.

be to the world what it is to-day, the emblem of a Christian Government. Wherever our good flag flies darkness and heathenism must be dispersed. It is Britain's glory that she exists as a nation "to right the wrongs of suffering humanity and to establish peace on earth."

CHAPTER IX

A TRAMP INTO THE UNKNOWN

Footprints of the lions Snake in the grass Ravages of the lions A narrow escape—Dry and thirsty land—I meet the Captain The Soudanese guard—Following the compass Hunting water-buck Between heaven and earth—A fine specimen—A picturesque camp—Elephants- Carving our way Up a tree—Patience rewarded—Tropical vegetation—The Captain and I part company We camp in the wilderness Mount Edwin Arnold Mpanga river A hostile people Heathen sacrifice—Home again to Toro.

NOT being content to follow merely in the footsteps of other men in Africa, and to keep to the old beaten tracks, I took a most interesting journey through the south-eastern portion of Toro, which might well be described as a tramp into the unknown.

I left the capital of Toro with a few strong porters for my things and the biggest of my boys, including my faithful old friend Mika. It was a glorious morning, and as we set off on this another tramp, one felt a kind of exhilaration of freedom which can be experienced nowhere, but in Africa. Our road lay to the south, and we had the advantage of a fine, wide, well-kept road for some little distance. On each side of the path was a high wall of tiger grass 10 to 15 feet, which completely shut out the view, and we felt something like the Pygmies must do as they tramp through their mighty forest.

We soon became aware that the path had been recently traversed by other strangers, for there were huge footprints right along, conspicuous among them being the elephant's. But by a little close inspection we found that there were scores of lion footprints. I loaded my gun, and we had to walk close together, as they were evidently in the near vicinity. Presently I was startled by the unexpected appearance of a large puff adder just in the path, not a yard in front of us. It was coiled up in some dead cut grass, and fortunately for me my little

A TYPICAL ROAD.

dog, who was at my heels as usual, first saw it and gave a short, sharp bark, and I knew that something was wrong. At that moment the reptile reared its head close before me. I was too much taken by surprise to kill it and it made off into the high grass.

We were now passing through entirely uninhabited country, and the path was still covered with lion spoor, and we expected every moment to meet with the animals themselves. Suddenly a boy who was walking a little ahead of us came running back; he said he had seen some lions, and there was something lying in the pathway. I pressed forward with my rifle ready; there, about fifty yards in front, I saw the body of a man lying across the path. I hurried up, followed closely by the rest of the party. The man was quite dead, but had evidently only been so a very short time. Footprints were all around, and blood smeared over the grass in the vicinity, but the lions were nowhere to be seen. We walked slowly on, and less than three hundred yards further on we came to the body of another man, frightfully mauled and quite dead. It was a ghastly sight, and made us wonder who might be the next to be seized. No doubt the lions were somewhere near, and had only been temporarily frightened from the path by our approach. We therefore kept a sharp look-out both before and behind, but saw nothing, and after about four hours' walk sat down by one of the beautiful mountain streams, cooked some food, and generally enjoyed ourselves for half an hour.

Another four hours brought us to a very large village called Butanuka, which is the country seat of the Katikiro (Prime Minister) of Toro. We were most heartily welcomed by the chief and the people. The former sent me a fine goat and plenty of food. After an excellent meal and a little chat with the chief and the people, we all retired, I to my little tent and the boys and porters to the native huts.

The following day was Sunday, and I spent it amongst my good friends, visiting the houses, and holding services in the church, which the Christians had built for themselves. Two young Waganda teachers were working here and doing really good service. The chief, an avowed Christian, is very true to his faith, and nothing seems to please him more than to sit with his Testament in his hand, reading the Gospels to his people as they gather around him. Another poor woman was the victim of the lions while I was at this place. She had gone into the garden to pick some bananas for the midday meal when she was seized and devoured within sight of her companions. One man who saw it all came running into the village giving the alarm, and a large number of the warriors went to try and drive the lions off. There was extraordinary excitement in the village, and every one seemed scared and frightened, but in the midst of it all I heard some little boys singing, "Go to Perati [French priest] and he will give you a medal, but if you go to Lloyd you will get a New Testament." I asked one of the little chaps if he knew what the New Testament taught us, and he said, "Yes, I do, I know a lot about it." "Tell me what you know," I said, and he answered very promptly, "I know that God loves me, because He says so." I thought that if every man on God's earth knew even that much, how blessed it would be.

The next morning I made a bold resolve to hunt the lions, but alas! it came to nothing, for they were nowhere to be found; the warriors had driven them right away. We had a tremendous walk, however, following up one track after another, with always the same result.

I had one narrow escape that day, about which I must write. Walking in front of the men and boys who had followed me, I heard one of them utter a most awful yell, and turning round saw them all running away into the long grass. What could the matter be? I called to one of them, but could not hear what he said, he was too far off. Another, who was nearer to me, seemed too much startled to speak at all. So I walked back to find out for myself what was wrong. The cries of the boys became louder and I found out that it was a snake that had alarmed them. I laughed and was passing on, when they called me back. Mika, who by this time had caught us up (he having been some distance behind) now came forward and asked where the snake was. One of the men pointed with his stick to the very track in the grass that I had made. He said nothing, but with his eyes almost starting out of his head gazed at the spot. Mika and I went forward and then—what a sight! There, coiled up in a tuft of grass and partly hidden from view, was the largest snake I had ever seen. It was a python. The middle of its body was, without doubt, a foot in diameter, while the length of this awful reptile must have been at least 20 feet. Oh, horrors! I could have faced a lion without blinking, but this terrible monster made me quake, especially when I found that I had put my foot down, as I passed, less than three inches from its head! As Mika approached it lifted its head, and made a low, curious sound, its little black eyes sparkling like diamonds. How it glared at us! I almost felt its fascination. Brave old Mika, never afraid, and always ready, saw in a moment that to hesitate would be fatal, gave me a push backwards, and lifting the big knobstick that he was carrying rushed at it, and jumping skilfully to one side as the reptile prepared to spring, brought down the stick like a sledge hammer right in the middle of its body, and before it had time scarcely to move he was round the other side and had dealt another blow. But he might as well have slashed away at a huge oak-tree as to try and make much impression on this roll of muscle. Another blow, and another leap by Mika, and away dashed the snake into the thicket, feeling no doubt that it had met its match. As it went it reared its head and shot back deadly glances at brave old Mika, but it did not return to the fight, and we heard it plunging along through the undergrowth, making a noise like some large four-footed animal, and we saw it no more.

As we retraced our steps we were surprised to find how

far we had wandered from camp, and I have seldom suffered so much from thirst as I did that day. We had at least five hours' walk through a scorching sun, and nothing at all to drink. However, just as I was beginning to feel I could go no further without water, we came to some damp earth; but what good was this? We very quickly dug a hole about a foot deep, and then to our joy saw the water just beginning to come; drop by drop it oozed from the sides of the hole. I first put a leaf at the bottom, and when it became damp, sucked it, then when a little more had come I scooped it up with the leaf, and at last, after much patience, the hole filled up, the mud sank to the bottom and a delightful pool of pure, clear water appeared. I put my head down and took a long, long draught, and never did water taste so sweet. Then the boys and men drank, and all were satisfied.

We got to our camp about 4 p.m., had a little rest and refreshment, and then a short walk brought us to a place where Captain Sitwell was camped on the top of a hill, surrounded by a banana grove. We had previously arranged to meet at this place, and journey together into the unknown. My tent was pitched by the side of his, and in a very short time we had dinner together. The Captain had brought with him six cows for milk, and several sheep for killing, and quite a lot of home comforts. He also had with him an experienced Indian cook, who had travelled with him from Uganda. We sat and chatted together after an excellent repast, till nine o'clock and then separated for the night.

As Her Majesty's Vice-Consul in Toro the Captain travelled under an escort of Soudanese troops of the Uganda Protectorate; they were a very fine set of men and seemed to be much attached to their commanding officer. At night two of these fellows acted as sentries at the door of our tents, and a small camp fire was kept burning.

This certainly gave to me a sense of security that I had seldom felt in Africa, and I enjoyed a good deep sleep for once in my life. As a rule I slept so lightly that the sound of a night bird, or a bat as it fluttered past my tent, would always rouse me, and it was a relief to feel that there was some one outside who would be awake all through the night and give prompt intimation to us if

SOUDANESE SENTRY.

anything went wrong. However, "Put not your trust in princes, nor in any son of man," is good advice, and once, with the sentry actually standing a few yards from the tent door, a leopard entered the tent of my friend, and carried off a dog that was quietly sleeping on the chair by the bedside, and the sentry was utterly ignorant of the fact until he heard the dog yell, which was then, of course, too late.

IN DWARF LAND. 183

Early the next morning our walk into the unknown commenced. The Captain determined not to stick to paths, but just to proceed by compass, and very soon after we had struck camp we made due east, and for three hours were simply cutting our way through the country, with axes and swords; such dense thick undergrowth, it was hard work for the soldiers who did the cutting, and seldom could we see more than a few yards in front.

HAPPY NIGGERS, PLENTY TO EAT.

In the evening we reached a small village and here camped. The chief brought us plenty of food, which we distributed to the porters and boys. During the evening I visited some of the people and had chats with them, and I found that here also the lions had been making great ravages. One poor woman that I saw had been terribly torn about by a lion, the whole of the flesh on one side of her face being literally eaten off, and the greatest wonder was that she escaped at all.

We started off very early the following morning, but we could find no path leading in the direction we desired, so again we went by compass. This time long, tangled grass impeded our progress, and made walking most difficult. The country looked very beautiful, much after the style of a big English park. The recent rains had had the effect of freshening up everything. After a little while we saw in the distance a small herd of water-buck quietly grazing on the hillside. I hurried off in front of the caravan and was soon fighting my way through the terrible long, rank grass, cutting myself all over with its knifelike blades. I was pushing my way rapidly through some of this long grass, with my eyes fixed upon a fine buck, about 300 yards off, when suddenly I felt my feet tread on air! and my next sensation was one of suspension between earth and heaven. Quite unconsciously I had come upon a deep gully, almost like a crack in the earth, with a lot of water at the bottom, which seemed about 20 feet beneath. My arms were held fast by some creepers above my head. While wondering what I should do to get out of this queer state, I was suddenly saved the trouble by the creepers giving way, and down, down I went with a whack, splash into the water, which was fortunately deep enough to break my fall. It was a good thing for me that I did not get a broken skull, for there were rocks sticking up here and there through the water. As it was I was not a bit hurt, only shaken and wet, and I therefore soon began to think again about that water-buck I had left up above. The question was, how to get up! I had my gun in my hand, and I was alone, and in front of me twenty feet of steep rocky bank. However, by clinging to the creepers, and holding on to little tufts of grass, I got up the other side quite serenely and looked about for my prize. There he was, reclining under the shadow of a big tree. I walked a few yards, and at about two hundred yards fired. He rolled over, but got up again and was off, but as he ran I put another shot into him, and this time it went through the heart, and over he went, not to move again. It was a very fine specimen with twenty-seven inch horns. The caravan came up, and the meat was quickly divided amongst the porters.

We did not go much further that day but camped on a hill overlooking the whole surrounding country—a most charming place. The wildness of it was enchanting. We were on ground that no white man had ever trodden before, and possibly no black man either. All around us were beautiful hills and deep valleys, some of the former thickly wooded, and lovely little rivulets running through the latter.

As we sat at lunch just outside our tents we saw quite close to us a large herd of elephants ; we counted about thirty in all. They were quietly feeding upon the grass and tender shoots from the trees.

We left this charming spot at six the next morning, and after a short walk came to the thickest and tallest grass I have ever seen. Every foot had to be cut by the Soudanese with their sword bayonets. For three and a half hours we toiled on, and it seemed to get worse and worse at every step. The men were at last tired out with the hard cutting, and we all sat down for a rest by the side of a very high tree. The Captain called for several of his men to climb up and look out for a path or village, or some means of getting out of this horrible jungle. Man after man tried to climb and failed, at last I made an attempt. I found a long thin creeper hanging down through the branches of the tree, just like a very thick rope. I tested it to see if it would bear my weight, and then commenced to swarm up. For about 60 feet the creeper was separated from the tree, and when I got up about two-thirds of the way I looked down, and I was literally hanging in space. Up and up I went, until I reached the huge bough from which the creeper hung, scrambled on to it, climbed a little higher up the tree, and then looked round. But while doing so I became conscious of a terrible pricking sensation all over my body and which I found was caused by thousands of little black ants. I was simply smothered. It was frightful agony; I hastily looked round, but the branches were too thick, I could see nothing, so I climbed out on to one of the boughs, broke off a few of the smaller ones so as to get a view, and then at last I was rewarded by seeing a little way to the north, a forest, which would, I thought, be much easier to walk through than this awful grass. I then came down the creeper and got a few boys to pick off the little pests that had by this time bitten me in every part of my body, easily finding their way under my loose clothing. The Captain agreed with me that the forest would be preferable to the high grass jungle, and so we changed our direction a little, and soon came to it, and found as we expected that it was much easier to walk through. The tropical vegetation was magnificent: tree ferns on every hand, cabbage-like lichens of immense size on almost every branch, trees and twigs all covered with thick green moss, and creepers festooned from branch to branch. Monkeys screamed amongst the leaves of the giant trees 150 feet in height.

We, however, were too tired to take much notice of the forest beauties, we wanted water and a suitable camping-ground for the night. We sent off men in all directions to look for water, and after a time one man came running back with the tidings that a river ran not far from where we were resting. There it was quite close to us, a beautiful stream flowing silently through the forest, winding its way in and out like a snake. By the side of it we camped. It was well for the porters that I had been successful in killing the water-buck, as we had hoped to reach a village where they could have procured food instead of thus camping in a wild forest. We struck camp about 5 a.m. the next day. It had been a terribly cold night, due to a damp river mist. We walked another four hours through the forest and then struck a path which led us to a village, and here we camped again. The Captain returned to Toro from this place, but I determined to go on a little further.

A big chief came to see us in the evening, and on the morning of the next day I went at this chief's request to visit his village, stayed a few hours with him and exchanged presents. He was a prince of Toro, Kaibari by name, and used to be one of Kaba Rega's old supporters, a most untrustworthy fellow. He was very kind to me, however, giving me a large quantity of food to take on with me.

We went on for another three hours, and at 5 p.m. camped out in the wilderness by the side of a tiny stream close to a thick forest. The boys built rough huts around my tent, in which to sleep. I shot two large golden-crested cranes for meat, together with a red-tailed monkey, and these, with the food given us by the old chief, met our requirements. Just before dark I had the good fortune to kill a very fine specimen of Colibus monkey, which was sporting about amongst the trees within sight of my tent.

It was bright and fresh the next day when we started, and we had the most majestic country to pass through. On our right was the big mountain called Mount Edwin Arnold, beautifully covered from base to crest with bright green grass; in front of us was another large range of hills, not marked on the map, but called by the natives Lubala Mountains; and behind us in the dim distance we could just see the snow-capped peaks of Ruwenzori some forty miles away, and all around us were the most lovely trees. Being very short, soft grass we did not keep to the path, which seemed to wind about a great deal.

At about eleven o'clock we reached the banks of the Mpanga river, a stream that has its source in the eternal snows of Ruwenzori, winding in a horseshoe shape to the east on to the great plains, and finally into the north-easterly arm of the Albert Edward Lake. The

MPANGA RIVER.

water was deep and the current strong, and we had some difficulty in finding a place where it was fordable.

Having crossed the Mpanga river, we at once entered into a new country, and at 3 p.m. approached a large village. It was built on a hill, and we could see that all the men were collecting together around one man, who was dressed in long, white flowing robes. All were armed with spears and knives, bows and arrows, &c. Not a pleasant sight for a harmless individual like myself. However, one has to face such things in Africa, and so I told the boys who were carrying my sporting guns, and who were very frightened at the turn of events, to fall to the rear, while I went on alone, unarmed, to see what was amiss and try and make peace. As I climbed the hill I heard the war-drum beating, and great excitement seemed to animate all. At last I reached the summit and was immediately surrounded, and not a word was spoken, but every man grasped his spear ready for instant use. I went straight up to the chief without showing any sign of fear or suspicion, although I confess to a little dryness of the throat and palpitation of the heart. As I approached him I kept my weather eye fixed upon one great fellow who had a very big spear, and who seemed to be edging his way towards me. I put out my hand to greet the chief, smiling pleasantly, but he refused to answer my salutation, and said, "Do you want to steal my sheep and my goats?" I answered him that nothing was further from my thoughts. "You are a liar," he politely said; "I *know* this is what you have come for." I replied, "Should I have come into your presence, and into the presence of these your armed warriors, unarmed and alone, if I were going to fight and steal?" He then said, "But your soldiers may be hidden in the forest, waiting for you to call them to your assistance." "No," I said; "all the men I have are just now coming up the hill; look at them, and you will see that they are unarmed, except my two boys, who are carrying my two guns I use for killing game to eat." At this he seemed more satisfied, but asked me a few more questions, and then withdrew his men into his own enclosure, having pointed out to me a spot where I might pitch my tent. This happened to be very close to a most strange spectacle, a bird sacrifice. A dead fowl was hanging by the neck from a long pole, which was festooned with plaited grasses, &c. This was a propitiatory offering to the spirit of evil, that is supposed to destroy their cattle, sheep and goats, &c. When I had pitched my tent the chief came again to see me with all his spearmen and asked me to show him various things my guns, my brush, looking-glass, field glasses, &c. I took one thing after another and explained it carefully to him and he was much pleased, and I soon felt I was gaining his confidence; and by and by the spearmen dispersed, but not before I had spoken to them of the one great Sacrifice, once offered, for the sins of the whole world, and of the loving Father of us all. One sincerely trusts that the good seed sown by the wayside in these wild, dark hearts may bear fruit after many days.

Up to that moment no food had been brought to us, but now it came in great abundance, and all the porters had plenty and to spare. At night I went into the chief's house and sat and chatted with him till bedtime. The house was all decked with charms and fetishes of every description, in all of which he seemed to put implicit trust.

In the morning I bade an affectionate farewell to the people, the chief showing the wonderful change of feeling toward me by accompanying me a good part of the way *alone*. We were now on our return journey, and I intended visiting a large village called Karumuli, about twenty miles distant.

The second day we left Mount Edwin Arnold to the north; the base of the mountain was quite invisible, but the summit was very distinct, and one could easily see the trees, &c., on the very top. We stayed at Karumuli two days, and then made our way home by one long, forced march to Kabarole, reaching the Mission station about 5 p.m., just eleven days from the time we left it.

CHAPTER X

AT HOME IN TORO

Climate of Toro—Brick-making—House-building—A tornado—A disaster—The Government fort—Missionaries and the Government officials—A Christmas feast—The Mission garden—My first elephant—The Batatela rebellion—Adventures of a French priest—Belgian officer takes refuge in British Protectorate—Fort George attacked—A splendid victory—Death of Rev. John Callis—Lions again—A lucky shot.

THE climate of Toro is very different from that of Uganda, no doubt by reason of the mountains and their snow-capped peaks. In Toro rain falls much more frequently, and during the first year I spent there it rained on 272 days out of the 365. In the early morning the wind seems to blow always from the west, a keen, cutting blast which makes one very reluctant to leave the warm blankets. Very often the wind brings with it clouds of thick mist, and it is not an uncommon occurrence in Toro to get up and find the whole district in a thick fog. It is often 11 o'clock before it clears up.

Even in the middle of the day the heat is never what it is in Uganda and other countries nearer the coast. I have known the thermometer to be as low as 65° at 12 midday in Toro, and much lower than that at night and in the early dawn, but I have never seen it below 40°. As a direct result of these cold mornings the people are not early risers like the Waganda, excepting perhaps in the dry season, which lasts for three months only—December, January, and February.

The ordinary reed houses, as built by the Europeans in Uganda, were not sufficiently warm in Toro. I therefore commenced to teach the natives to make sun-dried bricks. I had never done anything of the kind before myself, but, as I have said, a missionary must be prepared for anything. I made a wooden mould out of old broken clothes boxes, and commenced operations. The bricks were larger than the ordinary burnt brick of the Old Country, but my

BRICK-MAKING, TORO.

idea was that it would take less bricks if I made them a good size. Very soon the native boys whom I employed at one shell per brick were able to turn out sixty bricks per day each, and in a short time my yard was stacked with good strong material for a new house. But boys will be boys, and black boys are no exception, and every few minutes these little blackies were flinging mud into each other's faces. They are terrible little creatures, and take the whole thing as a huge joke, and if a stray cow or goat came walking leisurely amongst the wet bricks, trampling them all out of shape, perhaps spoiling a whole day's work, they simply laughed, jumped and shouted with delight, and thought it great fun.

At last I started to erect what was to be the most wonderful house in Toro about the beginning of January, digging out a 3-feet foundation. Having got the building well started, laying every brick myself, I thought I would try and teach some of the boys to be bricklayers. My man Mika offered to try if he could do it. I told him what to do and left him. I came back in about two

POLES FOR BUILDING PURPOSES.

hours' time, alas! to find that, although the good-hearted fellow had put down some hundreds of bricks not one was laid straight, and the wall was crescent-shape, and had to be pulled down. I tried again and again, but without success, and so made up my mind to do the whole thing myself. I laid some ten thousand bricks, and two-thirds of the walls were finished, and then a terrible thing happened. It was the middle of the dry season, and we expected a good six weeks more without rain; but one morning while I was very busy, all bespattered with mud, laying brick after brick, I saw a great, black, lowering cloud come sailing up from the southeast, which was always our rainy quarter; then distant thunder was heard, and the women in the gardens and the men in the fields all ran to their houses, and in a very few moments the storm burst upon us. It was an awful gale, a regular tornado. The wind was so strong that it carried away part of the roof of the house in which I lived; the plantain gardens were laid low, trees were uprooted, and many of the native huts were demolished.

MISSIONARIES' MUD-HOUSE, TORO.

In the midst of it all I heard a crash, and running to the window I saw, to my great sorrow, that my hard work of the past six weeks was all destroyed in a moment. The temporary roof erected to protect the sun-dried bricks while the walls were built, was blown away, and then the full force of the gale fell upon the walls and down they came. The storm lasted about two hours, and seemed rather to increase in violence towards the end, and very much damage was done.

In consequence of the destruction wrought upon the

banana groves there was a famine, which lasted two or three months, and some of the people suffered very severely. The brick-house, or the remains of it, had to be cleared away, and I built a mud-house in its place, and with the rest of the bricks, which were in stock, I constructed a smaller house.

The Government fort of Toro was only a quarter of an hour's walk from our Mission station, and we constantly exchanged visits with the officer in charge. Fort Gerry, as it is called, is one of the best in the whole Protectorate. Built on the top of a hill, it commanded the district for miles round, and no native force could possibly have stormed it with any success. A ditch 10 feet deep surrounded it, which was usually partly filled with rain-water. The fort walls were of mud, and high Maxim bastions were at the four corners. There was only one entrance, with a small bridge built across the ditch. The Vice-Consul's house stood in the centre, with a fine, well-kept lawn in the front. The military officer had his dwelling next door, and officers' stores, magazine, and servants' departments, &c., were the only other buildings inside. The chief aspect of the place was its neat, business-like appearance. The company of Soudanese troops had their quarters outside.

During the two years I spent in Toro the intercourse which was maintained between the missionaries and the Government officials was of the best possible kind. At least twice a week we exchanged visits, and tried to be of mutual help in every way. Sometimes we tramped together through the country, each performing in his own way the duty allotted to him by his calling. If one had tea and the others had none the more fortunate would share what he had with his companion, and although our work led us often in different directions, he as an official of the British Government and we as missionaries, it was the object of both to improve the state of the country—the one dealing with its political troubles, the others with its social evils. So should Government officials and missionaries work hand in hand, in every way possible helping each other, but in no way whatever the one hindering or discouraging the other, as, alas! is sometimes unfortunately the case. It can never be said, however, that this was so in Toro, at least during the term I spent in residence there, or

THATCHING.

even in Uganda, where the happiest relations have always existed.

Christmas, 1896, was a day of much rejoicing in Toro; the king, Kasagama, wishing to introduce the good old Christmas custom of a feast on that great day, offered two bullocks towards a big festival. Fisher and I gave a bullock and some sheep, several of the chiefs gave sheep, goats, and fowls, and after a short, bright Christmas service in the Church of St. John, Toro, the people went off to their huts to prepare the "Mbaga" (feast).

At 2 p.m. the drum began to beat, and the crowds collected on the open green in front of the church. Some seven hundred people all arranged themselves in little groups; each under-chief had about twenty men to look after. The King and five of the biggest chiefs, together with the Queen Mother and ourselves, formed a separate group. When all were seated the baskets of food were brought, one hundred baskets of all kinds of luxuries, including bananas, potatoes, yams, millet, and many other sorts of native food; meat, broiled, stewed, and curried, and large calabashes of sweet banana wine, unfermented and harmless, with a few luxuries such as biscuits and tea for the king's special benefit. All the food was distributed, and then the King stepped forward and in a loud voice, while every head was bowed, said: "O! great God, our Father, we praise Thee for Thy goodness to us and for this food; may we eat it with thanksgiving, through Jesus Christ our Lord. Amen."

It was a wonderful sight in the midst of this dark land there to see the king of the country, who so lately had emerged from heathenism of the lowest type, surrounded by hundreds of his subjects, most of whom were still heathen, giving praise to the great Father of us all through Christ, the Saviour of the world. It was a sight from which might well be learned a lesson, by many a man in this civilised land who never thinks of offering to the great God who made him the thanks due unto His name.

The following day another feast was given to the sick patients, and about three hundred partook of it. Captain Sitwell very kindly gave two fat-tailed sheep towards this feast, and right glad were the poor creatures to enjoy the privilege of sharing in the Christmas festivities. Of course only the convalescent among them could take part, but the others were not forgotten, and little luxuries were taken to them in their huts, which, as I have mentioned, were built just outside of the Mission compound.

We were able to enjoy in Toro the best English vegetables, and our Mission garden always provided us with new potatoes and green peas all the year round; in addition to these cabbages, turnips, radishes, cauliflowers, French beans and broad beans, carrots and lettuce—in fact, everything seemed to do well excepting wheat, and this, most precious of all, could not be reared to any perfection in Toro. We tried at all seasons of the

GARDENING IN TORO.

year, and would reap about as much as we had sown, but usually less, and often none at all. Therefore when the English flour ran out we had to content ourselves with maize bread or banana flour cakes.

There was plenty of game of all sorts close to Toro, and very occasionally when a change was necessary (for missionaries are human and get tired in their work sometimes) a run through the country, enjoying freedom from work for a few days, soon puts a man on his feet again. Such a little relaxation I had early in

1897, on to the Semliki plains, crossing the mountain at the north end. The plains were simply covered with antelope, chiefly cobus cob and reed-buck, but buffalo and elephants and water-buck were also to be found; gazelles and wild pigs too.

Returning from one of these expeditions, I came to a village the people of which were in great distress, as they said a large herd of elephants was in the district, destroying all their gardens. They pointed out to me their potato gardens, with the potatoes all rooted up, the plantations also were torn up and spoiled, and several houses had been demolished.

I had never hunted these colossal beasts before: in fact, I had always looked upon elephant hunting as being all right for those who were tired of life and longed to be freed from its worries, but not quite the thing for a missionary who desired to live long in the land of his adoption. But here was an occasion when one might be doing the natives a real service; and when I looked at it in that light, I decided at once to make my first elephant hunt.

I first cleaned my rifle, which was of small (·303) calibre, selected three of my most plucky boys, asked the chief of the village to give me a man to guide us to the herd, and when he was forthcoming we started off. It was not long before we were pushing our way through long tiger-grass towering away about 6 feet above us. In front, advancing noiselessly, was our native guide, twisting himself in and out amongst the tufts of thick jungle, sometimes creeping on hands and knees, and ever keeping eyes and ears well on the alert, for not only elephants but lions also were about. Then I followed much more clumsily, I must admit, but as quietly as possible. Occasionally I would fall full length, having tripped over some hidden stump or caught my foot in a creeper, and each time I did so the guide would stop and gravely shake his head, meaning, I suppose, to show how much he pitied me for my clumsiness. A quarter of an hour's progress of this kind brought us to an open patch of land covered with much shorter grass. Here the guide stopped and told us to wait while he went forward a little to scout. We waited in breathless excitement, for somehow we felt sure we were very near to the herd. After a time the guide returned with a beaming countenance, which denoted that he had seen the elephants. He beckoned to me, and I followed again with my three boys at my heels, all in a state of suppressed excitement. Then the guide stopped and with his spear pointed to what looked to me like a great granite rock about forty yards away. Then, without a word, he fell back to the rear, and I became "boss" of the situation. I crept a little closer to get a better view, and then I saw about six great trunks go up to sniff the air, but none of the herd attempted to run away, for they had not seen us. And now the supreme moment had arrived. There before us, not thirty yards distant, stood an enormous bull elephant. I raised my rifle, a fly popped into my eye and obscured my vision; I cleared it out, then again raised my rifle. Yes, my hand was steady, but my eye was full of tears resulting from the fly. I pulled the trigger, there was a squeal and a shaking of the earth, and I saw the great bull racing round and round with trunk in the air, and mighty ears flapping at his sides. He was looking for us. Could I have missed my aim? I lay flat down in the grass, and my boys did the same. My rifle was at full cock ready for the next shot. It was a rifle with a magazine for five cartridges. At last he moved away, following the rest of the herd, which had run off when I fired, and very cautiously we followed in his track, which was now a good one, comparatively speaking, that is, it was about 4 feet wide, and the grass was all beaten down, but the jungle was like a mighty wall on either side of us. We followed the herd for about half an hour, when suddenly, as we turned round a corner, I saw the bull standing facing me, not twenty yards in front. For a moment I was taken by surprise, then I saw he had discovered me, and with trunk in the air he came charging towards me. I knelt down and rested my arm upon my knee, took very deliberate aim at a spot between the eyes. I only had a few seconds to aim, for the speed of an elephant is tremendous when he is on the war-path. I pulled the trigger, and almost simultaneously with the report of the gun we heard a terrific thump, and the earth literally shook beneath us, as only ten yards in front of me that huge beast fell dead. The bullet had first entered the trunk, piercing that, and then into the centre of the skull, between the eyes, passing through the brain. It never moved again, and we walked up to the carcase and congratulated ourselves.

We were sitting resting upon the dead body of the elephant when we heard something coming towards us through the jungle. At first I thought it was some men coming to see the result of the shot, but no, the tread was too heavy. It was another elephant making straight for us. I filled up my magazine, shot a cartridge into the breech, and waited; my boys also, who were armed with old Snider rifles, loaded up, and I ordered them not to fire till I told them. The suspense seemed awful as the elephant, very slowly and with measured tread, came towards us. We could not see a sign of it; we were in the midst of the thickest of thick jungles. At last the crackling of the twigs seemed close to us. I raised my gun to my shoulder. Another second, and an enormous head came pushing through the wall of thick vegetation just by the side of the dead elephant. I fired point blank, and my boys followed suit. Down went the second elephant like a clap of thunder, kicked about for a moment, and then sprang up again, and started off, only to fall a few hundred yards away, stone dead. He was a much bigger animal than the first, and carried immense tusks, each weighing about 60lbs. The first pair of tusks I kept as a souvenir of my first elephant hunt; they were not very large, although the animal was full grown, both weighing about 36 lbs. One of the tusks of the second I gave to the Queen Mother, who owned the district in which the elephants had been killed, and the other I sold.

In the spring of the year 1897 a mutiny which occurred in the Congo Free State caused a great deal of unrest and apprehension in Toro. The native troops engaged in an expedition under Baron Dhanis, an officer of the Congo Free State, revolted in February, and, it was reported, killed no less than fifty-nine Belgian officers and soldiers. It appears to have been quite unexpected, and the rebellion was one of great treachery. The mutineers were natives of the district to the north-west of Lake Tanganyika, and were called the Batatela. Their desire, after rebelling and killing as many of their officers as they could lay hands on, was to make good their escape to their own land, but to do so they had to first travel as far west as the British territory to get out of the terrible forest, and to procure food. They therefore came right to the banks of the Semliki river, some of them, it was reported, having crossed over. Wherever they went they attacked the natives and destroyed the houses, causing great disturbance, especially at Mboga, a large country within the British Protectorate, on the west of the Semliki river.

Unfortunately it happened that one of the French fathers of the Roman Catholic Mission in Toro was visiting that country just at the time, and he suffered much discomfort at the hands of the rebels. I met him just after he had escaped, and he told me the story. It appears that he was staying with the chief of Mboga when the rebels crossed the frontier, and hearing that there was a European in the district immediately sent some men to catch him; he was therefore brought up before the head officer. "There sat these men," said the priest, "in European clothing, with their tents and

FRENCH MISSION, TORO.
(The priest who fell into the hands of the Batatele is in the foreground.)

camp furniture just as they had been stolen from the murdered officers. They were smoking European pipes, and eating European provisions, and every now and then calling out 'Boy!' to their servants." The French father was most roughly used, pulled about and bullied by these fellows, his clothing dragged from his back, and every incivility possible shown to him. One man pulled his beard, others went and ransacked his tent and took all his things. He managed to make them understand by speaking in Swahili that he was not a Belgian, nor was he an official, but merely a teacher; otherwise there is little doubt but that they would have killed him. As it was they robbed him of everything he possessed and then presented him with a large tusk of ivory as compensation for what they had taken, so that the priest might not tell the English that the Batatela had stolen his goods, but merely bought them of him. They then sent the priest about his business, giving him time to get out of their way; and poor Père A—— arrived in Toro in a most dilapidated condition, half clothed, and with nothing but what he stood upright in, but fortunate indeed to get off as easily.

The rebels then moved south along the Semliki valley. At Karimi was stationed another Belgian officer, whose men remained loyal to him, and when he heard that the rebels were advancing towards him he escaped into British territory, and took refuge in Fort George, the frontier fort of the British, to the extreme north of Lake Albert Edward. When the rebels reached Karimi they crossed the river and advanced towards Fort George, no doubt having heard that the Belgian officer was there. The fort was in charge of a young Soudanese lieutenant, with a small section of about eighteen Soudanese troops. These, together with the few faithful followers of the Belgian, were all that could be mustered to resist the coming attack of about five hundred Batatela, all armed with Albini rifles, and who had plenty of ammunition. But the gallant few held the fort, and it was a most creditable victory.

The next move of the rebels was to cross the Semliki and make off down south to their own country. However, soon after they crossed they were met by the relief party of Belgian officers and troops, and sustained a very heavy loss, being scattered in all directions.

We in the British Protectorate were free from their presence, and heard but little more about them.

It was reported that I left the country on account of its disturbed state, and fled into Uganda. I would here like to refute that, and state that I did not leave the country at all, nor was there any need whatever to do so. It is true, however, that in April of that year I was obliged to leave Bamutenda, the capital of Toro, to nurse my companion, the Rev. J. S. Callis, who had lately joined me in Toro, and who had gone to Mwenge, about twenty-three miles distant, to visit, and had been taken ill. This may have given rise to the report that "I had left the country so as to escape disturbances." I may add that Mr. Callis never recovered from his illness, and died only ten days after I arrived at his bedside.

About the same time fresh ravages by lions were reported, and every evening at about 5 p.m. we could hear them roar. They seemed to be quite close to the station, but the men assured us they were some distance off.

One afternoon, while we were all sitting in the church, we were suddenly alarmed by hearing a great shout quite close to the church, and rushing out the foremost were just in time to see a lion carry off a poor fellow who had been sitting outside, not many yards away. I rushed off for my gun, and with my man, Mika, followed up the track made by the lion as it carried off its prey. We followed it for nearly an hour, and then Mika, who was just in front of me, stopped, and pointed to a dense piece of jungle and said, "Here is its home." There was just a low entrance into what looked like a cave, but what in reality was merely thick jungle, and the track of the lion led right to the entrance. Mika declared that the lion was inside, and urged me to go forward to shoot it. But this was not an easy task; in the first place, it was too dark to see anything, and then it would be rather a risky business to advance upon a lion without seeing it. However, I went a little nearer and tried to peer into the hole, and then I could distinctly hear the low, cat-like growl of the lion as it devoured its prey, and I could even hear the crunching of the bones. I then made up my mind to fire in the direction from which the sound came and hope to hit the beast. So, going almost to the mouth of the den, I fired. There was a roar and then a scuffle, and then all was still. I crept inside the den with Mika, and after a moment or two our eyes got more accustomed to the darkness, and we could distinguish the mangled remains of a man on the floor, but no lion could we see. We found after a while that there was a back way to the den, and that the lion had left the lair that way. We followed the track for some distance, but darkness came on and we had to return to the station.

About six days afterwards news was brought to us that a dead lion had been found not far from the spot, and I therefore take it for granted that this was the one I had shot. The body was by that time all decomposed, and I could not make any examination, but the bullet evidently struck some vital spot, and the animal must have died the same night.

CHAPTER XI

RAMBLES ROUND ABOUT TORO

Visiting the craters—A day on the lake—A bicycle experience—Lion in the path—Visiting Mwenge—The "Speed-away"—A swollen river—Exhaustion—Kindly help—Fever—I am hailed as a "rain producer"—I go to see Prince Matu—I overhear an interesting conversation—Sally to the rescue—A would-be assassin—To the Semliki Valley—A black man's gratitude—A magnificent view—Albert Lake—Hunting reed-buck—I start for Mboga—Elephant hunt—Over the Mountains of the Moon—Fresh meat—Among the Bamba—The hot springs—Crossing the Semliki—Elephant camp—A morning call—Alive with game—Mboga—Church history.

SOME of my rambles round about Toro were of an interesting character, and I propose in this chapter to give a few of my adventures and experiences during these little trips.

About five miles from the Mission station of Toro is a very beautiful lake called Kijongo. It is only about two thousand yards long and eight hundred wide, but it is so beautifully situated at the foot of the great Mountains of the Moon that it was well worth a visit. On the eastern side of the lake were a number of conical-shaped hills, covered with bright green grass, but each one looked as if the top had been knocked off. I climbed to the summit of one of these hills, which was rather steep, and to my astonishment found it to be an extinct volcano, a huge circular hole, extending into the very heart of the hill and having a deep pool of clear blue water at the bottom. On the sides of the crater were most beautiful trees and all kinds of tropical vegetation. I climbed down to the water's edge, and found it to be quite warm and beautifully pure. There were wild geese swimming about on the water, and monkeys playing in the trees. I got the boys who were with me to light a fire by the water's edge, and here we boiled some of the water and made tea, roasted some potatoes, and generally enjoyed ourselves.

I paid a second visit to the Lake Kijongo, accompanied

CRATER OF EXTINCT VOLCANO, TORO.

by Lieutenant H——, when we embarked on its waters in a native canoe, with the purpose of finding out its extent, and if possible of shooting some of the wild geese which live thereon. But being unable to procure paddles, and the wind being too strong for punting, we failed in our object.

A bicycle which had been sent to me during my stay in Uganda was constantly used by me in taking my journeys abroad, and often I have had most exciting times when on the wheel. One morning I started off to visit a village some few miles away from the Mission station. The road was well cultivated, and about 5 feet wide. It was, in fact, the main road leading to Uganda. I had reached the top of a long hill, and on the other side was a gentle slope into the valley beyond; I knew the road well, having often passed that way, and I therefore prepared myself for a "coast." Near the foot of the hill

CRATER OF EXTINCT VOLCANO, TORO.

was a slight turn in the road, and as I approached it I put my feet again on to the pedals. I was going at a great speed, and as I rounded the corner an awful sight met my gaze; not twenty yards in front there lay in the centre of the path a huge lion, with head down upon his paws, facing the direction from which I was coming. It was impossible for me to stop the machine, the speed was too great. To the left of the path was a high wall of rock towering some 20 feet above my head; on the right was a steep incline, down, down, down, for 100 feet to a river. I had scarcely a second to take in the situation, and to make up my mind as to what course of action to pursue. It was a critical moment. What *could* I do? To turn to the right down the steep incline would have meant almost certain destruction; to attempt to stop, even if successful, would have meant pulling up at the entrance to the jaws of the King of the Forest. I therefore did the only thing that was possible—I rang my bell, and shouting at the top of my voice, then let the "bike" go at its topmost speed. As I shot into view, the lion raised his huge shaggy head, and seeing this unearthly creature come racing towards him making so strange a cry, he lifted up his voice and gave forth a most blood-curdling yelp. The apparition was too much even for him, and when I was about five yards from him he leapt on to the right of the path, and I just had room to scramble past him. Once beyond, I pedalled away as I never had before, not even looking round to see what next happened to the startled lion. But such an experience, if it happen once, is quite enough, and I learned the lesson not to "scorch," even in Africa, where there are no policemen.

I had promised the Prince of Mwenge that I would pay him another visit, and towards the end of the year I did so, starting from Toro at 8 a.m. on a lovely morning, with clear blue sky overhead, and a soft, cool breeze. I mounted my "speed-away" (as my bicycle was called) and was soon spinning along at a nice even pace; but alas! it did not last. A stump of a tree, completely hidden in the grass, caused the "speed-away" very suddenly to stop, and the rider very suddenly to dismount, who, when he picked himself up out of a bed of thistles

IN DWARF LAND.

into which he had alighted, saw to his great sorrow that one of the cranks of his faithful "bike" was badly bent. And so the "speed-away" had to be sent back to the Mission station, and I had to proceed on foot. This was a great disappointment, as I had anticipated a magnificent ride. However, it was all for the best, as I found out afterwards.

At ten o'clock I noticed strange black clouds gathering in the east, the direction we were going, and slowly but surely they came towards us; then very suddenly, without a minute's warning, there was a terrific flash of lightning, followed immediately by a perfect deluge of rain. There was nothing to do but to walk on, no houses were anywhere near. It lasted till eleven o'clock, and then a slow, drizzling rain till twelve, and another storm followed, if possible, of greater violence than the first. I shall never forget it. We were descending a valley, at the bottom of which was a stream, and over which our path led, when the second storm came on. Before we reached the water we could see that it was only a few feet wide, but so terrific was the downpour that in less than five minutes it was a torrent one almost shuddered to look upon.

Here was a pretty fix, eight miles at least from any inhabited place, and this torrent in front of us; every moment the stream increasing in dimensions, and we were shivering with cold. Some of the boys began to cry, and the men gave in and sat down, and my teeth chattered so that I could scarcely speak. It was no use sitting down, however; that would mean being starved to death with the cold, and so I seized the donkey that I had with me, and by sheer force thrust it into the stream to try the depth, but what was my horror when I saw the poor creature completely disappear, and it kept out of sight for some moments, coming at last to the surface some distance down the stream, and then swam to the opposite bank. At any rate, it was impossible for us to cross at that spot. I started off down the valley, telling the men to follow me, and after a toilsome walk through long, rank grass and tangled vegetation, we came to a place where the water seemed much shallower, although it was much wider. I plunged in, and found the water reached my chest, and when I got to the middle it was much deeper, and but for a fallen tree it would have been impossible to cross. As it was, the current was

SWAMPY GROUND.

so strong that I was completely thrown off my legs, but hung on to the tree, and finally dragged myself across. When I reached the shallow part again I waited for the men and boys, and with the greatest effort helped them all safely across, none getting more than a severe ducking, and few less. By this time I was so cold I could scarcely walk, my limbs were shaking so violently. The rain continued for three hours, the whole time coming down in sheets. On and on we went, and it seemed as though we should never reach our journey's end, and night was fast approaching. At five o'clock, two of the boys completely knocked up, and fell by the wayside unable to move, quite numbed with cold. Dear old Mika and another of the boys remained with them, and by short stages carried them the whole way. At six I was nearly done, and we were still some hours from the place, so I fired two shots in succession, hoping that as we were on a

MWENGE.

hill the people might possibly hear us and come to our relief. Happily it was so, and although we were so far away, the shots were distinctly heard. I reckon the angels ministered to our need and carried the sound a little bit further than usual. We shuffled along again for another half-hour, and all was pitch dark, and we could hear no sound but the howl of a hungry hyæna, somewhere in our rear following us, and no doubt anticipating a meal. Then came the sound of human voices, which grew louder and louder, and we knew that help was coming.

Suddenly three men sprang out of the darkness, challenging us with loaded guns. I replied, "Peace, I am the European teacher." Then such a shout went up, and we found that about one hundred armed warriors were all around us. But it was a shout of joy as they recognised me. Two powerful fellows seized me round the waist and lifted me like a baby in their arms on to their shoulders and carried me the rest of the way. How I did thank God for their help! Similar help was also given to the porters and boys, and several bands of men set off to assist those left behind. Thus I reached Mwenge in a sort of dream, borne upon the shoulders of my two stalwart friends, in the midst of this great band of warriors. I learned afterwards that the reason for this great display of arms was, that when they heard the reports of the gun they thought it was an attack upon their country by some enemies.

They brought to me some food and made a big fire in the house in which I lay. I had had no food since six in the morning, and it was 9 p.m. when we arrived. I stripped off my wet things and rolled myself up in a native bark cloth, but very soon fever came on and I was tossing about on my hard bed with aching limbs and throbbing head. About midnight I heard a soft step in the room, and then I felt a beautiful warm blanket thrown over me. I thought I was only dreaming, but in the morning I found that my boy Elisa had gone off and helped the porter who was carrying my blankets, and, tired out as he was, carried them in, and while every one else was asleep he covered me up and then sat by my bedside till morning. It was some days before the fever left me, and during it all, this boy Elisa sat by me; sometimes he would fetch cold water to bathe my fevered brow, or feed me with spoonfuls of soup, never leaving me for more than a moment or two. It was not the first time that he had showed his devotion to me. It was perfectly wonderful to note how this untutored lad, not long emerged from heathenism, had learned the art of lovingkindness. With this devoted attention and nursing I recovered in a week's time, and was able to proceed with my work as a teacher at Mwenge; and it was most encouraging to me and worth all the trials of the road

OFF TO SEE PRINCE MATU. (REFRESHMENT BY THE WAY.)

to see the real earnestness of the people to imbibe the blessed truths of the Gospel.

From Mwenge I journeyed to another place, hitherto unvisited by a European, and again my experiences were of a very lively character. We tramped due south for two days, passing through very wild but beautiful country, almost entirely uninhabited, and finally arrived at a large village. The gardens all seemed to be in a very dilapidated condition, and I found that famine was rife in the district, as there had been no rain and a terribly hot sun for some long time. By some strange coincidence soon after my arrival the rain came down in torrents. The chief and all his people then came to me in great state, and with much rejoicing, and *thanked me for bringing them the rain*, and I was immediately hailed by all as a great rain-producer, and people came from all quarters to see the wonderful white man who had brought the rain! I tried to tell them that it was not I but God who gives the rain and the sunshine and all things beautiful; but they said, "Who is God? We don't know, but we know that you are a great white man who has given us the rain!"

Another day's journey brought us to another large village, the capital of the district, with its prince, called Matu, and here I had another adventure.

When I approached the village I saw all the women leave it and the men only collect upon a hill. I took no notice of this, but went straight into the village and sat down. Presently the men all came towards me, and I greeted Prince Matu and asked him if I might spend the night in his village. After some little whispered conversation with his chiefs he consented, and took me to a small hut on the outskirts and told me I might sleep there if I liked. As it was tolerably clean I decided to sleep in the hut and not put up my tent. The people were not at all friendly and kept out of our way as much as possible. I put it down to the fact that they had never seen a white man before, and were very naturally afraid of him. It was about seven o'clock, and I had just finished my evening meal and was walking about in the banana garden in the moonlight, when some little distance away I heard some people talking very eagerly together. I crept up as quietly as possible and listened to their conversation. I was thunderstruck! What was this I heard? Sitting on the ground before a small fire were two men; the one I thought I recognised as the chief, the other was one of his followers, a great fellow with massive shoulders. The purport of their conversation was this: "How can we kill the European and possess ourselves of his two cows?" I was completely taken aback as I listened, and my first idea was to spring out upon them both and accuse them of their intention of taking my life. However, so fascinating was the conversation that I kept perfectly still and listened intently. I could not catch all that was said, but I most distinctly heard the man who was talking with the chief say, "I will spear him through the side of the hut when he is asleep." This was quite enough for me, so I returned noiselessly to my little hut. My boys had placed my bed on the right side, close up to the wall of the hut. My first precaution, therefore, was to get the boys to move the bed to the opposite side of the hut, without telling them my reason for this alteration. I took it for granted that the man whom I had heard talking to the chief had actually been to the hut to see upon which side my bed was put. I next tied up my little dog Sally to the doorpost, and finally rolled myself up in my blankets, lay down upon my bed, and waited. Somehow or other, as is so often the case, the very suspense made me sleepy, and I dozed off quite peacefully. Suddenly I heard Sally growl very quietly, but quite loud enough to at once arouse me. I listened in breathless excitement, and then Sally gave one of her short, sharp barks and I was out of bed in a twinkling, deliberately pushed open the door, and walked out into the moonlight. There stood my would-be assassin with spear upraised, just by the very spot where my bed had originally been placed. When he caught sight of me he seemed to gasp and then to vanish into thin air. I listened, but not a sound could I hear, so I returned to my hut, closed the door, and again flung myself down upon my bed and was soon fast asleep. Morning came, and when I got up and went out into the village there was not a soul to be seen anywhere. The chief and all his men had fled; having been discovered in the very act of attempting to take my life, they naturally thought I should wreak my vengeance upon them in the morning, and so they fled and I saw them no more.

This is not altogether an uncommon way the people of these districts have of attempting to put a person to death. My former colleague, Mr. A. B. Fisher, who left Toro at the end of 1896, was visiting one of these places round Toro, and had pitched his tent in the centre of a village, when, in the middle of the night, some ruffian thrust his spear right through the tent, the very side where Fisher was sleeping. It pierced the fly of the tent and the tent itself, right through the two blankets that were covering him, and stuck into the bed, and yet by a most merciful Providence did not even scratch the occupant of the bed. So we, who choose the wilder parts of Africa in which to live, that we may do what we can to dispel the darkness, must go forth with our lives in our hands, trusting only to the All-Seeing One to protect us from dangers which we ourselves are helpless to avert. But even a visit such as I have just described to Prince Matu, although apparently such a failure, was by no means so. When I got back to the Toro Mission station about a month afterwards a messenger came to me from this very man Matu, asking that teachers might be sent to himself and his people, so that they might learn to read the New Testament.

I did not return immediately to the station, as I have stated above, but after visiting Matu took a journey to the Semliki valley. There are living upon these plains a lot of wild fellows who live upon what they can hunt, and we were desirous of getting to know them. The first place I came to was Nsororo, which in the early days was a fort (Wavertree) occupied by a small section of Soudanese for the protection of the country of Toro from raiders from the north. Nothing of this fort could we see, but there was a very large garden with lots of people. Here I found one of the porters who had accompanied me to Mwenge when we had to go through the rain and storm, and whom, as he reminded me, I had helped over the swollen river, carrying his load for him. He brought me two eggs, saying that he was very poor, but that I was his dear friend, and he felt he must bring me some small present.

The next day we had to cross a low range of hills which overlook the great Semliki plains. For three hours we were going up and up very gradually, and all through thick mist, so that we could only just see the path a few yards before us. Quite suddenly we came to a sharp edge, and the path seemed to disappear at our very feet; and then the mist lifted and a magnificent view presented itself. Right before us, and yet seeming to be miles away, was the great plain stretching away to the Congo Free State. There in the dim distance were the indistinct outlines of the Barega Hills. Through the very heart of the valley flowed the great river Semliki, winding its way in and out like a great red vein; a little to the north we could see the beautiful Albert Lake, its waters sparkling in splendour with the reflected sun rays, like a sheet of burnished silver. Our path, as I said, seemed to disappear at our feet, and we now had a rare stiff bit of work in descending. Sometimes very steep, always rocky and rough—down, down we went for another three hours, when at last we stood upon the plain, and one hour's walk brought us to a large village on the banks of a beautiful river, a tributary of the Semliki. I pitched my tent close to the river-side under the shade of the lovely trees. Here were all kinds of birds and the air seemed filled with the music of their song, mingled with the gentle ripple of the stream as it raced along over its pebbly bed.

We were off again at six the next morning, and soon became aware that all around us were the graceful antelope, just waiting as it seemed to tempt us to shoot them. It was only a very tiny village that we reached, inhabited by a dozen or so hunters. I therefore spent a little time hunting, and without much difficulty brought down three fine reed buck, which I deemed sufficient for our immediate need. Another tramp across the plain for about three hours, passing through beautiful green pastures stretching away to the north, and as far as the eye could see, dotted all over with many kinds of antelope, elephants, &c., but there were very few people. Once we came upon a little hut, but it seemed to be occupied only by an old hunter, who spent a week or so hunting and then returned to the haunts of men.

Having reached the banks of the Semliki river, and not desiring to cross to the other side, we retraced our steps, and in six days reached the Mission station again without any further adventure.

My next trip was to Mboga, a large country to the west of the Semliki river, and about six days' march from Kabarole. I left about 4 a.m. with four of my boys and about a dozen porters.

Our first camp was in a village at the foot of the Chwantegi Hills. About four in the afternoon, as I sat in my tent, I heard a great yelling and crying, and climbing a tree which grew close to my tent, I soon found out the cause. A huge elephant was having a game in the gardens and houses of the people. Now, I thought, here is a chance to distinguish myself: I have only got a Martini rifle, and if I can kill an elephant with *that* what a great Nimrodic act it will be! At that moment the village people came racing to me and begged of me to go and shoot the beast ; and so, seizing my gun and with a look of determination which seemed to startle the natives, I set off alone after this gigantic creature. I first found the path it had made through the forest, and very gingerly I picked my way after it (for it had finished "making hay" with the houses for a time and retired into the bush). I said I was alone, but it is true that I was followed at some distance by half a dozen shivering blackies armed with spears. On I went as steadily as possible, and then suddenly there stood the leviathan of the forest, not ten yards in front of me, but all that I could see were its hind legs and its tail. One of the boys who had got near to me now immediately said in a husky whisper, "*Gite! gite!*" ("Kill it! kill it!"). Yes, that's all very well, but I think the sight of that huge monster was quite enough to settle for me, that to attempt to shoot with a Martini, would be about as much as my life was worth. The fact is, I came to my senses at that moment and felt just a "pygmy with a pop-gun," for, good as a Martini is, elephant is big meat to knock over, and he does not die too quickly, but has a kind of way about him when wounded which would make the fleetest pray for wings. So what I did was to stand and look at him, and no more dreamed of firing than of flying. It was not long, however, before my presence was observed, and a terrific crash, which seemed like a young earthquake, forcibly reminded us that something bigger than a dormouse was about. Fortunately he took a forward movement, and ploughed his way through the forest, huge trees snapping like matchwood against his colossal sides. My mind was then fully made up that it was time to return to camp.

The next morning we pursued our journey, and our path led up the mountain-side. We had to pass over the Mountains of the Moon, and although we crossed at the most northerly extremity, the highest point we reached was over 6,000 feet above sea-level. At the summit just before we descended a very large water-buck dashed out of the long grass in front of me, and stood about 150 yards off, to see who we were. It was standing a second too long, for a bullet from the Martini laid it low, and the meat was divided amongst the hungry porters.

At the western side of the mountains of the

BAMBA.

Moon we found ourselves among an entirely different tribe of people called the Bamba. Wild, and grossly ignorant, men and women alike practically nude, adorned with numberless charms, and some with bits of wood pierced through the nose protruding at either nostril, others with pieces of wood sticking upright in the upper lip. All the women seemed to wear iron rings round their necks, some had six or seven of them, which must have weighed at least 5 lbs. These rings were curled like a watch spring at each end, and were quite artistically made. The men, and some of the women, have their teeth sharpened to points, very much like shark's teeth. Their food consists of native beans and potatoes; rats and snakes, lizards and frogs being counted as luxuries.

Through the kindness of their chief I was taken to see the wonderful hot springs of the Mountains of the Moon. They are situated right at the base of Mount Gordon Bennett, and present a most remarkable appearance to the traveller. Nothing could be more strange and fantastic than the approach to these wonders of Central

HOT SPRINGS.

Africa. The chief promised me a guide to direct me to the place. About twenty young Bamba warriors, all armed with their spears, presented themselves to me, as being prepared to take me to this strange place.

We first climbed the mountain some hundreds of feet, and then one of the men pointed out to me in the distance what looked like a beautiful feathery cloud resting just above the earth's surface. This I was told was where the springs were. We made our way down the hill again and entered a thick forest which runs all along the western base of the mountain. We followed a tiny path winding in and out amongst the dense undergrowth for about three-quarters of an hour, and then we suddenly came upon a large well-made road, evidently much used, and along this we tramped. I asked what made the path so big, and was told that it was constantly traversed by numbers of sick folk who came every day from the districts round to bathe in the springs.

Suddenly we were made aware of a distinct rise in the temperature and also of a nasty sickly odour.

NATIVES WASHING IN HOT SPRINGS.

The vegetation very rapidly became ultra-tropical, and ferns, which in other places were small and stunted, here were large trees. The whole scene was changed. The path led through this most beautiful vegetation for about a quarter of an hour, and then we entered a thick cloud of highly odoriferous steam, and then into a wide, open space all over which were little bubbling springs of boiling water. Some were much bigger than others, the largest was throwing up water to about a foot in height. A thick deposit encrusted the whole area. The water

BAMBA WARRIORS AT THE HOT SPRINGS.

tasted of sulphur and potash, and was quite unpalatable. All the water as it bubbles up passes into one large stream and this is again lost in the forest.

We crossed the Semliki in a small canoe that was at hand, about 20 feet long and 1½ feet beam, cut out of a solid tree. The river at that point was seventy yards wide and the current was very strong. This brought us to our next camp, another Bamba village. All night long

TABALO, CHIEF OF MBOGA.

we were kept awake by the tramping and trumpeting of innumerable elephants. I never heard such a row, there must have been at least fifty of them. While we were sitting outside a hut about 9 p.m. roasting native potatoes by the camp fire, a big herd of them came charging towards the village. Fortunately their course was turned by the yelling of the natives, and we again sat down to roast our suppers. Early in the morning, just as I got out of bed, the boys came to me and said some water-buck were close to the house. I took up my rifle and went outside, and there, not fifty yards away, quietly feeding in the garden upon potato tops, was a small herd. I was able at once to replenish our larder for the day without any difficulty. The village people begged me to shoot some meat for them as they said they were half starved, and seeing a herd of cobus cob a little way from the village I went after it and brought down nine full-grown bucks in less than an hour. This greatly rejoiced the hearts of the poor hungry folk.

CHURCH AT MBOGA, WITH TWO WAGANDA TEACHERS.

After six days' tramp we arrived at Mboga. Here we were most heartily welcomed by the people. This little church has suffered no little persecution. When Christianity was first introduced by Waganda teachers the chief of the country strongly objected to his people imbibing its teaching, and when he found that in spite of his threats they continued steadfastly to believe, he did his utmost to stamp out the new religion from the country. He adopted all the most horrible tortures he could think of, killing some of the converts, burning down their houses, thrashing the teachers, and finally driving away into the forest all who had in any way attached themselves to the new faith. But it was all of no avail; the little band of Christians met day after day in a secluded spot in the forest and there continued to offer to God their praises and their worship. Finally, the chief himself admitted that Christianity had conquered, and he began diligently to search himself to see what kind of religion it was that made his people so different, and that made them able to suffer and even die rather than give it up. It resulted in his conversion, and he welcomed back his teachers and his people, rebuilt their houses and their church. But then came the Batatela rebellion, of which I have spoken in the preceding chapter, when the rebels again hunted down the Christians and drove all the people into the forest. In spite of all this trouble the Christians stood firm to their faith, and at the present time the Mboga church stands as a witness, on the very confines of the dark forest, to the power of the gospel of Jesus Christ. I spent a week with these whole-hearted, simple folk, then returned to Toro.

CHAPTER XII

SOUDANESE REBELLION

Political troubles—Mwanga's flight—Major Ternan wounded—Mwanga's capture by the Germans—Uganda regents—A record journey—Major Macdonald's expedition—Soudanese rebellion—Its causes—British pluck—Battle of Luba's Hill—Murder of Major Thurston—Disarming the Soudanese in Mengo—Native auxiliaries—Night attack—Battle on the plain at Luba's—Some one has blundered—Reinforcements—Destroying banana gardens—Death of George Pilkington and Lieutenant Macdonald.

THE year 1897 was filled with a succession of unforeseen political troubles, and since the occupation of the country by the British there has never been so much cause for anxiety in Uganda.

In the spring of the year, as I have already mentioned, the Batatela rebellion which occurred in the Congo Free State, although doing little damage in the British Protectorate, caused much unrest and serious apprehension, especially in the western provinces of the Protectorate, and the Government did not know how soon it might be necessary to have to meet an attack upon its possessions from that quarter. In May of the same year a plot was discovered by Mr. George Wilson, officer-in-charge at Kampala, in which three chiefs of Uganda were implicated.

Fortunately it was brought to light in the nick of time, and two of them were sent as prisoners to the

Eldoma Ravine, but the third Gabriel, the Roman Catholic Mujasi (head of the army), managed to escape.

The king was suspected of having had something to do with this attempt to bring about the rising against the Government. Knowing that he was suspected, and ever being a most arrant coward, he ran away from Mengo in July and escaped to Budu. It was rather an ignominious

MWANGA, EX-KING OF UGANDA.

flight for a king; he could not even find friends enough in Mengo to make his escape worthy of a king; not even being able to trust his gate-keepers, he actually cut his way through the great fence that surrounds his dwelling, and was accompanied by only one chief. He fled to the lake-shore, and there procured three small canoes.

His reason for running away would seem undoubtedly

to have been his fear of the consequences of his connivance with the other three plotters. But for some long time he had been dissatisfied with the restraint that was laid upon him; no longer could he carry on his old evil practices of murder and bloodshed and crime of every kind, and he disliked the moral restraints that the British Government naturally imposed upon him; of course many of the heathen most deeply sympathised with him in this.

Dr. Cook, of Uganda, writing on July 12th, says: "Nearly all the police have deserted; they went off with guns last night to join Mwanga. The Katikiro (Prime Minister) wrote rather a gloomy letter to Walker, saying he does not realise how serious a matter it is, and that the people hate and detest the conquerors. . . . The King hates the Europeans because they stopped his gross immoralities; the chiefs hate us because a Christian is expected only to have one wife, and because no slaves are allowed; and the people hate us because they say they are obliged to carry loads and make roads (measures adopted by the Government for the good of the country), and because the old heathen customs are dying away. The worst of it is the Katikiro says half of the Waganda, when they get to the scene of war, are likely to desert to the King's side. *The only faithful natives are the Protestants.*"

It is also stated that Mwanga, before running away, had sent to all the feudatory states—to Busoga in the east and Toro in the west, to Kaba Rega, ex-king of Unyoro, asking them all to join in a revolution, drive out all the Europeans from Uganda, and restore their old heathen customs.

When the King reached Budu most of the important Roman Catholic chiefs joined him, and the French priests who resided there, fearful lest they should be captured, were escorted by a small force of Soudanese troops to the borders of that province. Active measures were at once taken to suppress the rising, and Major Ternan, the acting Commissioner, with a small force, routed Mwanga's army in Budu, which then consisted of several thousand guns, beside thousands of spearmen. Major Ternan received a wound in the shoulder, but it was only slight, and did not incapacitate him for renewed efforts against the now scattered foe. This smash-up of Mwanga's forces at the very outset rather discomfited the King, and he fled into German territory. But it was an unlucky move for him. The German officers, who were on the alert, pounced upon him when he was quite unprepared, and took him prisoner to Mwanza towards the south end of the Victoria Lake. He was proclaimed an outlaw, and his infant son, Daudi Chwa, was placed upon the throne of Uganda on August 14th. Three regents were selected to administer the necessary Government matters, Apolo Kagwa, and Mugwania—the Protestant and Roman Catholic Prime Ministers, or Katikiros—and the Kangao, a leading Protestant chief.

The same month the rebels in Budu again collected and fought, with great loss to themselves, against the troops under the command of Lieutenant Hobart and Mr. Grant. In reply to a letter of thanks sent to Major Ternan, upon his arrival in England, by Sir John Kennaway, " for the consideration and active concern he had shown for the safety of the missionaries during these native rebellions," Major Ternan said : " It has been a great pleasure to me to have been of use to my friends of the Mission of Uganda, and I had the pleasure of drawing the attention of Lord Salisbury to the really excellent example set by the C.M.S. missionaries in Uganda. At a very critical moment they remained at their posts, though surrounded by rebels, and by so doing reassured the native chiefs in their vicinity, and were able to furnish us with valuable information when most needed. I am very glad I should have this opportunity of bringing to the notice of the Society the very high opinion that we have of the members of the Mission in Uganda."

Early in September I left Toro on a visit to Mengo, in order to settle certain matters with reference to our work. Of the troubles recorded above we in Toro were practically

DAUDI CHWA, PRESENT KING OF UGANDA.

ignorant. We had heard vague reports that Mwanga had fled, but had put them down as merely native stories, and it was only as I approached Uganda that I found in what a very unsettled state the country was.

I made a record journey into Mengo, accomplishing the whole distance (close upon two hundred miles by road) in eight days. Nothing of any importance occurred during the journey, but soon after I arrived most alarming news came to us.

In the middle of 1897 Major (now Colonel) Macdonald, R.E., was sent out by the Foreign Office to conduct an exploratory expedition in the districts adjoining the Italian sphere of influence, to the north-east of Lake Rudolph, and the authorities in the Uganda Protectorate were instructed to supply him for this purpose with three

SOUDANESE TROOPS.

hundred Soudanese troops and a number of porters. Major Ternan having left for the coast, Mr. W. F. Jackson took over the duties of Acting Commissioner of the Uganda Protectorate. Just as Major Macdonald was about to start northward a large portion of the Soudanese who were supplied to him by the Protectorate deserted. Mr. Jackson immediately followed them to their camp, after their desertion, at the Eldoma Ravine, and asked their reasons for deserting, which they readily gave. *First*, they were tired of being sent on successive expeditions while many of their companions-in-arms were comfortably settled in stations. *Second*, they were not allowed to take their women with them.* *Third*, they were going to a foodless and waterless country, where in all probability they would die. *Fourth*, the old complaint, that they were underpaid and insufficiently fed. Their grievances were undoubtedly of some weight, especially that concerning their pay. Five rupees a month is hardly the rate of pay one would expect to be meted out to a regiment of native troops of the British Government. They had been introduced into Uganda by Captain (now Colonel) Lugard in 1891 and 1892, being remnants of the old force used by Dr. Emin Pasha in the Equatorial Province, and left by him at Kavali's on the south-west shore of Lake Albert; and from the time of their entrance into the British Government employ, their pay had been but slightly raised. It is always a mistaken policy, and an expensive one too, to try and run a Protectorate like that of Uganda on insufficient means. But it is not for me to enlarge upon the right or wrong of the Soudanese complaints, but merely to tell the plain facts as they occurred.

A very grave mistake was made at the very outset of the mutiny, which no doubt made it a far more serious business than it otherwise would have been. Captain Kirkpatrick, of the Uganda Rifles, after trying to get the rebels of No. 4 Company to lay down their arms, ordered the Maxim to be fired upon them, having given them five minutes in which to comply, and they having refused to do so. This action made it then quite impossible to expect them to quietly talk the matter of their

---

* The Soudanese women always carry the cooking-pots and food, &c., of the men, and prepare the food for their husbands when they arrive in camp at night.

grievances over with their officers. They immediately marched westward to Nandi, and were joined by other companies. Most of the Nandi garrison joined them, taking possession of all the ammunition, and making a prisoner of Captain Bagnall, who was in charge there at the time, but finally left him unhurt. The Soudanese, who were at the other station called Mumia's, also joined them, and Mr. Tompkins, who was in charge, had a most marvellous escape, and it was only sheer British pluck that saved him and preserved the fort from the hands of the rebels. When he heard they were coming he at once put into the fort a mixed lot of Swahilis who were untrained soldiers, and by showing a bold front, in spite of the weakness of his garrison, turned the tide.

At the time this happened I was staying at Ngogwe, a large place between Busoga and Mengo, where the Church Missionary Society had a flourishing station, and it was here that I met brave Major Thurston on his way to Busoga to try and negotiate with the rebels before they committed themselves further. He was at the time suffering very considerably from illness, and we tried to urge him to stay a day or two to recruit his strength, but he evidently knew more than we did of what had happened, and how important it was for him to push on without delay. Alas! when he reached Luba's Fort in Busoga the Soudanese who were garrisoned there joined the rebels and made prisoners of Major Thurston, Mr. Wilson, and Mr. Scott, the last named having been sent from Mengo by lake with a fresh supply of ammunition and a Maxim gun for Major Macdonald when he arrived. The main body of the rebels had reached Busoga by this time, and the whole party fortified themselves in Luba's Fort. Major Macdonald and Mr. Jackson reached Luba's on October 18th, and immediately fortified themselves in a strong position overlooking the fort by the lake shore, which was occupied by the rebels.

The whole of the Major's force consisted of ten Europeans, eighteen Sikhs, and about 340 Swahilis—a mixed crowd, most of whom were new to arms; and he also had but a very limited supply of ammunition. The first real fight took place on October 19th, the rebels coming up to Major Macdonald's position in great force, and as they approached they shouted out that they had come for a "parley," and at the same time it was clearly seen that they intended an immediate attack. It was a very severe fight, Lieut. Fielding being killed, Mr. Jackson severely wounded, and Dr. Macpherson slightly so. Of the troops sixteen were killed and thirty wounded. At one time it looked as if the British must be defeated, but the battle was finally won, and the Soudanese suffered defeat, returned to their fort, and at once murdered Major Thurston, Messrs. Wilson and Scott.

That same morning a different scene was taking place in Mengo. At 6 a.m. messages came from Kampala to the missionaries at Namirembe, asking some to go up at once well armed, as there was to be an attempt to disarm the Soudanese garrison, which was then at Kampala. I was one of three who went. Upon our arrival there we soon saw how things stood. At the bottom of the hill were the Soudanese, all armed, and in the fort were about a dozen Europeans, each with a rifle; over the fort wall was pointed a Hotchkiss gun, but the whole of the breach was out of working order, and it could not possibly have been used even if an attack had been made upon us. A Maxim also was close at hand; this the gunsmith had in pieces, as it had jammed, and therefore that also was practically useless. A deputy from the officer in charge was then sent down to try and negotiate with the Soudanese, and, if possible, get them to lay down their arms peaceably, and warning them that if they refused we should open fire upon them. After half an hour's conversation they consented to do so, and it was a great relief to us all to see them bring their guns and ammunition and lay them down. All were then collected and brought into the fort, and the danger we so much dreaded was averted for the present. Native auxiliaries were then sent off from Mengo to help in the suppression of the rebels at Luba's, between three and four thousand

KATIKIRO OF UGANDA, WITH HIS SON.

Waganda, under their own chief, the Katikiro being in command.

On October 26th they had their first engagement, and fought most nobly, charging right up to the fort walls, alas! only to meet with an awful slaughter from the reserved Maxim fire of the wily rebels. Dr. Cook and Mr. Geo. Pilkington offered their services to the Government, the former to the wounded, and the latter to help in interpretation work, that there might be no misunderstanding between the European officers and the Waganda auxiliaries.

On the 26th and 28th of October the Waganda lost twenty killed and fifty-four wounded; on November 24th their losses were sixty killed and 280 wounded.

On October 31st Mr. Wilson, of Kampala, sent and asked if more of the missionaries would offer to go to the front. Three of us at once volunteered our services, and started off, viz., Messrs. Fletcher, Wilson, and myself. The first day we walked about thirty-four miles before 7.30 in the evening, and the following day reached a place called Mondos, and the third day reached Busoga, climbed the hill, and were most heartily welcomed into the fort by Major Macdonald. Mr. Jackson, who was severely wounded in the first fight, was taken into Mengo the same day, and Dr. Cook accompanied him.

It was a novel sensation to be aroused at daybreak by the bugle call, and one had to rub one's eyes a second time before one fully realised the position of affairs.

The fort which we occupied was built on a hill overlooking the lake, and commanding a complete view of the rebel fort, which, as I have said, was built on the shores of the lake. The fighting force at the command of Major Macdonald was not sufficient to make any definite attack upon the rebels, whose position was an exceptionally strong one.

However, on Tuesday, 9th, a half-hearted attack was made upon us; all was peaceful when we retired to rest, but about twelve o'clock a gun was fired, followed immediately by twenty or thirty others. As soon as I heard the first shot I was out of bed; there was a tremendous storm of rain, which made it almost impossible to see anything. All I could find out was that around me, on every side, volley after volley was being fired, and the bullets were whizzing about my head. I staggered through the blinding rain to the fort wall, and then found that an attack was certainly being made, but a very feeble one, and our men were just recklessly throwing away their powder. Then the Maxim commenced, and some twenty or thirty rounds were fired; what at, I could not imagine, for I could not see the sign of anything living outside the fort. The fight, or fusilade, lasted a quarter of an hour, but it seemed much longer;

A FAITHFUL UGANDA CHIEF.

the enemy then apparently withdrew. Several of our men described narrow escapes they had had, but there were no casualties to record. One of the Sikhs, however, who was standing on the Maxim bastion declared that one of the rebels rushed up within ten yards of the fort wall and fired at him point blank, the bullet just missing him, going over his shoulder. When all had quieted down we retired again to rest, leaving an extra guard in case of another attack. In the morning the friendly Waganda made an attack upon the Soudanese, but could do very little. The rebels held their ground, and nine Waganda were killed and twenty badly wounded. During their attack the Hotchkiss gun was fired on and off into the enemy's fort, but whether any damage was done is very doubtful.

On November 24th a severe fight took place. Being unable actually to storm the fort, on account of the smallness of our force, it was decided to advance within five hundred yards of the rebel fort and set up a strong position there, while the auxiliaries built a fort on the plain within eight hundred yards of the enemy's fort; this to be occupied by a strong force so as to make it impossible for the Soudanese to leave their fort to procure food. Major Macdonald, having gone into Kampala, Captain Woodward was put in charge. In the very early morning with a force of about two hundred Swahilis and two Maxim gun detachments composed of Indians, we moved from our fort on the hill to attack the mutineers and to take up the position above named. The Waganda guns were ordered to carry on operations on our right and left flank, the entire force to advance simultaneously. Unfortunately the Waganda, in their eagerness for the fray, and being quite unaccustomed to the ordinary methods of European warfare, rushed forward and commenced a heavy fire upon the rebels, who were in the wood just to the right of the fort. This was kept up the whole time that we were getting into position, namely, till 7.30, when the Soudanese were obliged to retire, and we advanced to within 250 yards of their fort, and held out for nine hours. The mutineers made several counter attacks upon our flanks, and twice the Waganda retired, leaving our lines exposed, but our Swahilis behaved splendidly, and repulsed the attack.

While this position was being held Captain Woodward pointed out a spot and gave instructions to the Waganda to build a small fort, but through some extraordinary mistake the fort was built in a hollow, being completely overlooked on two sides, and a thick wood being but a hundred yards away from the third side. Therefore, when evening came it was found to be utterly

MY PERSONAL ESCORT DURING SOUDANESE REBELLION.

untenable, and it was evident to all that " some one had blundered." Consequently that day's fighting was absolutely useless in hastening the termination of the affair, as we all had to retire to our fort at the top of the hill.

The Waganda loss was very heavy, no less than 340 being killed and wounded, and the Swahili loss was twenty-four, but no European was touched. Personally, I was here, there, and everywhere while the fight continued. In the first place I was sent to look after the stretchers and assist the wounded. The stretcher carriers, however, ran off, and so these were useless. Then in interpretation work I was kept fully occupied.

About the middle of the day one of the officers in charge of a company of Swahilis fell sick, and I was sent to take his place; and it was then that I had a very narrow escape. I was standing by my men, who were firing volleys at intervals under a very heavy return fire from

MIKA, MY FAITHFUL GUN-BEARER.

the rebels, when a bullet struck my hat, piercing the crown, and just missing my skull. Then a rush was made upon the left flank, which was occupied by the Waganda, and who retired. It was with the greatest difficulty that I got my men turned in time to meet the attack. My boys, who had accompanied me on this occasion, also displayed great bravery. I was next sent up to the right flank to look after a Sikh who had been badly wounded. I found the poor fellow dying, and while I was by his side another rush was made upon us, and about twenty desperate fellows came charging down upon us, firing as they advanced. However, our Maxim was turned upon them, and they retired a little, only to renew their efforts in a similar way; this time the Maxim jammed, and had to be carried to the rear; we turned our flank, and a second time repulsed them.

On one occasion, while sitting eating a little food, a bullet struck the ground not six inches from me, and flung up the dust over my repast.

On the 30th of November reinforcements arrived that greatly cheered our drooping spirits. Captains Harrison and Bagnall, and Corporal Brodie, and 295 Swahilis and a Maxim.

Major Macdonald again took the command at Luba's on the 5th of December, and on the same day Lieutenant Macdonald, with fourteen Sikhs and fifty men of the expedition arrived, with an additional supply of ammunition.

On the 7th another fight took place; three hundred and fifty men, with a Maxim, under the command of Captain Woodward, went down on to the plain to construct a new work within nine hundred yards of the enemy's fort. A fierce attack was made upon us, and for some time the issue seemed uncertain, but the steady volleys from Captain Harrison's well-trained men finally caused the rebels to slacken their efforts, and at 4 p.m. the new fort was so far completed as to be quite defensible. A garrison of some two hundred men was put into it for the night. During the day our losses were not heavy, the Swahilis losing five wounded, and the Waganda three killed and four wounded, but it was estimated that the rebel loss was heavy, probably thirty killed and wounded.

The same night the mutineers fired about two hundred rounds at the fort, wounding one man.

On the 10th of December a covering party was sent out under Captain Harrison, while the work of destroying the banana gardens, from which the rebels obtain their food, was carried on, but only a few shots were exchanged, and there was no serious loss on either side.

At one time during the day we began to wonder what the rebels were up to, as there was no response to our shots, and so to get a better view of the fort I very quickly climbed a tree, with the intention of spying out the land. I had climbed about 10 feet when, whiz-z-z came a bullet just above my head, breaking the small twigs close to me, and I hurriedly descended. The man who fired at me was on the rebel fort wall, with several others. Captain Harrison, having seen this, took twelve picked men, and one other European, and crept up in the grass to within about one hundred and thirty yards of the fort, and commenced sniping. But a party of the rebels, seeing that the captain was right away from the rest and had only a small number of men with him, made a charge at them, and when within about thirty yards fired a volley; but it was done hurriedly, and the bullets missed their mark; this necessitated a very speedy return of the snipers.

However, on the following day, when Captain Harrison again took out his covering party, that the Waganda might continue their work of cutting down the banana gardens, a most furious attack on the front and left of our force was made. Mr. George Pilkington took up his position close to Captain Harrison, to superintend the cutting down of the bananas, and no sooner had he done so than his boy Aloni saw a company of Soudanese concealed in the grass close at hand, and fired at them. Captain Harrison and Mr. Pilkington, thinking them to

HARD AT IT.

be Waganda, reprimanded the boy for firing without orders, but his fire was responded to, and one of them took deliberate aim at Mr. Pilkington and fired several times, hitting him in the thigh and breaking the femoral artery. He was carried to the rear and back to the fort, but died in a few minutes after reaching it. Lieutenant Macdonald was also shot dead at the same time, a rush having been made upon the left flank which he was commanding.

Again and again the enemy made most desperate attacks upon our men, sometimes getting up to within twenty yards of our firing line. The Swahilis fought most bravely, considering their inexperience as soldiers. All day long the killed and wounded were being brought in until the total had reached thirty.

The man who shot Pilkington, after seeing him fall, fired again at the native officer (captain) of Captain Harrison's regulars. He was a fine fellow, a Soudanese, but was loyal to the backbone. Alas, the bullet took effect, hitting him in the arm below the elbow, and smashing the bone. The man who shot him then cried out, " What are you doing here, Bilal? I know you; have you come here to kill your brethren? Go back to Egypt." To this the officer replied, " Yes, we will wipe you all out, for you are rebels," and with that he drew his revolver with his left hand and shot him; and thus Pilkington's murderer fell.

After the fighting was over we all withdrew to our forts, some to the one on the plain, others to that on the hill. The Major, on hearing of the death of Pilkington and his brother, was much overcome, but he bore it like a soldier and a Christian. He said to me that he felt the loss of Pilkington most keenly, " My brother," he said, " was a soldier, and he died as a soldier expects to die, but this could not be said of Pilkington."

Just before sundown a little band wended its way out of the fort, along the ridge of the hill, every head uncovered, and every heart bowed low. Fifteen Indian Sikhs in double line marched slowly and with measured steps in front, then I followed, reading aloud the solemn words of the Burial Service; next came the body of Lieutenant Macdonald carried by six of his fellow officers, and behind him was the broken-hearted Major. Then came the second bier, that of dear Pilkington, carried by eight devoted Waganda chiefs; and lastly followed the other Europeans and a number of Waganda and Swahilis. The solemn procession at last reached a spot on the crest of the hill, overlooking the beautiful Victoria Lake, into which the glorious sun was just sinking; and here upon this hallowed spot, being that whereon Bishop Hannington was murdered, we laid our brethren down to rest with a sure and certain hope of a glorious resurrection on the great Easter morning.

On Sunday, December 12th, one of our party, Mr. Allan Wilson, who had joined the forces of Major Macdonald at the same time as myself, was taken seriously ill with dysentery and fever, and it was arranged that I should take him in to Mengo. It was a most difficult and responsible task, but I decided to do my best. I left Luba's on the following morning, and got a number of men to carry my patient in a hammock, and when we reached the lake shore I procured a canoe, and making it as comfortable as possible with an awning to keep off the sun, we started to cross to the mainland of Uganda. Arriving at the other side in safety, we met two Government officials, who had been instructed to protect the landing-place with a small force of Waganda. At 8 a.m., the third day we got to Ngogwe, where Mr. Baskerville, of the C.M.S., was at his post, in spite of the troubles all around, and here at this station I left my charge, going on alone into Mengo to deliver letters entrusted to me by Major Macdonald. I reached Mengo at midday, having tramped about fifty-six miles in two days.

On the 16th of December I was on my way back again to the front, in charge of a steel boat which was wanted by the Major to rig up as a miniature gunboat; and on the 19th arrived once more at Luba's. The Major greeted me very heartily, and expressed his pleasure at my return.

Mr. Fletcher and myself were now the last of the missionaries at the front, and the duties of the day fell very heavily upon us. We attended to the wounded, took our turn with the others as night and day watchers, and in addition to this we were constantly called up sometimes at midnight to act as interpreters.

CHAPTER XIII

SOUDANESE REBELLION (*continued*)

The major leaves for Budu—Christmas Day in camp The mutineers raid the gardens –Vigorous attack upon the Waganda camp—Mwanga's escape from Germans- Evacuation of rebel fort- I am sent to Ripon Falls- Attempts to blow up the dhow—Fort building—Rebels attempt to cross into Uganda Indian troops arrive—All into Mengo—With Major Macdonald to Kabagambi -A responsible charge –A night scare—A brush with Mohammedans- Off again to the front Rifle-stealing –A kind offer –More fighting Severe struggle at Kabagambi—Death of Captain Maloney.

NEWS of further troubles in Uganda having reached us, Major Macdonald, with five other Europeans and about two hundred soldiers, left on the 20th for Budu to endeavour to smash up the rebel king's army, which had again collected, and which was doing considerable damage in the country. We now received the good news that the Indian troops that had been sent by Sir Arthur Hardinge from the coast were to arrive in another month.

On the 23rd a skirmish took place at Luba's. I was the officer on guard when about eleven o'clock I saw a lot of the rebels leaving the fort and coming in our direction; this I immediately reported to the officer commanding, and a hundred of our men were sent off to meet them under Captain Austin. The Waganda, seeing that our force was rather a small one, and thinking that our men would be driven back, dashed down the hill about three hundred strong and charged the mutineers, reserving their fire until at close quarters. The Soudanese turned and fled, and the Waganda, not knowing when to stop, rushed after them, and it came about that when they were tired of chasing them the rebels suddenly turned round upon them. The Waganda were tired, and, what was worse, their ammunition was nearly done. The mutineers soon found this out and in their turn charged down upon them and drove them back with considerable loss; ten Waganda being killed and fifteen wounded, while in Captain Austin's force only two were wounded. At first the Waganda leaders were much discouraged and inclined to blame the Europeans, as they said that we left them to it, that they had come to our assistance, and when we saw them come we stopped advancing. But after all they were in the wrong, as it would have been impossible for us to have followed them, going, as they did, at full speed close at the heels of their foes.

Christmas Day, with all its holy memories, was spent in quietness, at least so far as the rebels were concerned. They kept themselves shut up in their fort, and we did in ours. The flies were our greatest enemies on that peaceful day; the heat was terrific, and this, combined with the horrible state of our camp, attracted millions of these awful little pests. They would settle on one's nose and mouth and eyes, and were so anxious to procure the little moisture which was secreted from one's brow on a hot day like this, that they could actually be picked off with the greatest ease, and they did not seem to think of flying away. In the evening of the day we tried hard to get up a little amusement. One commenced to sing "In the dear homeland," and immediately another fellow jumped up and said "Look here, H——, you just shut up; I can't stand that. Would to God I *were* in the homeland and somewhere near my dear wife!" Another commenced soon after to him "The Star of Bethlehem," and this was taken up by one or two more, but it was very evident that everybody felt rather *down*. At last, when a few lines of the "The old folks at home" were sung, several got up and went to bed, and this crushed everything, and so the day closed.

The mutineers were now getting very short of food. As described in the previous chapter the banana gardens from which they had procured their support were destroyed, and they had to either starve or constantly go further afield for the necessaries of life. In the daytime they could not leave the fort, as our men were ever watchful, and at once sent out forces to stop them if they attempted to do so; but at night it was more difficult to put a check upon them, and night after night they would go out into the darkness and raid the villages, killing the inhabitants and stealing cattle and food. Once they went out in canoes they had, to a place on the mainland where there was plenty of food, and there in the night they murdered the inhabitants, set fire to their houses, and took everything in the shape of food that they could lay their hands upon.

One morning as I went on watch I saw a most exciting finish to what had been an exciting chase. A number of the rebels had crossed by canoe to a headland just opposite their fort, apparently for the purpose of obtaining food, when they were discovered by the Waganda, who had a force on the western bank of the Nile, and who immediately manned several canoes and chased them. I was just in time to see the finish. Two of the rebels' canoes arrived back at their fort in safety, but the other two foundered, and the occupants were thrown into the water; some were drowned, and others, while clinging to the overturned boats, were captured by the Waganda and taken ashore. Several other of the

Soudanese were caught on the land and immediately taken prisoners and subsequently executed.

On New Year's morning we had a little bit of excitement. Our big gun (2lb. Hotchkiss) was fired to usher in the New Year, just at twelve o'clock. The shell was directed to fall into the rebel camp, and I believe did so. At 3 a.m. the mutineers, thinking they would return the compliments of the season, came up, 150 strong, and made a very desperate attack upon the Waganda camp. The firing lasted about an hour, and at times we thought from where we were that the rebels were in possession. At daybreak, however, we found that the Waganda had most successfully repulsed the attack, one only of their number being killed and three wounded, while it was estimated that the Soudanese lost at least four killed and six wounded. There is no doubt that the Waganda defended their camp most bravely, reserving their fire till the last moment. It was thought that the Soudanese expected that we should come out of our fort in great numbers to help the Waganda, and it was found that a large number of the mutineers had been hiding just a few hundred yards from our fort, ready no doubt to attack it, and, if possible, take possession as soon as we should leave it. They had counted without their host, and we felt sure the Waganda could defend themselves in camp without our aid.

Then came the most startling news, that Mwanga, the rebel King of Uganda, had escaped from the Germans, returned to his country and was collecting an army in Budu to join forces with the Soudanese. Major Macdonald, who was in Mengo, at once started off with a large force to meet him. Everything was looking very black at this time. It was half expected that the Soudanese garrisons of Unyoro, Toro, and Budu would join the rebels, and that Mwanga, being still recognised as king by the common people, would have a very large following. If this were the case nothing but a trained regiment could ever win back the country.

A very fortunate capture was made at Fort Alice, when two of Mwanga's boys, bearing one hundred letters, written by Mwanga to different chiefs asking them to help, were discovered by the aid of friendly Waganda, and thus did not reach their destination. This was most fortunate, as these letters, if distributed through the country, would no doubt have led to a general rising amongst the disaffected Mohammedans and heathen.

The siege of the mutineers' fort had lasted nearly three months when the rebels, reduced to but a fraction of their original number, evacuated their fort during the night of January 9th. Their intention undoubtedly was to join hands with the other Soudanese who up to that time had remained loyal.

The Indians had not yet arrived, and our force was not large enough to split up. The rebels had a large Arab dhow and several native canoes, the former being at the fort when they first occupied it. The Waganda, under the command of one of the Europeans, made several attempts to stop the crossing of the dhow, but the Wasese boatmen were not to be relied upon, and whenever the enemy opened fire upon the canoes they paddled away as hard as possible for the shore. On January 7th I left the fort on Luba's Hill, in the company of Mr. Fowler (late R.N.), with orders to follow up the rebels and prevent them, if possible, from crossing the Nile. A large escort brought us down to the lake shore, where we embarked in two large canoes. I was in one and Fowler in the other; both of us had a Maxim gun fixed to the bows of the canoe. Fowler set off by lake to try and capture the rebels' dhow, which had been sighted in the act of taking provisions, &c., to the enemy's camp.

while I proceeded with greatest possible speed to the Waganda camp at Lugumba's, to help the two Europeans who were in charge there.

Fowler seemed to have had a pretty hot time of it, as the rebels, when they saw him coming towards them, opened upon him a very heavy fire, and he was obliged to retire on account of the unwillingness of the boatmen to advance. As soon as I arrived on the mainland I went up to see the fort that was being built on the hill, overlooking the lake, to protect the crossing; here I was put in charge for the night. But about midnight Fowler turned up with letters, stating that the rebels were making for the crossing above the Ripon Falls, which was entirely unprotected. We were both ordered to set off, taking our Maxims and a couple of canoes, to stop them if possible. All night long we wandered about in an open boat waiting and expecting every minute to come up with a canoe full of Soudanese. Just at early dawn a terrible storm came on and made it necessary for us to take shelter. Fortunately when we put in to shore we found ourselves near a small village, and into a house, small and filthy dirty, we crammed ourselves; it was a case of "any port in a storm." We were both hungry, having had little or no food all the previous day; fortunately I had with me a small tin of potted meat which we ate with some hard ship's biscuits. We then stretched our legs on two native beds in the hut, and I blush to confess that we turned out two poor innocent darkies on that cold night to get into their beds, while they sat by the fire and shivered. The live stock was far too busy to allow us to sleep, and in half an hour we had had quite enough, and as the storm had abated, and the sun was up, we got into our canoes, and in about half an hour reached the crossing above Ripon Falls, with the satisfaction of knowing that we were there before the rebels had crossed. About three hundred Waganda had come on by land in the night and were there waiting for us.

The next two days we spent building a fort to command the crossing; and then received instructions from the officer in charge at Luba's to try and blow up the dhow under the cover of night. At 1 p.m. we once more mounted the Maxim on to a large canoe. Our plan was as follows: Fowler was to go off in a small canoe with four picked men and was to proceed along the shore towards the rebel fort, and in the darkness to creep near enough, and throw a charge of dynamite into the dhow that was supposed to be moored off the land close to the camp. I was to follow behind him in the big canoe with the Maxim and a few of our best and most reliable men, and as soon as he had thrown in the bomb, to open Maxim fire upon the rebels to cover Fowler's escape. Our plans seemed beautifully laid out and we looked forward to our task with a great deal of eagerness. Alas! we wandered about up and down the shore all night and no dhow could we find. Instead, however, of returning direct to our fort at the Ripon Falls we first visited the big fort which the rebels had evacuated, and around the walls of which all our fighting had been carried on. There was not a soul to be seen; the earthworks erected by the rebels were most interesting; the whole place was honeycombed like a rabbit warren, and holes that the mutineers had dug to use as rifle pits, were everywhere, and we at once saw what a terrible disaster it would have been had we, with our weak force, attempted to rush the fort; for even if we had succeeded in getting inside we should most likely never have got out again alive; every man would in all probability have been shot down by unseen marksmen.

Again we spent the day searching about the lake for any sign of the enemy, and at midnight orders came to us from the commanding officer to return to the fort at Ripon Falls. Fowler was then recalled to Luba's Hill and I was left in charge of the fort until further notice, with about five hundred guns and a Maxim. I immediately set about strengthening our position, so as to make it possible for us to withstand an attack from a superior force of the enemy. The walls of the fort were made thicker, and were loopholed for rifles all along. At three corners we built Maxim bastions, and all round the fort wall at a distance of five yards we put a thick bush of thorns two yards wide, which would be an additional protection in case of attack.

One day, a party of rebels were seen on the opposite bank, and we prepared to give them a hearty reception if they attempted to cross, but when they saw our fort and the Maxim guarding the crossing, they thought better of it and went off in another direction. This news I sent off to the chief officer, and he at once despatched reinforcements to join me—Captains Harrison and Austin, and Lieutenant Malcolm and Corporal Brodie.

Captain Harrison then took charge. I had already sent out scouts all over the country to get information, and soon after the Captain arrived one of them came back bringing word that the rebels had gone into North Busoga, and had abandoned the idea of crossing at the Ripon Falls. In the meanwhile the first company of the Indian troops, under Lieutenant Scott, had arrived at Luba's and were immediately despatched by Captain Woodward into Mengo to help garrison the capital; he himself accompanied them, as he feared the Soudanese in Unyoro would now join the rebels and advance against Mengo. When he arrived there with the Indians, he found all peaceful, and heard that the garrisons in Unyoro were still loyal, and his former information was false. He then set off along the west bank of the Lwajali river, to try and prevent the enemy from crossing into Bukoba, and thus to get a free passage into Mengo.

While this was going on Major Macdonald, who was in Budu, had a most successful fight against Mwanga's army, gaining a most complete victory, with only the loss of five killed and twenty-one wounded, while the enemy left twenty-five dead upon the battlefield and thirty-five dead were found in the pursuit which took place afterwards, and forty wounded. This victory did much to re-establish confidence amongst the natives in Budu.

Strange to say, the garrisons in Unyoro, &c., did not show any further signs of rebelling, and were apparently waiting to see what would be the next move of the mutineers. A very small force was now left at Luba's and at the Ripon Falls, and the rest marched into Mengo, and then on in a northerly direction, down the left bank of the Nile, to try and stop the crossings; but as we journeyed we heard that it was too late; the enemy had already crossed, and were in the country that lies between the Lwajali river and the Victoria Nile. It was evident that the mutineers wanted to get to Mruli, where there was a large force of their companions in arms, who were up to that time loyal, but who, they seemed to believe, would join them upon their arrival at their fort; but to accomplish this they first had to cross the Lwajali, and this was a difficulty, the river being choked up with thick papyrus growth, and only very narrow channels being cut.

After his victory over Mwanga's army Major Macdonald again turned his attention to the Soudanese rebels, and with a large force of Swahili and Waganda he followed after Captain Woodward, who, as is stated above, was on the west bank of the Lwajali.

I was with Major Macdonald, and by this time was getting quite used to the military life, and much as I disliked the whole business, it was clearly my duty to stick to it to the bitter end, or until it was possible to completely smash up the rebel force and put Uganda in safety.

Although it was distasteful, one felt sure that one was of some little value as an interpreter, if in no other way, and I willingly agreed to continue with the army. Up to that time I had taken part in practically all the engagements at Luba's; had often been three nights a week on watch duty, had helped to attend every day to about fifty wounded men, and in addition to all this had acted as interpreter at all hours of the day and night. Mr. Fletcher, the other remaining missionary, who had similar duties to my own, was at this time with Captain Woodward.

By forced marches, Major Macdonald very speedily caught up Captain Woodward, who was moving very cautiously and slowly along the banks of the river. After joining forces with him, the Major selected Lieutenant Scott, Lieutenant Malcolm, Mr. Fowler, and Mr. Fletcher to proceed at once by forced marches to Mruli, and if possible to disarm the garrison there, which consisted of Soudanese troops; then to proceed to Masindi and Hoima and do the same. Upon the success of this mission everything depended. In four days this flying expedition reached Mruli, and Lieutenant Scott was able with great tact to rescue the Soudanese garrison; he then marched to Masindi, the headquarters of the Unyoro command.

On February 4th the Major went on an exploring tour as far as Kabagambi, reaching there about 12 midday, and then procured a canoe to go out on to the Lake Kioja. It took us at least an hour to push our way through the papyrus which thickly fringed the bank of the lake ; then we saw that it was next to impossible for a large force to cross the lake at this point, and if attempted a few determined men armed with breech-loaders would well be able to stop them.

The Major then directed that all the other canoe crossings should be blocked, and finally left a party of Waganda to guard the spot. Captain Woodward, on account of ill-health, was ordered into Mengo, and I was sent to look after him, and also to take charge of fifty boxes of ammunition which were not needed at the front. He being unable to walk, I had a hammock constructed for him, and we marched only in the early morning and also in the evening, when the sun had less power. But it was a most difficult journey. To protect the fifty boxes of ammunition we had only twenty armed Swahilis and the porters to carry it, and some seven days' journey before us. This in itself would have been responsibility enough for one so inexperienced as a soldier, but added to this was the care and constant attention necessary for a sick man.

For five days all went well, and we arrived at a place called Kitibwa, a few days' journey from Mengo, and then our troubles commenced. Late in the evening the chief came to tell me privately that the Mohammedans had rebelled, and had joined the mutineers; that his own followers, a great number of whom were Mohammedans, had suddenly disappeared, whither he knew not, but suggested that, having seen the great quantity of ammunition that I had, and the small force to protect it, they had arranged to attack us and possess themselves of it.

To add to this, I received a letter from Mengo, even while the chief was talking to me, giving me information to the effect that there was a general rising of the Mohammedans in Mengo and elsewhere, and telling me to protect myself accordingly. I did not wish to trouble

Captain Woodward in his weak state with these matters, but unfortunately he overheard the conversation, and I told him all; he was much upset. I suggested that we should at once raise some works to protect ourselves, in case of an attack, and send off into Mengo for reinforcements. It was midnight when we came to this decision, and right on into the morning we worked away our hardest, making rifle pits for the men to surround the ammunition. The Captain was greatly excited and caused me much anxiety, for although he was an experienced officer I had been put in charge of the caravan, and in his weak state of health any excitement would be dangerous. At daybreak our work was done, and after sending out scouts in all directions we tried to get a little sleep. Again letters came in to say that five hundred Mohammedans had collected at a place not a day's journey from where we were camped, and in a direct line between ourselves and the capital. There was nothing for it but to remain where we were, using every precaution, and I was not without hope that we should be able to resist an attack.

At midday a report reached us that a European from Mengo was coming towards us, and would arrive before nightfall. Very patiently we waited, and sincerely hoped he had a good number of men with him to reinforce our small escort. About 4 p.m. a fusilade of musketry was distinctly heard not far from us, and we at once sent off scouts in that direction to find out the cause. In an hour they came back, saying that a large party of Mohammedans had attacked a loyal chief with his following, and had beaten him off, killing several of his men; but the scouts also said that the enemy had gone on to the north. Strangely enough, these men had actually passed within an hour's march of our little camp, probably having heard of the approach of the European from Mengo, and being afraid to attack us on that account.

Just before dark the European arrived, but to our astonishment had only a dozen recently raised native troops. However, we had to make the best of it; all night long we maintained a very careful watch, and kept sending in all directions small skirmishing parties, so as to give us immediate warning of any approach of the enemy.

The night passed by in safety, and before daybreak we started for Mengo. At 10 a.m. the sun was so hot that I felt it would not be right to keep Captain Woodward exposed to it longer; we camped by the roadside on a hill, but unfortunately all around us was the high tiger grass, capable of hiding a whole army, and completely obscuring our view of the surrounding country, there being no better position anywhere near. We cleared as much ground as possible, and stacking all the ammunition in the centre of the camp pitched our tents close by and arranged the small forces at our disposal in a complete circle round the camp. When night came on all seemed quiet, and the scouts which were constantly coming and going reported no appearance of the enemy. The others retired to rest, but I remained on watch through the night.

I had entered my tent about 2 a.m. to sit down for a moment, having just inspected the guard, when a great cry arose close to our camp and a shot was fired. I ran out immediately and inquired of the sentry what was wrong, and he reported having seen a large party of the natives on the northern side of our camp and one had fired at him. The men, by this time, were all at their post ready for action, but no enemy appeared, and I began to think that the sentry had been dreaming, and had discharged his own rifle. As a last precaution I sent off in the direction he indicated a small skirmishing party of picked men. They had just disappeared into the darkness when a fusilade commenced from that quarter and they returned.

My man Mika, who had accompanied them, told me that they had met with a party of Mohammedans lying in the grass only one hundred yards from camp, and they had fired upon them and then chased them as they fled. He, Mika, had caught one of them, and was in the act of bringing him into camp when the fellow had suddenly produced a knife which was concealed in his cloth, and slashed out at Mika and unfortunately, in the struggle that ensued, had made his escape. However, he brought into camp the fellow's cloth which he had been wearing and had slipped out of when he escaped, also a small bundle, containing, amongst other things, letters of an incriminating character written by some chief to incite the Mohammedans to rebel. There was no sleep that night, all had to keep ready for immediate action; but as is so often the case when all is ready for giving the enemy a warm reception, he keeps away; and he did so that night.

We got safely into Mengo the next morning about eleven o'clock, and I confess it was a great relief to me to see that ammunition stacked up in the fort at Kampala, and to know that there my responsibility ended. Captain Woodward was little the worse for his journey from the front, but was invalided home a week after his arrival in Mengo.

I had one day in Mengo to rest, then was again despatched to the front to catch up the Major, who was somewhere in Bugerere. A very large caravan, consisting of about three hundred loads of provisions, &c., was put under my care. I was the only European, and I had an escort of forty Swahilis armed with Martini rifles. As we could not leave till 2 p.m. we were obliged to camp within five miles of Mengo, but even here enemies were met with. I had arranged sentries at different points to guard the camp, but Swahili sentries are not at all particular about keeping awake, and one of these gentlemen went to sleep, to find in the morning that his rifle had been stolen. Another fellow, against orders, had left the camp late in the evening with the pretence of buying food, when he was set upon by two Mohammedans; he fired at them, but missed, and was then overpowered and his rifle taken, together with his belt of ammunition, and he himself left senseless by the roadside.

The following day, while performing a very long march, I was seized with fever, and in a short time was quite incapacitated for walking. The men made a rough stretcher, upon which I was carried to Nakanyonyi. When I arrived there I was more dead than alive. At last the reaction had come; up to that time, through all the horrible scenes of war and bloodshed I had come in perfect health, never getting even a scratch, although I had taken part in no less than eleven engagements; at last to be laid low, by the most subtle of all foes—malaria.

It was very fortunate for me that at Nakanyonyi there resided a C.M.S. Missionary, Rev. G. R. Blackledge, one of the three who had accompanied me up-country from Zanzibar to Uganda. Most tenderly he nursed me, putting me into his own bed, and himself taking charge of the great caravan that I had brought. All that night I lay in a critical condition, and the next morning I was not much better. It was imperative that the caravan should proceed at once, as much depended upon maintaining a constant supply of food at the front.

Mr. Blackledge most nobly offered to take my place, and go forward with the caravan. I was deeply grateful to him; for it would have been the death of me to move again for a day or two.

He reached Major Macdonald on the 18th of February, just in time to join in a most successful skirmish with the enemy. While in the act of pitching camp a strong force of the enemy advanced against them with flags, but our men met them with a terrific fire; then fixing bayonets they charged, and the enemy fled, leaving their dead and wounded behind them. Several were taken prisoners, and a number of rifles captured. Our total loss was fifteen killed and wounded and the enemy's at least twenty-five.

In the meantime Lieutenant Scott with his contingent of Indians had been completely successful, and now all fear as to whether the Unyoro garrisons would join the rebels had vanished and strong hopes were entertained that the whole affair would speedily be brought to a close. As a matter of fact another fight took place at Kabagambi, where the enemy had built a strong fort, but were completely smashed up by Captain Harrison's force, after one and a half hour's fighting of the severest character. When the fort was captured one of the enemy's officers and two sergeants were taken, and no less than 514 women and children who had followed the rebels, and the majority of whom belonged to companies in Mengo who had not mutinied. The enemy left one officer and thirty-two men dead about the fort, and their total loss was probably not far short of a hundred men. The British loss, however, was heavy: ten killed and seventeen wounded; amongst whom were Captain C. A. Malony, R.A., who subsequently died of his wounds, and Lieutenant P. B. Osborn, Oxfordshire Light Infantry.

But here my connection with the rebellion came to an end. I know it was but an insignificant part that I played, but most gladly I did what I could, and although the honours and distinctions that were showered upon the military section did not reach the missionaries, still our ample reward came with the knowledge of the fact that we had done our duty as Englishmen.

Some have severely criticised us missionaries for taking any part whatever in the suppression of the rebellion, and others have even looked coldly upon us and condemned us; but we can only hope that our example will have no harmful effect upon the tender consciences of such, and will stimulate others to act upon the principle contained in the words—

> "Where duty calls, or danger,
> Be never wanting there."

N.B.—Subsequent events have shown that the fight mentioned above was practically the finish of what has proved the most serious affair in the history of the Central African Protectorate of Uganda. The rebels were then driven into the Bukedi country, and their leader was killed. Mwanga, the rebel king of Uganda, and Kabarega, of Bunyuro, were captured in April of this year, 1899, and have been transported to the coast. Peace was then finally established in the country.

PART III

UGANDA TO THE WEST COAST

CHAPTER XIV

UGANDA TO CONGO FREE STATE

Westward Ho—Uganda escort—An alarm—Blackened ruins—Elephants—My reasons for journey through Pygmy land—The Bishop's consent—Preparations for the start—Farewells—Escorts—The start—Violent earthquakes—Elephants again—A glorious sight—A faithless donkey—Sally submerged—An elephant hunt—Another snake story—Wakonjo village—Kikorongo—Chased by a hippo—Katwe—Hospitality of No. X. Company—Their loyalty.

THE illness which I mentioned in the previous chapter continued with great severity for a month, and when convalescent I had a fortnight's cruise on the Victoria Lake, visiting Kagei, at the south of the lake, which is two hours from Nasa, and also calling at the two German stations of Bukoba and Mwanza. I was very soon active and strong once more, and the cruise on the lake was most invigorating, and blew away all the traces of fever.

When I got back to Mengo I went straight to Her Majesty's Commissioner in Uganda and asked his permission to proceed at once to Toro. To my great joy he consented, providing that I had with me a sufficient escort, as it was supposed that Mwanga was still about the neighbourhood of Ankole. Of course to this I readily agreed: the officer in charge at Kampala kindly gave to me three Snider rifles with which to arm my boys. I next visited the Katikiro of Ugando and asked him to levy for me fifty Waganda guns to accompany me to Toro.

About a week from that time all was ready: thirty Waganda guns instead of fifty, but quite sufficient I judged for anything we should want.

The first day out from Mengo I had a review of all the men, examined their arms, and to my amusement found that not more than fifteen of the men had more than one charge of powder and two caps, and only twelve men had bullets of any kind, but they seemed perfectly satisfied, and told me that if the enemy heard that there was a party of Waganda with a European at their head, there would be no possible chance of their being so foolish as to attack us. There being a certain amount of truth in what they said, I allowed the matter to pass, and my warriors and I proceeded.

The second day, however, we had a little alarm; a man met us with a letter which had been written by one of the European officers in Bulimezi, a few days' journey away, and it was addressed to the officer in charge at Kampala. In troublous times like these I did not hesitate to open it, and was somewhat startled at its contents. It stated that from a very reliable informant the writer had been told that a large force (about five hundred) of Waganda guns, under the leadership of Gabriel the rebel, were coming from Ankole, on their way to Buzinde, to attack the outpost there. I knew at once that I was on the very road that they would in all probability be traversing for some little distance. I called together a few of the most reliable men and asked their advice in the matter; they all agreed that it was best to go forward, the report might not be true. We therefore pressed on till 5 p.m. and then camped in a tiny village. I told the men to form a guard for the night, but I fear my instructions in this matter were not carried out. However, nothing happened that night, and we left the village early in the morning. We had not gone a quarter of a mile when we met some people who were in a great state of excitement, and who informed us that a very large army of the rebels had

A WILD COUNTRY.

passed by in the night, had burnt their village and murdered some of the people. All this had been done within a mile of where we were camped. Had they got to know that we were so near there is little doubt but that they would have attacked us, and with their very superior force would have soon made an end of us. A watchful Providence protected us. In a very short time we crossed the track made by the army, and saw the devastation that it had wrought. Our safety now lay in pressing forward with all possible speed to Toro.

The sixth day from Mengo we had a very long march of twenty-six miles, hoping to reach Nakabimba where there was a large garden with plenty of food. This latter we much needed, our men having been unable to procure any on the journey on account of the deserted state of the villages. As we approached Nakabimba we were surprised to find no one about, and when we finally got up to the chief's enclosure we saw that all that was left of a beautiful village was blackened ruins on every hand; not only so, but the gardens also had been destroyed. Part of Mwanga's army had been there only a few days before, and there was not a sign of food anywhere, excepting a few wild tomatoes. To add to our discomfort rain commenced to fall as soon as we reached camp. Some of the men wanted to push forward, but I was far too tired and so also were the porters. I hunted about in the rain to try and find something I could shoot for the poor fellows, and good fortune led me down to the banks of a small stream, and there I found a flock of guinea fowl, and was able to bring down quite a large number of these birds and distribute them amongst the men. Still, fifty hungry fellows take a lot of satisfying, and they had to be content with a light repast.

It was only just early dawn when the boys awoke, one declaring that "hunger was hurting them," and that we must push on. So on we went, through the wild, uninhabited district between Nakabimba and Mwenge. About half way there we passed through the very midst of a large herd of elephants. I never saw so many together, there were quite two hundred of them, and some were carrying enormous tusks. I did not attempt to hunt them, time was precious, and they did not seem at all disturbed by our presence.

The last day into Toro was without adventure, but full of interest to us. We were met by hundreds of the people, who had come out to greet us and to welcome us back to their country. Reports had spread that I had been killed, and our party broken up, and other reports said that I had returned to Europe; so when my friends the Watoro actually saw me, their rejoicing was very real.

My stay, however, amongst them was to be a short one. In August Bishop Tucker and Dr. Cook visited Toro to inspect the work, and after consulting the latter concerning my state of health, he decided that it would be well for me to leave for Europe without delay. The privations and exposures I had experienced during the time of war had left rather more than a passing impression upon my physical well-being. I was not ill, but I cannot say I was well. The slightest worry upset me and caused headache. Sometimes for days I was incapable of doing anything on account of a singularly depressed feeling, and many such signs distinctly told me that I needed rest. It so happened that a Belgian officer visited Toro in September, 1898. He had come in the wake of the Batatela mutineers with a large force of native troops to establish a fort on the Belgian frontier.

Now it occurred to me that a journey home *viâ* the Congo would be of great interest to me, and of profit to the Mission to which I belonged. For some time we had been wanting to start work amongst the wonderful people, the Pygmies, if such a tribe actually existed. We had heard much about them from the natives, and vague reports concerning them had come to us from European sources, but we were still a little sceptical as to whether they actually existed; and I judged that if by passing through the forest I could settle once and for all this uncertainty, and if they really *did* exist, communicate with them in some way or other, I should have done a certain amount of good and have made it possible to proceed to evangelise them. Add to this desire of extending the missionary work, a very natural one for adventure, which is inbred in the breast of most true Britons, and one has in a nutshell my reasons for undertaking the journey that I am about to describe.

I called upon the Belgian officer at an early date after his arrival in Toro, and asked him for full particulars of the route. He described the way he had come some months before, and declared that I should experience no difficulty whatever in getting through. First he thought a thirty days' tramp through the forest on to the Aruwimi, then by canoe for fifteen days or so; reaching the Congo, I should find a service of steamers running between Stanley Falls and Leopoldville; and have no difficulty in obtaining a passage to Boma; where I should catch a Belgian mail boat. The only difficult part was apparently the first thirty days through the forest. I might discover the tracks made by his caravan overgrown, and it might be necessary to cut a fresh one. There was another route which was being constantly traversed, and which would be more likely to be in good condition and easy to follow, but it did not pass through the centre of the forest inhabited by the Pygmies, and this is what I was most anxious to do. I therefore decided that, even if I had to cut every mile of the way, I would make the attempt.

Bishop Tucker being in Toro, I consulted him and asked him to sanction my proposed journey. At first he did not seem at all inclined to do so, thinking the risk too great, not only that which would come from contact with wild men, but more especially that from malaria: for the Congo has a very bad name for being anything but a health

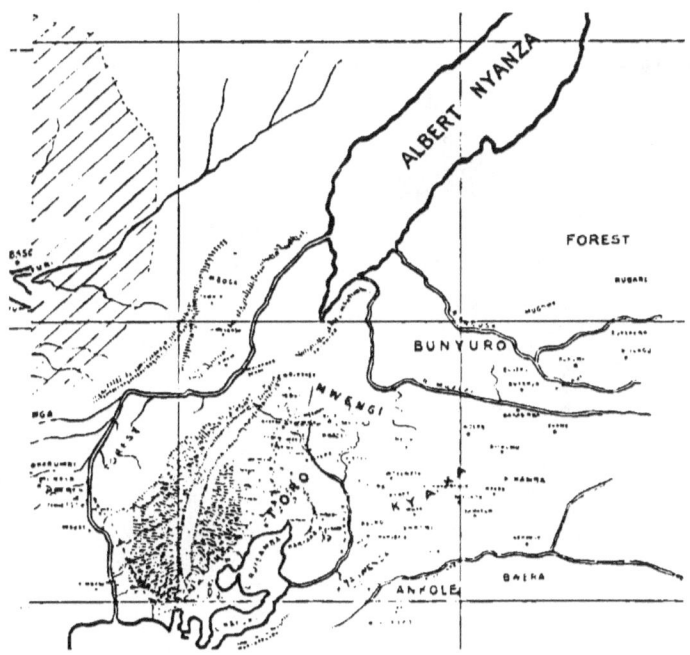

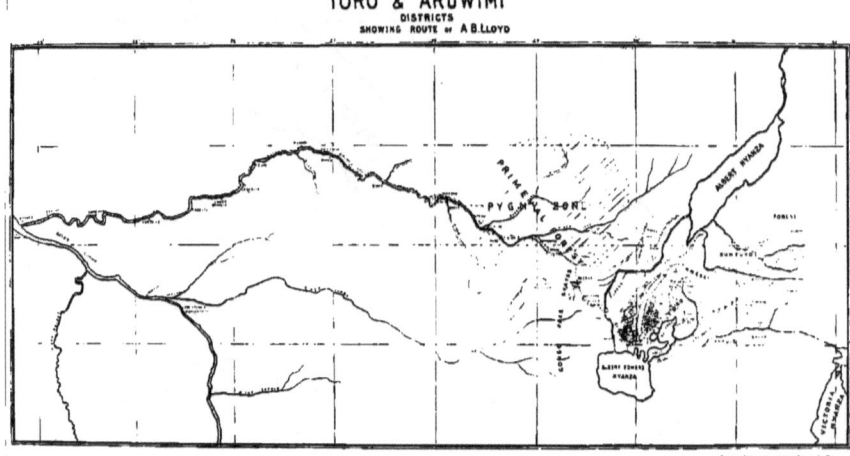

resort, and certainly the name could not be too bad, for it undoubtedly merits it.

However, I heard from my Belgian friend that it was highly probable that he himself would be journeying homeward to the West Coast about the time that I intended going, and then, when Bishop Tucker was told of this he with some reluctance gave his consent, telling me I must go entirely at my own risk, if I went at all. I was of course perfectly willing to do this—in fact I never expected anything less. It was therefore finally decided that I should start as soon as I was able to get together what was necessary for the journey.

I had first of all to settle upon what should be taken with me, and what best could be left behind; not an easy question to answer. I knew nothing of the country or of the facilities for procuring food—in the forest at any rate. I believed there were none, but on the river I did not know what to expect. Then the quantity of supplies. Could the number of days given me as likely by my Belgian friend be relied upon? I at length decided that it would be best to take a good supply, sufficient to last at least three months.

Then, as to porters! I again visited my friend, and he soon set me right on this topic. Watoro porters, he said, were necessary as far as Mbeni, the Belgian frontier fort, and from thence the people of Mbeni would carry my things through the forest. This was perfectly straightforward.

But about a guide through the forest! Oh yes! even he could be found for me at Mbeni; a man who had once passed through the forest could be secured to guide me through. In fact, everything seemed easy. Consequently I packed up my things into as few loads as possible, making each as light as I could, so that none exceeded 50 lbs. in weight.

But another difficulty presented itself, what about personal attendants? Again I applied to my friend, and this time the difficulty seemed a real one. He could suggest no other way than to take boys from Toro as far as the Congo. But where were the boys to come from? Were there any who would be willing to follow me into so wild a place? I called together my ten boys and asked them; the first to offer, almost as soon as I had asked the question, was Mika, but I told him no; he had married a wife, and therefore he must not go, his wife required him. Then two other of my Waganda boys offered, Elisa and Alberto; both were lads of a fair age, Elisa being about seventeen and Alberto fifteen, and were most capable servants, and I was much attached to them. Very readily I accepted their offer. Another boy, a native of Toro, Mufumu, also offered, and I gladly agreed. "And now," I said to them, "let us arrange about wages." "What!" said Elisa, "are we *slaves* that you should pay us for helping you? We will have no wage; you are our father, we love you and trust you; we need nothing but our clothes to wear; we will accompany you as friends." I was very much touched by these loving words. They meant something to me, a missionary, just leaving the country where he has striven to live for the people, and to do them good, is, of necessity, somewhat sad at parting with those whom he has learned to love; and if he finds that *some* of them, although they may be but few in number, at least *some* have learned to love him too, what a pleasure it is to him; none but those who have passed through it can realise what it means. One could not help looking back over the past years and think of so many things one might have done that were still undone, and of the very many imperfections even in one's best efforts and of the selfish motives that, alas! so often had prompted those efforts. All this made it hard to go away, perhaps never to have these opportunities again.

I arranged to start from the capital of Toro on September 19th; the latter rains of Toro had commenced, and the rivers were fast filling up, and in a little while some of the small mountain streams would be huge torrents which it would be impossible to ford.

When I told the King of Toro my intention of going Westward Ho, he laughed at me, and then said, "You must not think of going." "Why?" I asked. "Simply because the Pygmies will kill you; or if you escape them the cannibals will eat you." But when I told him that I had made up my mind most thoroughly to go, in spite of all, he simply said, "*Ofude*" ("You are dead").

The day before I arranged to start news came in from Mengo to the effect that Gabriel had been to Bulimezi, and was returning to Ankole, and the captain at the fort immediately gave orders to the King to collect an army to go out and intercept his escape into Ankole. The 19th of September therefore was a day of greatest excitement amongst the Watoro. On the one hand all was rush and bustle to get ready for the anticipated fight with Gabriel, and on the other the bidding goodbye to their teacher.

Many most embarrassing farewells were taken of me, and some were most pathetic. One incident in this connection impressed me much. A little princess, about twelve years old who had been rescued from slavery by my colleague, Mr. Fisher, when in Unyoro, and had been brought to Toro, where we had taught her to read and write, came to me crying most bitterly to bid me goodbye. She stood before me a moment, and then drew off a little native-made bracelet from her wrist, and sobbingly handed it to me and said, "Take this bracelet, and when you look at it you will think of me, and when you think of me you will think of all my people, and you will long to come back to us again." I think this little bracelet will always have an influence upon me, and if for no other reason than that I fancy I should be obliged to return.

At last the goodbyes were over, and my porters were impatient to start; the escort that had come with me from Uganda had of course returned, and on this journey I was to have no escort at all. I did not think it would be necessary, chiefly because the escort itself would in all probability cause trouble. Untrained natives with guns are most dangerous beings, and one is much safer without them. When a black man has a gun in his hand—especially if it be for the first time—he becomes at once the vainest creature on God's earth, and he has such an inordinate opinion of himself that if he wants food, he expects the heathen—as he will promptly call his fellows—to supply him. I also believed that by wise and judicious treatment of the natives of the forest, and of the river districts, I should be able to gain their confidence and escape the difficulties arising from the fact of having with me a large party of men, all dependent upon me for food.

As I have said, the porters that I took to the frontier fort of the Belgians would return from thence, and then the rest of the journey I should be practically without a following, excepting for my two faithful Waganda boys and the one Watoro lad. I should rely upon procuring porters from village to village, changing them at every place. This I know was rather a doubtful policy, as upon the event of any chief refusing to give me porters I should be stranded, and this might occur in the forest, where to wait would mean slow death by starvation. However, there was no help for it, as it would be impossible to get the Watoro porters to proceed the whole distance with me, and even if they were willing their return journey would be a serious difficulty.

And now, with bicycle and donkey, both well groomed

and ready, and nineteen stalwart Watoro porters, each man with his 50 lb. load, and with a party of my faithful boys to accompany me as far as the frontier, and my little dog Sally at my heels, we left the fair capital of Toro, with all its memories of sacred scenes and of adventurous life, and faced about to the south-west. Our first task was to get round the Mountains of the Moon. There were three distinct tracks—the one crossing the mountains to the north, the second passing right through the range, and the third to the south of the mountains, between them and the Albert Edward Lake. I chose the latter, as being the easiest, from the porters' point of view, as both of the other routes were difficult, on account of the steepness of the mountain paths, while the road to the south merely skirted the base of the mountain range, and there was a good cultivated road as far as Fort George on the lake shore.

For a long distance the first day our path, as usual, led through the huge tiger grass, which literally formed a barrier 15 feet high on either side of us, and entirely shut out any view, excepting when we reached the top of some lofty hill. The path ran along the eastern ridge of the mountains, and was, therefore, through country of an undulating nature, and the porters soon got tired of going up and down the sides of the valleys, and of crossing swamps and rivers at the bottom of each. We pitched our camp about three hours after the start in a very pretty spot overlooking a beautiful valley. As I sat in my tent, I could see the elephants sporting about in the swampy ground at the bottom of the valley, and could hear quite distinctly their childish trumpetings as they enjoyed themselves in the water.

In the evening I was sitting in my tent writing my diary and weaving plans for the future, and for the journey that lay before me, when suddenly, without the slightest warning, a violent earthquake took place. Everything in my tent began to jump about, and it was most difficult to keep oneself perpendicular. The porters were alarmed, and declared the earth would crack and swallow us up; some of them even went so far as to roll up all their earthly possessions into their sleeping-mats and make off, to try, I suppose, to reach a spot where the earth was steady. Although it only lasted a

EARTHQUAKE CAMP.

few moments, it was, for all that, most alarming, and we were glad when it had passed.

Some very curious ideas existed amongst the natives, I found, as to the cause of the motion. Some, indeed the majority, declare it to be an evil spirit trying to break loose from a cavity in the earth; others said it was the angry spirit of the great mountain, and that it brooded evil for the country, and many other strange ideas one heard of. A return of the shock came later on in the night when all were asleep, and it was quite as violent as the first, but most of the men were too soundly sleeping to be aware of it, and only a few of the more wakeful ones felt it. I had experienced many earthquake shocks since going to Toro, but none had ever been of such violence as this one.

The following day I came in closer contact with the elephant herd that I had seen. There were about twenty in all, and it was a very fine sight; some had huge tusks and were but little concerned by our approach, and one might judge from their behaviour that they were not quite sure what we were, and whether we were harmless or otherwise. I walked quite close up to them to get a better view, but had no intention of firing on them. At first they did not seem to mind a bit, until one big fellow became a little uneasy about my presence and proceeded towards me; I then thought it was time to show him that although harmless while he left us alone, we might be just the opposite if he did not, and I am sure he thought so when he got a Martini bullet into his ribs. He fell over and kicked about a little, and then suddenly remembered an engagement he had elsewhere and went off with the rest at a trot. Elephants are usually very harmless excepting when interfered with.

Our next camp was on the banks of the beautiful Rwimi river, a little stream that comes down from the snows and broadens out into a very powerful river. As I stood on its banks gazing up at the immense sides of old Ruwenzori, with the clouds that seem for ever to be hovering about the crest, the sparkling snowy peaks towering away into the blue sky were gloriously visible; it was a magnificent sight. I have never seen a better.

My dear old donkey " Lady " came into my tent in the evening, poking her nose all over the table, and gave me most loving caresses. I could not understand this spontaneous demonstration of affection at the time, but I did so the next morning when I got up and found that she had made off back to Toro. Two of the boys went after her, but did not catch her up until they were almost within sight of the capital. In the meantime we had come to a river the current of which was very strong and the water deep. One after another of the boys made attempts to cross and failed, and then my little dog Sally thought she would try, and this attempt nearly cost her her life, for the current simply tossed the poor little creature about like a cork, dashing her against the great boulders and rushing off with her faster than we could

RWIMI RIVER.

run. However, to my great delight, in about twenty minutes she came pushing her way back through the long grass and making the best of a bad job by coming to her much-distressed master. Several of the porters, who, being Watoro, were more accustomed to rivers, next made attempts to cross, and one after the other succeeded, and then helped over the boys, and I finally got across after the donkey had been captured again, riding upon her back. In another hour we came to an equally strong river, and poor old Sally, thinking that this time she would have better luck, simply took a "header" before any one could stop her, and of course with the same result as before. We waited and waited, but no Sally came, and I then went sadly along the bank searching for the least sign of my poor little companion. After walking for some distance I got into the water and waded about expecting to find her dead body, and I began to feel very much like a little boy whose mother has taken his marbles away; when suddenly I heard some one calling me from the bank, and turning round to see who it was, there stood one of my boys with the best of all doggies by his side. She was looking at me in such a cheeky way, as much as to say, "Well, you must think I'm a poor case if you have the notion that such a paltry thing as that river can make an end of me after all I've passed through." She had climbed up the bank some fifty yards farther up the river, and had come with my boys to look for me. It is a strange fact that a dog can be so companionable, but that little creature had become to me a friend that seemed indispensable, and my joy at thus seeing her alive when I thought her dead can better be imagined than described; and I promptly gave her half my lunch.*

Another three hours brought us to camp, a most charming place, the country all around covered with game, and the grass, instead of being long, was short and soft. The plain was studded with low trees and bushes, making excellent cover for shooting. Just as we had reached camp I noticed at a short distance from us another large herd of elephants. I counted twenty-six in all. After a cup of tea I went off after them and had a most exciting time. We first came up with two,

* It may be added here that, in spite of many narrow escapes, Sally finally accomplished the journey with me, reaching the west coast in perfect condition; but, alas! only to meet with an ignominious death in the jaws of a Congo crocodile at Boma.

one a veritable monster, I never saw his equal, but he had evidently seen mine, and before I had a chance to fire he turned tail and bolted as hard as he could. We went on a little further into a valley where the grass was much longer, and quite suddenly came up with about a dozen, all standing together with trunks in the air; one very large one which was nearest to me, only fifteen yards off, was evidently thinking of other things, and little expected the sudden end that awaited him, for after a careful aim I fired, hitting him between eye and ear, and down he fell like the side of a house. I had used my Martini, and the bullet passed right into the brain.

But while we stood there a strange thing happened. From out of the long grass just to my left a female elephant dashed, and came straight for me, and I being occupied with the other did not see it at all, and but for my boy it would have been upon me before I knew of its existence. He seeing it coming, and having an old Snider rifle, fired at it, and although he did not hit it the report frightened it; but it did not turn till it was within five yards of us. As I have said, I was fully occupied with the other. When the one I shot fell, a big female elephant walked leisurely up to it, looked at it, and then put its trunk round it and lifted it up, and at the same moment another of the herd came the opposite side, and between the two they dragged it off a few hundred yards, and then apparently finding out that it was dead, simply left it, and with terrific trumpeting made off after the rest of the herd. Had I not seen this with my own eyes I should most certainly have doubted the possibility of such sagacity, but the whole scene was enacted before me, not twenty yards away. We were very tired and left the elephant where it lay and returned to camp, arranging with a native chief who was close at hand to take care of the ivory for us and send it into Toro.

Those who wanted elephant steak helped themselves, for there was plenty for all, and none need have been without a substantial supper.

Another snake story may be interesting. After the encounter with the elephants we were walking along by the side of a river when, without a moment's notice, a huge snake seemed to leap out of the grass, knocking over my boy Alberto into the river, and the snake itself disappeared into the water. The whole thing was so sudden, I hardly realised what had happened. Fortunately the boy was not bitten, although badly drenched, but it was a narrow escape both for him and myself, as he was only two yards behind me, and it leapt out immediately I passed.

That night the hyænas had a great holiday over the carcase of the elephant, and their angry yelps as they fought each other over their feast were most distinctly audible in our camp.

On the following day we camped in a village called Mwoikya, amongst an entirely different race of people called the Wakonjo, the mountain tribe. They are a very harmless kind of folk who live at peace with all men. These people have few ambitions—a hut in which to sleep and plenty of food to eat, and they are quite satisfied. They despise clothing, and prefer to remain in Nature's own garb. Some of their villages reach an altitude of about 10,000 feet above sea-level, and only a few thousand feet from the eternal snows. The cold at that height is intense, but these hardy mountain people seem not to notice it, as for hours after sunset they sit outside their huts before large fires smoking their rank tobacco and drinking their "maruwa." The chief of the village was not a very nice man, and seemed to have an immense opinion of himself and of his elevated position as chief over about one hundred people. However, he brought us

food enough, and we had all we needed. At this place
I found two soldiers waiting for me; they had been sent
by my friend the Belgian officer. They had a letter for
me in which he told me that he did not now expect
to journey with me on account of fresh orders he had
received from his Government. I was thus deprived of
the European's company that I had counted upon during

WAKONJO VILLAGE.

my difficult journey. Still I determined that this would
not in any way deter me.

The next camping-place was Kikorongo by the side of
a small lake. Early in the day I shot two fine antelope
and rejoiced the hearts of men and boys, who immediately upon their arrival in camp lit a fire, and, sitting
round it, each one with a lump of meat stuck on to

a stick roasted it before the fire, chattering away the whole time like a troop of monkeys, as happy as possible. In the little lake was a quantity of hippopotami, large and small. In the afternoon I sat by the shore and watched these curious creatures sport about in the shallow water. They did not seem at all afraid of me, and some came right out of the deeper water to look at so extraordinary a creature as I must have appeared to them. In the evening one of my boys went to the lake for a bathe, and while he was in the middle of his wash a huge hippo came floundering after him. To see the little fellow run was a sight indeed; he yelled and yelled, and did not stop running until he got safely amongst his companions in camp. Of course the hippo had long since given up the chase and returned to the water, apparently well satisfied that it had done its duty in driving off the intruder.

On September 24th we reached Katwe. This is the last British station of the Uganda Protectorate to the west. We arrived rather late in the day, as it had been very hot, and a long march with no water all the way after leaving the lake. I was most kindly welcomed by the Soudanese who were posted there, about fifteen all told; they soon procured me plenty of food, and I was allowed to sleep in the officer's house in the fort, which was a pleasant change after tent life. Fort George is situated at the top of a cliff overlooking the Albert Lake to the south; to the north is the famous Salt Lake, which looked to me like a large crater of an extinct volcano. The fort walls were built of mud and stones, and were of a very substantial thickness, and one could see at once how it was possible for the small force of Soudanese in command to make so singular a resistance to the five hundred rebels of the Batatela in March, 1897. These Soudanese belonged to No. 10 Company, which had remained perfectly loyal during the whole rebellion, under Captain (now Major) Sitwell of Toro. When there was disaffection and rebellion among the others, this company only, remained loyal to the British. This was due to three causes: First and foremost, to the most excellent treatment they received at the hands of their European officer, whom they loved and respected and in whom they had implicit confidence; secondly, to the faithfulness of their native officer, Rahan Effendi; and

SALT LAKE.

thirdly, to their ignorance of the movements of the rebels occasioned by the great distance between them and the seat of the rebellion. Whether these be the real reasons or no, suffice it to say that, instead of displaying any signs of mutiny, they actually caught three Mohammedans who had brought letters from their Soudanese friends in Uganda, urging them to rebel, and handed them over to their commanding officer. He sentenced them to death, and a section of the Soudanese themselves performed the execution. In addition to this they built a large bridge over one of the Toro rivers, just to prove their willingness to obey their commander; and also had several most successful engagements with Mwanga's army in Budu and elsewhere. It is to be hoped that this company was suitably rewarded for its loyalty when there was so much inducement for them to rebel.

CHAPTER XV

KATWE TO KILONGA-LONGA. THE GREAT PYGMY FOREST

The boundary river—Lions—Meeting with the Belgian officer—We have a little hunt—Sporting yarns—Frontier settlement—Women slaves—Abundance of game—Traces of Mr. H. M. Stanley—Crossing the Semliki—Fort Mbeni—Preparing for the plunge—The forest—Its extent—Pygmy area—Vegetation—Clearings—Animal life—Rivers—Birds—Insects—Darkness—An Arab settlement—Cutting our way—Sakarumbi—Our camp in the forest—Elephants—Wading through rivers—Red ants—Adventure with a snake—"A man-monkey!"—Visit from the Pygmies—Friendly intercourse—Mode of life—A Pygmy hunt—An attempt at photography—An Arab chief—Tippu-Tib—Kilonga-Longa.

ON the 25th of September I crossed the boundary river Nyamagasani, into the Congo Free State, and pitched our camp on its banks. We had scarcely done so when some people came to us and said that there were a number of lions in the neighbourhood, would we go and hunt them? I declined with thanks; my experiences at lion hunts had not been of the most charming character, and never once have I really got a clear shot at one of these animals; I have hunted them times without number, but, usually speaking, they keep out of the way. Perhaps the nature of the country in which I had hunted made it more difficult to come up with them, the grass being long and rank, and capable of hiding an elephant a few yards away, much more so a lion; so I did not accept the invitation to hunt. The boys built little huts around my tent, so as

IN DWARF LAND.

to be close at hand should any of these creatures attempt to harm us, and large fires were lit at dusk. As we sat around them just before turning in, suddenly rolling out like thunder through the silence came the deep roar of a lion, apparently not more than two hundred yards away. We all sat with mouths open, listening and expecting every moment to see one or another of the party carried off. I kept my gun loaded and close at hand, and ordered the fires to be kept up all round the camp and a watch to be set. How many of these precautions were observed I

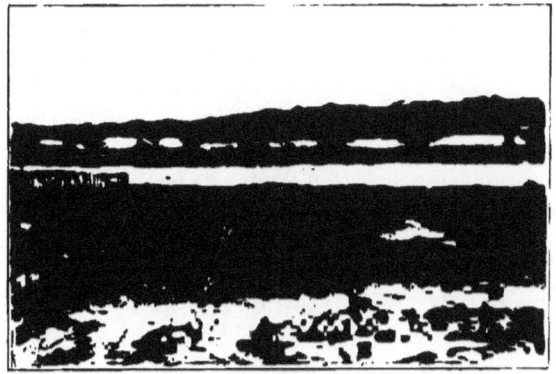

THE ANGLO-BELGIAN FRONTIER.

cannot say, for I was too sleepy to keep awake. But fortunately all was well when morning dawned.

The following day we met a Belgian officer with about forty soldiers. When they saw me coming the soldiers lined up on either side of the path, and when I was about fifty yards away the bugles sounded, and the troops all saluted. Not being by any means a French scholar myself, and the Belgian being quite ignorant of English, we had to resort to the black man's language and engage in conversation in Kiswahili, of which we both knew a little. I first told him my business, where I was going, &c., and he explained that he had come to take the place of the officer whom I had met in Toro and was then at Mbeni, the frontier fort of the Congo Free State. We had lunch together, and then as we were nearing the great forest, where there was a doubt about getting any food, I decided to spend a little time shooting on the plains, to collect a good quantity of antelope flesh which we could dry into "biltong," and which would last us many days. My friend the Belgian officer also said that he would accompany me, and help me to secure a good supply.

We started off together on to the grassy plains which lie to the west of the Albert Edward Lake, and which abound with reed-buck, water-buck, and cobus cob. On the way my friend was spinning some great sporting yarns, saying how he often went out in the afternoon and came back with a bag of twenty antelope to his account and occasionally an elephant or two. Presently he saw a small antelope, and immediately blazed away, one, two, three shots, and still the little creature went happily on its way. He remarked that he had not got his hand in yet, and I certainly thought so too. Another antelope appeared, this time a full grown reed-buck, and he asked me to take the shot and I did so, and brought the buck to earth at 150 yards. My friend began to look a little uneasy, but still went on with his sporting tales. A little further on another was seen—bang, bang, bang, went my little friend's gun, and this time the antelope did not think it worth its while to move away, but stood and stared at the mighty Nimrod. Again the bullets began to fly about, and still with no result. I then thought it time to leave my friend to it, thinking that perhaps my presence made him nervous. So I went off after a large cobus cob that I saw in the distance, and was again successful. In the meantime my friend had been "getting his hand in," but, as I found out afterwards, all his efforts had been in vain, and my two shots were the only effective ones that afternoon. Poor man, he seemed quite crestfallen, and absolutely refused to tell me any more of his little tales.

The next day we parted company, and I pressed on to Karimi, a small Belgian settlement which had been deserted after the Batatela rebellion, but was then in charge of a native officer. The house, once occupied by the Europeans, was in good condition, and in this I spent

KARIMI.

the night. Several presents were brought to me of sheep, potatoes, honey, salt, &c., and I was kindly received.

In the afternoon I was walking through the potato fields when I came upon sixty or a hundred women, all with hoes, cultivating the ground, and close at hand was a native soldier, with a rifle across his shoulder, acting as guard. I inquired where all these poor creatures had come from, and I was told a sad, sad story—alas! not an uncommon one in the Belgian Free State. A Wakonjo chief had been told to do some work for the Belgians, and when he refused soldiers were sent, and upon the least resistance the men were shot down, and the women captured as slaves and made to work. It was a sad sight to behold these poor creatures, driven like dogs here and there, and kept hard at their toil from morning till night. One of the Belgian soldiers told me that there had been many killed, including the chief, and when I said what a terrible thing it was, he merely laughed and said, "*Washenzi Bwana*" ("They are only *heathen*"). This is the usual way; because the poor wretches are low and degraded, it does not matter how they are treated! My faithful old Mika, who was still with me, when he saw these poor slaves came and said, "Why don't you tell these men to liberate the slaves, and let these poor women go back to their little ones?" I pointed out to him how helpless I was: that if the European in charge of this district commanded this, how could I interfere? But it made me sick at heart.

Leaving this settlement in the morning, we again crossed a large plain, upon which I shot some antelope for food. Upon the very spot where we camped that day were the remains of a very big camp, and the natives told us that a long time ago a number of Europeans, with a lot of soldiers, camped at this place. In all probability it would be one of Mr. H. M. Stanley's old camps when on his way across the Dark Continent.

At daybreak the next morning we crossed the Semliki river; at this point it is about a quarter of a mile wide, and a swift-flowing current. A small dug-out canoe was found near this spot, and into this we got, a few at a time, and made our way across. The boxes were placed in the bottom of the boat to help keep it steady, but in the rushing stream it was difficult to kept it afloat. All safely landed, and we next sent for the donkey. A strap was fastened to her neck and she was thus led into the water, and following the canoe swam across in fine style.

I arrived at Mbeni on the 29th of September, and was particularly pleased with the excellence of the fort, and of the buildings in connection with it. My friend, whose acquaintance I had made in Toro, greeted me most heartily, and at once extended to me the best hospitality of the place. He expressed very great sorrow at being

THE FERRY.

unable to journey with me to the coast, and asked me if I would wait for him, as in a month's time he would be able to go. But as I had made up my mind to go on in spite of being the only European in the party, I told him of my intention, and he assured me there was no danger of any kind, but if I liked he might be able to send with me an escort of soldiers, who would protect me in the forest and save me from the hands of any who might try to harm me. This kind offer I preferred to refuse, and explained to him that I was a civilian, and quite accustomed to going about without an escort; and would rather do so on this particular occasion. He seemed surprised, but no doubt felt himself that an escort was not absolutely necessary.

I now began to make my final preparations for the plunge into the forest. There on the horizon was the thick, black line which I was told was the commencement of the Pygmy forest, and after half an hour's walk we should enter its dark shades. My first occupation was to arrange all my loads in such a way as to make it possible for them to be carried with the greatest ease. All the large, bulky boxes I abandoned and chose small, narrow ones, that would be less difficult to manipulate in the forest, and I also reduced the weight of some of them to about 40 lbs., and a great many I did away with entirely. Each porter had to carry three days' rations of food in addition to his load, so it was necessary to have it as small as possible. I next procured from my good friends the Belgian officers three loads of rice, six sheep, twenty fowls, flour, cloth, and a few things for trade purposes. Nothing could exceed the real disinterested kindness shown to me by the officers. Anything that I wanted they most willingly gave me, including European provisions, such as biscuits, tinned meats, and vegetables, things that, as a rule, a European in Africa can ill afford to give away.

At this place I parted with my boys, excepting those I have already mentioned who were to accompany me to the Congo. These boys had been with me as my constant companions through my wanderings in Uganda and Toro. I had become much attached to them, and I naturally did not like bidding them farewell. They also had a long journey before them, for they were to return at once to Uganda along the same route that we had come. Before leaving Uganda in July, I had made an arrangement with one of the big chiefs to give me one of his numerous gardens, upon which my boys might live when I had left the country; and this he had most willingly done, so that the boys might have a home to go to as soon as they left me. Mika, being a married man, was to be in charge of the garden and was expected to look after the others. I had left with him a number of sheep and goats and a cow, with which they were to do as they liked, and no

FORT MBENI.

doubt they would make a big feast when they reached their new home, and kill the cow for that purpose.

After two days' rest and preparation, I again set out upon my journey, which now was to be of the deepest interest to me, and half an hour after we left Mbeni we had entered the dark gloom of the primeval forest.

The great forest of Central Africa has an area of no less than 300,000 square miles, and is penetrated to a very considerable distance by the two majestic rivers, the Congo and the Aruwimi. That part in which is found that extraordinary race of people known to the world as the Pygmies, is not more than one-thirtieth of the whole area, and it is with this particular part that I shall deal. Passing through as I did, not as a great explorer who has time, money, and patience at his disposal, whose hobby it is to pry into the secrets of Nature; but merely as a lonely traveller, bent upon reaching home in as short a time as possible, all my observations in the forest were necessarily very hurriedly made. But there were certain things in the forest that could not possibly escape my notice. So varied, and yet so uniform are its features, that it would require many chapters, nay volumes, to be written to give an adequate idea of its true character. The botanist would find new specimens of ferns and flowers almost every step of the journey; the geologist would have open before him a field for unlimited research, and the zoologist would find a storehouse of never-failing interest. As to the adventurer or sportsman, both would meet with all they could desire, and more than even their wildest dreams could depict. All is so beautiful, and yet so weird and uncanny: the majestic trees towering up to the sky 180 to 200 feet high, interlacing their foliage, and thus preventing even the tropical rays of the sun from penetrating, and shutting out the glorious sky from view; festooned in wild confusion, with giant cables from two inches to a foot in diameter, and these intertwined with the slender cords and creepers, until the whole is one dense tangle of vegetation. The ground is strewn with the empty pods of the giant tree beans, and dead leaves. Here and there a forest monarch has been uprooted, either by the force of tempest or through the decay of old age, and crashing to the earth it has drawn down with it a solid mass of twisted and contorted bushes, but it has let a little sunlight in, and dispersed the dark shades of eternal twilight. The space will soon be filled up again by the multitudes of smaller trees which in their turn will be numbered among the monarchs of the forest. Very occasionally a clearing is found, where at some remote period lived a few fragments of a tribe, long since moved to other quarters or become extinct. Here is found the coarse, rank grass which has flourished in the sun, and it is even more difficult to force a passage through. Cuts and scratches from the knife-like blades of grass, or the poisonous thorns, are the natural results.

One or two villages still exist in the midst of the Pygmy forest even to-day wherein live a few Arabs. These now are surrounded by a number of slaves drawn from the tribes that live on the river banks to the south, and there is little doubt but that they, the Arabs, are there for the purpose of procuring slaves. Right away, hidden in the dark shades of the forest, who would think of looking there for the wild Islamite?

Apparently a good feeling exists between these Arabs and their fellow denizens of the thicket, the former selling various kinds of good sweet potatoes, maize, &c., for fresh meat and honey from the bush brought in by the Pygmies. As to the animal life of the forest, what shall we say of that? it is a subject of all-absorbing interest. Elephants and buffalo are met with constantly, sometimes in herds, sometimes singly ; wild pigs and forest antelope, many species of gazelles, chimpanzee, gorilla, and vast quantities of monkeys of every kind are seen; leopards, panthers, wild cats, civets, hyænas, and reptiles. Deadly snakes will be found hanging from the branches of the trees, or curled up amongst the decaying vegetation beneath ; huge black adders, pythons, bright green snakes with wicked red eyes, whip-cord snakes which look for all the world like green twigs. The forest is threaded with a network of rivers and streams, and all seemed full of fish. There are also crocodiles and hippos, water-snakes and lizards, leeches and slow-worms.

Birds of every description and varied hue, abound, parrots undoubtedly predominating, paraquets, swifts, owls, guinea-fowl, kingfishers, fish eagles, divers, kites, hornbills in great variety; pigeons, doves, honey-birds,

MY CARAVAN IN FOREST.

and all kinds of night birds. In the daytime it is delightful to sit and listen to the singing of the birds, their songs are so different from the bird songs of Europe: some with deep musical sounds like the tolling of a bell. The black and white wagtail is so tame that he will sit within a few yards and pour forth his beautiful notes. The tiny honey-bird darts here, there, and everywhere, like streaks of light, issuing forth its twit, twit, as it alights upon some honey-bedewed blossom. Overhead the ungainly hornbill ploughs its way above the tree-tops calling to its mate, and the screaming of the parrots as in great flocks they make their flight along the river banks, or through the tangled mass of vegetation overhead, is almost deafening.

By the little streams are countless numbers of wonderful

INTERIOR OF ANT HILL.

butterflies, some as large as swifts, and all most gorgeously coloured.

The insect life baffles description. Everywhere there is life: insects dropping from above, crawling about on the earth, and flying in the space between, into eyes and mouth, recklessly committing suicide. No stick can be grasped without getting something in one's hand; no

tree climbed without being immediately covered with
ants or beetles. Cockroaches, centipedes, and crickets
were everywhere. At night the stillness was broken by
the incessant croak of the frogs, combined with the shrill,
perpetual noise of the cicada; the weird moaning among
the trees, or the sudden crashing to earth of some forest
giant, which perhaps had stood for centuries; or the
ghastly yelps of the leopard as it silently creeps from its
hiding-place in search of food. In fact, no place on
earth's surface could be more in keeping with the strange
little people inhabiting this dark forest.

For the first few miles after we had entered, a very good
road had been cleared which made walking easy, but I
must confess there was a very wild, almost unearthly look
about the forest that gave one a very creepy sensation.
Gradually the path seemed to come to an end, and only a
tiny track, like that of a wild beast, was left to indicate to
us the direction; then it was we experienced out first
feelings of dread. We had reached a very dark patch of
forest, through which no light at all seemed to penetrate:
we could have imagined it to be night time; although it
was only 1 p.m. Suddenly we heard a great noise not
far from our track as of a crowd of people talking
wildly together. Everybody looked scared, and I asked
the guide, who was to accompany us half way through the
forest, what the noise was about, and he said it was
"*Nkima Nkubwa*" ("large monkeys"). I had been told
by the Belgians that in all probability we should meet with
gorilla in the forest, and so I supposed these must have
been some: the chatter was certainly most human, and
sounded like a lot of people quarrelling. It added much
to the strangeness of the place.

Late in the evening we arrived at one of the Arab
settlements above mentioned. The old gentleman in
charge was extremely kind and attentive, and told me that

he had been placed there by the Belgians to keep the road through the forest cleared, but when I chaffed him about this and said, "Where *is* the road?" he replied—"You do not expect to find roads like there are in Zanzibar, do you?"

The following day we had a hard tussle with the forest; the path was very soon lost, and it became a hand-to-hand fight. I had with me an old sword-bayonet, and with this I chopped my way, making room also for

MY CARAVAN CROSSING RIVER IN PYGMY FOREST.

the porters who followed me with the loads. It was desperate work, and I kept turning to the guide who was behind me asking him the direction, and I soon found that he was hopelessly lost, and I had to produce my compass and follow that, taking a north-westerly course. My desire was to get as soon as possible to the Ituri river, and then follow along its banks until it became navigable, which was, I believed, a little above Avakubi.

Every now and then we found a small track, which seemed to lead in the right direction, and along this we wended our way, until it turned off to the right or left, and we then went straight ahead. Sometimes we came to deep gullies at the bottom of which were little streams, and the porters had great difficulty in making their way up and down the steep banks. Reaching a very high eminence there was a clearing where at some remote period a village had existed. I looked back over the country through which we had passed, and away there in the dim distance we could see the glorious peaks of Ruwenzori, quite free from clouds on their crest, and the glittering snows looked radiant in the sunlight. It was the very last glimpse we had of the mountains, which were then about fifty miles distant.

We at last struck a path that we found led to a village called Sakarumbi, where a small number of people lived.

The next few days were spent in cutting our way along through the undergrowth. What a terrible business it was! The forest seemed to get thicker and thicker, and even in the middle of the day it was like advanced twilight. At night we always cleared, as best we could, a little plot of ground where we might pitch the tent, and around it the porters built a strong fence or zareba, by driving stakes into the soft mud, and fastening on crosspieces with tough bark. The tent ropes were fixed to the trees, and the porters and boys built themselves little shelters with the small saplings and then thatched them with the leaves of the trees. Herds of elephants roamed about everywhere, and at night we often heard them quite close to our camp, breaking off the branches of the trees, trumpeting and squealing, and we sometimes feared they would come walking into our camp, treading us underfoot as we slept. I arose one morning and went outside of the tent, before the men were awake, and there I saw, looking over the zareba round the tent, a huge old tusker, evidently in deep thought, and wondering what on earth this could mean. When he caught sight of me he looked a little startled, but did not seem in a particular hurry to run away, and it was only by making a great noise of clapping and shouting that he condescended to move off while I performed my toilet.

The rivers were a constant source of trouble to us, and we had to cross sometimes as many as thirty in a day;

FIRST CAMP IN FOREST.

some were but small streams, but others great rivers, that were most difficult to ford. Occasionally we found a rough bridge made by a tree having fallen across the stream, and very gingerly we had to make our way across this; but it was not easy to keep the perpendicular, especially if the tree were but a small one and slippery, as they always were, and many a ducking I got. Rain seemed to be almost incessant — in fact, we hardly knew when it was actually raining and when it was not, as the thick tangled mass overhead was always dropping with moisture, and we were seldom dry. Most of the rivers, however, we had to wade through, and with water up to one's armpits, and a strong current, this was more difficult still. Often the water was very offensive, and none was safe to drink unboiled and without being well filtered. The donkey was constantly getting into trouble in these rivers, and we had to exercise great patience with the poor animal. I soon wished I had never brought her into the forest, as it was of course impossible to ride her, owing to the tangled undergrowth.

One night I had a rather trying experience. It was midnight and I was quietly sleeping, when suddenly I became aware of a most terrible pricking sensation all over my body. It was as though pins were being thrust into me in every part. Then I heard my dog Sally racing about the tent in a most frantic manner, knocking everything over, including my washing basin, which was full of water, and which of course came all over my bed. I thought it was time I got up to see what was amiss. I struck a light, when I had at last found those tiresome matches, and then beheld the tent simply besieged by red ants, the real biting kind. My word! how they did go for me! I rushed from the tent to call the boys and porters. They all brought fire and surrounded the tent, and commenced killing the myriads of pests that were inside, whilst I, shivering with cold, stood outside the tent in the rain, picking dozens of these dangerous vermin off my poor aching limbs. It was not till 2 p.m. that the place was tolerably cleared and even in the morning, when dressing, I found many of the ants on my clothing.

On the 6th of October we had two adventures, which I will proceed to relate.

In the early morning, while as usual I was busy chopping away at the tangled vegetation before me—we had long since lost all sign of a path—a huge black snake darted out just a yard in front of me, reared its head, and prepared for its deadly strike; for a moment I seemed paralysed and powerless to move, but I fortunately recovered myself, and jumped back a yard or two, only just in time, for almost simultaneously with my movement

CROSSING A RIVER IN THE FOREST.

it darted forward and only just missed my leg; I made a slash at it, but missed, and then it reared its head again and slowly glided away. What a horrible monster! as black as ink and 12 feet long at least, and as it went, it kept its little sparkling eyes fixed upon me; I was most heartily glad when it had passed. But the second adventure was of much greater importance.

We had now been in the forest for six long days,

and had never once seen the slightest sign of Pygmies, and I began to half believe that after all the Pygmy stories were not true; but on this particular day I was converted to believe most thoroughly in Pygmies. I was still at the head of the caravan, rifle in hand, looking out for a shot at some wild pigs that had been seen a little while before. The forest was not so dense as it had been in the earlier part of the day, and we were making our way along a small antelope track which was in the direction we were going. My boy, who was just behind me, suddenly stopped and pointed out to me what he described as a "man-monkey." I looked up the tree at which he was pointing, and there, near the top of a high cotton-tree, I saw what I thought must be from the boy's description a gorilla. In the thick foliage it was impossible to get a clear view, and I could only see that it was some creature of large dimensions, to be so near the top of a tree like that. I therefore raised my rifle to my shoulder, took steady aim, and prepared to fire. I had been unsuccessful in killing the wild pig, and I thought at any rate monkey would be better than nothing, and it would not have been the first time that we had been reduced to that. I had very nearly pulled the trigger, indeed my finger was actually upon it, when my boy, who was still carefully studying the creature up the tree, suddenly pulled my arm and said, "Don't fire—it's a man!" I almost dropped my gun, so great was my astonishment. Could it possibly be so? Yes, there he was; I could now clearly distinguish him. He had discovered us, had heard my boy speak to me, and while with breathless horror we stood there gazing, the little man ran along the branch on which he stood, and jumping from tree to tree soon disappeared. It was a Pygmy, and how nearly had he paid the penalty of climbing trees! What the result would have been if I had killed him I cannot say, for, as I found out afterwards, he was not alone, and had he been shot the whole tribe would have been down upon us, and with their deadly little weapons would soon have put an end to us. But now my boy was literally shaking with fear. " We have seen a Pygmy, we have seen a Pygmy; we shall now see sorrow." It was an old idea of the Watoro that the Pygmies were *Bachwezi* (devils), and they always spoke of them with bated breath, and declared that no one ever saw one and lived to tell the story; that to see one was to die. I laughed at him and told him it was all right; God would protect us, and we should get through the forest in safety; had He not preserved us thus far from dangers on every hand? and we must trust Him to keep us all the way.

Five o'clock came and it was time to pitch camp. We found a nice spot which was tolerably clear from undergrowth, although it was quite thick overhead, and here we put the tent, and the porters built their little huts. I then sat down at my tent door and tried to read. Presently, upon looking up from my book, I became aware of a number of little faces peering at me through the thicket. Just in front of me was the trunk of a huge tree and around one side of it there peeped a tiny figure. For a moment I was completely taken aback; it was like being in fairyland and having visits paid to one by the fairies themselves. My boys, who were sitting near at hand cooking some food for our evening meal, also caught sight of these strange little beings and came at once to my side. I told one of them to go and fetch the little people, that I might talk with them, but he was too much afraid, and refused to leave my side. Indeed I did not wonder at his fear, for I too began to have strange apprehensions as to the character of my visitors. I did not know whether they had not come to attack me, and how soon I might find myself pierced with a deadly arrow. At last I called out in the language of the people of Toro just the ordinary salutation of the country, and to my great astonishment and pleasure one little man returned my greeting. I then said to him, "Come here and let us talk together." This I shouted out several times, and then, very slowly and very shyly he came creeping towards me, followed by the others. When he got into the open space before my tent he seemed very unhappy, and stared at me in blank amazement and hid his face behind his hands. Some of his companions dodged behind each other, while the majority remained partly hidden in the jungle.

I now had a complete view of my visitors, and what struck me first of all was naturally the shortness of their stature. But, although they were so very short (about 4 feet, by subsequent measurement), yet there was a powerfulness about their build that is not often seen in African races. Broad chested, with muscles finely developed, short, thick neck, and small bullet head, the lower limbs were massive and strong to a degree. The chest was covered with black, curly hair, and most of the men wore thick, black beards. Each carried either bow and quiver of arrows, or short throwing-spears. Round their arms they wore iron rings, and some of them had these round their necks also. I chatted away to the little man who knew the Toro language, and I was very much amazed at the smart way in which he answered my questions. His knowledge of the language was not perfect by any means, and he often used words that were strange to me, and savoured of Pygmy Land, yet he spoke sufficiently well for me to be able to follow him.

None of his followers—for he was their chief—seemed to know the Toro language at all, and merely stood looking on, lost in wonder at the white man's appearance. He, the chief, had at some time or other come in contact

A VISIT FROM THE DWARFS.

with the people of Toro, possibly at Mboga, and had there learned their language. I asked him all sorts of questions relating to the forest and to themselves, most of which he answered with marvellous intelligence, speaking in a rapid, sing-song way. I asked him the extent of the forest, as occupied by the Pygmies, and he described the distance by telling me the number of days it would take to pass through: from east to west seven days, and from north to south about six days, and, roughly speaking about one hundred and forty by one hundred and twenty miles broad, that is, counting twenty miles as an average day's march, which would be fairly good walking even for a native in the forest. I next asked him the number of his people, and he took a piece of stick and broke it up into little pieces, about forty in all, and said that each piece represented a chief, and he then went on to tell me the number of followers of each: some had two hundred, others only fifty, and a few as many as five hundred. It was very simple then to calculate that the total number would be somewhere about ten thousand.

Then the Pygmy chief told me that he knew long ago of my coming, and I asked him, "How?" He said that several days ago he saw me. "Saw me?" I said, "when did you see me?" "I have seen you in the forest for six days." "But I did not see you," I said; and then he laughed most heartily and said, "No, I could not see him, but he saw me." Upon further inquiry I found that a large party of these little creatures had been watching our every movement all through the forest, while we were in the most blissful ignorance of the fact. At every camp they had hovered about us, peering at us through the thicket as we passed. Why did they not attack us? is the question that kept coming up into my mind. If they are the thievish, wicked little people that they have been represented, why did they not molest us? We were entirely in their power, and had been for the past six days. Perhaps it was our very helplessness that protected us—they saw that we were not as the other white men who had passed through their forest, armed with guns, and having a big following of soldiers; or perhaps I had been overheard speaking in the language of Toro to my boys, and this had given them confidence. I firmly believe, however, that they are not untrustworthy folk, as is usually supposed, but, like most Africans, when not interfered with they are perfectly harmless. I cannot say which of these answers meets the case: I leave the reader to judge for himself. At any rate, upon this and subsequent occasions when I had intercourse with them in the great forest, I was most kindly treated. The little chief brought me a forest antelope for food, also a large pot of honey, that I requested him to taste first. Before they retired for the night, I asked them to come again in the morning to see me, and the chief said he would do so, and the next day I therefore had further conversation with these strange little folk.

Their mode of living is extraordinary; they never cultivate the ground, but wander from place to place, gathering the fruit, nuts, &c., from the trees, and the wild honey. The animals they shoot with their bows and arrows, and the hunt was most graphically described to me. Often they follow a wounded elephant for days, shooting into it hundreds of their little iron-tipped arrows, until the poor creature dies from sheer exhaustion. They then make their little camp all round the carcase, and live upon the flesh as long as it will last, and then away they go again to seek other food. Their method of catching wild pigs and forest antelope is very interesting. Two or three of the more agile of the men are sent off into the thicket to search for the animal. These little fellows sometimes climb the trees, and move along the branches from tree to tree, peering down into the dense undergrowth. In the meantime a large net made out of creepers is held in readiness, and men, women and children alike, arm themselves ready for the fray, some with sticks, but most of the men with bows and arrows. After a little time a shrill, birdlike whistle is heard from the forest ; it is the signal from the searchers that game has been found. Away the little army goes, all noiselessly picking their way through the jungle and tangled undergrowth, in the direction of the whistle. As they get near to the spot they quietly surround it, each man or woman keeping within sight of the next ; the net is fixed up on to the bushes, in one part of the circle, and then when all is ready the whole party commences a great shouting, beating the thicket, and very slowly driving all before them into the net, where stand the men with bows and arrows. Into the net rushes the pig or antelope, which is immediately shot through and through by the expert marksmen, and the hunt is finished. The meat is carried back to the camp, the blood being specially preserved for the chief.

In the morning I tried to photograph my little friends, but it was quite hopeless. It was too dark in the forest itself, and I could not persuade them to come out into a clearing, where I might get light enough. I tried time after time, but always failed. I exposed nearly a dozen plates, but with no good results ; snapshots were useless, and I could not get them still enough for a time exposure.

At our next camp, a small village, I met many more Pygmies, and I was able by interpretation, to hold quite an interesting conversation with them. None of these could speak the Toro language, but in the village was a man who could speak the Pygmy language, and who also knew Kiswahili, and I was thus able to make myself understood.

The Pygmies seemed to roam about not far from these forest settlements, and keep in constant communication with them; for the plantains, potatoes, and other food the Pygmies give fresh meat and honey. But at one village that I came upon unexpectedly I had a singular adventure. The place was governed by an Arab, who had a large number of so-called Arab followers, but who in reality were only Wanyema. The Arab chief was most rude and inhospitable when I arrived; I could not make it out. Upon my entrance into his village he at once came forward with his men and challenged me as to my business, and I explained who I was, and where I was going, but my explanation did not seem to satisfy him, and he said, "You cannot go through here; this country belongs to the Belgians, and you are not a Belgian." I explained that I had permission from the Belgians to pass that way, and who was he that he should hinder me? Upon this he became angry, and said something in Arabic, which I did not understand, to some of his attendants. They ran off into the house, and presently returned with their guns, and surrounded me. "Now," said the Arab, "you are not going through here." I told him he had made some great mistake, and that we had better talk the matter over candidly together, upon which I sat down and he did also. My boys who carried my sporting guns, when they saw the Arabs arm themselves, immediately came running to me, and stood one on either side of me with guns in hand. I turned angrily to them, and asked them what they wanted with the guns, and sent them back to the caravan. I then turned to the Arab and asked him if he would allow me to spend the night here in his village, and go on in the morning without any interference? No, he would not; and then I did not know what to say. Suddenly I had a strange inspiration, and again addressing the fellow I said, "Do you know

Tippu-Tib?" "What?" he said in great excitement, "Tippu-Tib?" "Yes; do you know him?" "I should think I do," said he; "do you know him?" "Yes," I replied; "he is an old friend of mine; I met him at Zanzibar, and made his acquaintance." "Allah!" said the Arab, "you know Tippu-Tib? Tell me quickly how he is." I then said all I could about this distinguished prisoner at Zanzibar, explaining as fluently as possible in Swahili, his appearance, &c. I never saw such a change in any man, as came over this Arab. Instead of rudeness, he was now the essence of politeness. He extended his hand to me, ordered his men to make his own house ready for me, sent off for food, and, in short, treated me with the utmost kindness and consideration. It turned out after further conversation, that he was a near relative of Tippu-Tib's, and by my slight acquaintance with that gentleman at Zanzibar, I was saved from what might have been a most awkward business. His chief reason for not wishing me to pass through his village was undoubtedly, because the place was full of slaves, gathered from various parts. He evidently thought that if I got through, having seen all these, I should tell the Belgians of his existence in the forest, and they would send soldiers to capture him. Thus once more we had to raise the note of praise and thanksgiving; for the loving, all-watchful eye of our Father had been upon us, and we were again preserved from danger, and were able to continue our journey. Five more days in the forest brought us to Kilonga-Longa, now called Mawambi.

CHAPTER XVI

KILONGA-LONGA TO AVAKUBI

Kilonga-Longa or Mawambi—The donkey sold—Gymnastics in the forest—A narrow escape—Falling trees—The Pygmies again—Renewed friendship—Bows and arrows—A Pygmy settlement—Pygmy women—Pygmy temples—Fever—My black nurse—Elephant scatters the porters—Wild pig—Snake adventure—Fishing—Crossing river on fallen tree—The guide kills an elephant—A hungry panther—Two days through water—Pengi—Canoes awaiting us—Socks *versus* stockings—First experiences on river—Shooting the rapids—Canoe men submerged—Canoe smashed up—A miserable night—Avakubi.

KILONGA-LONGA is now not quite the place that it used to be. A few years ago it was merely a small settlement where lived the chief Kilonga-Longa, from whom it took its name, an Arab, whose real name was Uledi, and a company of people who had attached themselves to him; these consisted chiefly of Manyema. He was of course a slave raider and ivory collector. He had a great number of slaves, whom he used to pass on to others, selling them for ivory, of which he collected an enormous quantity. He had many dealings with the Pygmies, and they had a kind of alliance with him, bringing him ivory, honey, and meat in exchange for food of various kinds, such as rice, maize, potatoes, and yams. Kilonga-Longa had long since died, and another man, a Manyema, once a follower of his, had been made chief.

The name of the place had been altered to Mawambi, after its present chief, who had been placed there by the Belgian authorities, and he was instructed to do away with all slave raiding and trading of every kind. This man had done his duty and the district was now a peaceable one.

Much to my astonishment I met here two Europeans, both of whom had been with Baron Dhanis when the great disaster occurred of the rebellion of his troops. They were very much surprised to see me, and wondered where on earth I had sprung from, and when I told them of our battles with the bush and cutting our way through the forest, they informed me that the troubles were not all over yet, and that I had another eight days at least of the same kind of travelling. The great wonder to them was, how I was able to do it with so small a company of followers, and with no escort at all, and they at once offered to send men with me if I desired. I told them that I did not want an escort, but if they would give me a fresh supply of porters I should be glad, so that the men I had brought with me might return to Mbeni, as they were more or less tired out. This they willingly did, and sending for the chief instructed him to find me twenty fresh men.

At this station I parted with my donkey, Lady; the difficulty of getting her through the forest was so great, that when one of the Europeans made me an offer to buy her, I readily accepted it. Several times she had got stuck fast in the bush, and once in thick swamp, when I had made up my mind to shoot her, and was indeed preparing to do so, when the poor creature made one last supreme effort and released herself.

Leaving Mawambi after a very short rest, we crossed the river Ituri, and then made our way along its banks. At first the path was very good, having been completely cleared of undergrowth and of the stumps, but we all knew it was too good to last. Narrower and narrower it became, and the bush got thicker and thicker, and then the path disappeared and only a tiny track remained, and once more we were cutting our way along; climbing over fallen trees, struggling amongst the creepers that seemed ever and anon to literally bind themselves around one, tripping over hidden stumps, crawling under reclining trees, wading through water, clambering up and down steep river banks, and all the time realising that a few dozen little people were hidden among the branches of the trees watching our gymnastics, and perhaps laughing at our carelessness. Occasionally one would sit down, half wishing that one had never been born, to pass through this terrible place. On the way up from one of the river banks, we had to crawl under a huge tree that had become uprooted and had fallen across the track, but was kept from reaching the ground by another smaller tree. I had just passed under with two boys when crash it came down across the track, a weight of many tons; a moment sooner and it would have been on our heads.

Sometimes at night we would hear these forest giants fall; it was like thunder, and in the stillness of the night to be suddenly aroused by such a crash made one turn cold all over. I expected every night that one of these trees would fall across my tent. Why not? they were falling all around us. What was to prevent their falling upon us? Once a tree fell so close to my little tent that the leaves that were dislodged by its fall, were scattered all over the tent. In the middle of one night a huge bough came down from a tree and actually fell across one of the huts in which some of the porters were sleeping, and by a miracle did not injure one of them, although one end of the bough was completely broken.

The storms, that came on nearly always during the night, were accountable for these falling trees, otherwise it would be difficult to discover why they should have the knack of coming down just after dark. Perhaps it might have been that during the day, with all the talking of the men, the noise of the birds, and the chatter of the monkeys, we did not hear them descending; but however that may be, we certainly heard them at the night season, and often dreaded lest they should demolish us.

One day after leaving Mawambi we met another little troop of Pygmies. They were not at all surprised to see us; they said that they knew of our coming and had been told about us by their own people. I was greatly surprised at this, and asked to see the man that had spoken about us, and he was brought—the very same little chief who had treated me so kindly before. He was so amused when I told him of my astonishment at finding him here, and he laughed most heartily and seemed to thoroughly enjoy the joke. I believe it was Dr. Moffat who once said that whenever he found a native in Africa who could *laugh*, he had hope for that man. A native who can see a joke and enjoy a laugh is usually a man who has not lost heart and become entirely absorbed in the problem of life, as to how to procure for himself a sustenance. And so this little Pygmy greatly enjoyed the simple joke of having passed us in the forest without our having seen him, and of being able to tell us of all our experiences since he left us; even the places where we camped he knew, and the animals we shot *en route* for food. Again the little man showed his good feeling towards me by presenting me with two bows and a quiver full of arrows; to some of which the deadly poison was still adhering. The arrows were of great variety, the simplest being merely sharpened sticks of hard wood, and these I found were the poisoned ones. Others were made with iron heads of different shapes, from the simple leaf shape to the six-barbed arrow; one or two I saw had double heads, and some had instead of sharp, *rounded* tips; others had two long barbs, one on either side, both at least half an inch in length. The poisoned arrows are no doubt used when at war, while the others are reserved for the hunt. All had, instead of a feather, a leaf fixed at the end of the shaft. The quivers in which they were kept were made some of antelope hide, and others of monkey skin.

In addition to the arrows, I procured from the Pygmies a horn of ivory used in the chase, a whistle made of wood for the same purpose, and two throwing-spears. All these articles, made by the Pygmies themselves, show a certain amount of skill and intelligence. The horn, for instance, is nicely carved out of the solid tusk of an elephant, and the spears are slightly ornamented on the blades.

I asked these little people to take me to one of their encampments, but they said they could not do so, that they never liked strangers to see where they lived. However, quite by chance, one day while out hunting in the forest with one of my boys, I came upon one of their settlements. It was in a very dense part of the jungle, and I could see at once that it could belong to no other tribe of people under the sun than the Pygmies. There were very tiny little huts or shelters, varying from three to four feet in height, thatched with giant leaves from the trees of the forest; a few broken clay pots, evidently used for cooking purposes; and scattered about the place in all directions, were the husks of a tree bean and the stones from the forest fruits. Apart from these few signs of human habitation, there was nothing to denote that here the Pygmies lived. I moved away from this strange, deserted camp, feeling as if I had reached a corner of fairyland.

I now had the opportunity of seeing some Pygmy women; hitherto I had seen only the men, but now, so very friendly were they, that they brought even their women to see me. They were very comely little creatures and most attractive, with very light skins, lighter even than the men, being a light tan colour; the usual flat nose and thick lips of the negro, and black curly hair;

BISHOP TUCKER AND PYGMY LADY.

but their eyes were of singular beauty, so bright and quick and restless they were, that not for a second did they seem to fix their gaze on anything. They were smaller than the men, and would average about 3 feet 10 inches in height. One of the women had a little child fastened to her back with a bit of bark cloth—a pretty little boy. I wanted to nurse him, but she very quickly turned away and took the child from out of my reach. She was only a Pygmy, but she had a mother's heart; she loved her babe, and feared lest I might injure it.

One of the Pygmy women was found at Mboga by Bishop Tucker when he visited the place in 1898, and she was photographed by his side. Her height was just under 4 feet; she had well-developed limbs and a bright, intelligent mind. She had lived for some years amongst the people of Mboga as a slave, but seemed to be quite contented with her lot.

Strange as it may seem, these Pygmies have their religion; it has been said that they have *none*, but in passing through the forest I often found signs of Pygmy worship. At the foot of some of the huge trees I picked up several times little bundles of food neatly tied up in rough bark cloth, sometimes a few forest beans, or a little handful of rice. I also saw little pots of honey placed at the foot of these forest giants. It seemed as if the Pygmies venerated the spirit of the great trees amongst which they made their home. I also found some little temples very neatly made that could not have belonged to any but the Pygmies. Upon their arms and round their necks some of them, especially the women, wore charms—little pieces of carved wood from some sacred tree, or else a leopard's claw or tooth. The latter I learned were to ward off the leopards which are roaming in the forest, and with which the Pygmies constantly wage war; the former to keep disease away, especially small-pox.

Arriving in camp one day after a hard day's fight with the bush, I found that fever was upon me. It was 5 p.m. and pouring with rain; my body ached as though every joint were dislocated. I flung myself upon one of the loads while the boys put up the tent, and then into bed I tumbled, and there I stayed for two days. I had many apprehensions as to whether I should be able to move for a month. My temperature was so high the first night that I fear I lost consciousness for a little while. How helpless I was, there in the very heart of the most solitary place on God's earth with, humanly speaking, none but a few black natives to look to. Never was I so thankful as then that I had two boys whom I could implicitly trust. Elisa had nursed me before through fever, and knew exactly what to do, even being able to inject quinine hypodermically. I did not have to tell him my requirements; he knew them beforehand, and never was any man better waited upon in sickness than I was in the forest. Night and day he never left

PYGMY TEMPLES.

my side, while the other boy, Alberto, made soup from the flesh of a wild pig that was as delicious and as palatable as Liebig's extract of beef. So well was I attended to that after two days the temperature had been reduced, and I decided, for the sake of my porters, who were getting short of food, to push on.

The next day's tramp was refreshing to me, and although I was very weak indeed, I managed to get along with the help of a stick. We now came to a district where elephants were more numerous than monkeys, and several times large herds passed close to us. Occasionally a huge rogue would dash in amongst the porters and scatter them in all directions. At such times I trembled for my "kit"; one could not expect a porter to keep his load on his back when getting out the way of an elephant; but I did fervently hope that the man who was carrying my photographic apparatus would not throw the box anywhere near the elephant's "trotters." Alas! the mere dropping of it was sufficient to smash some of the plates, and in this way I lost many valuable pictures that could never be reproduced.

On the 15th of October we reached a beautiful place, where there was a deserted settlement on the riverside. There was a very good house in first-rate order, and although we arrived at the place at 9 a.m. I decided that we would spend the day there, and have some hunting and fishing. I went off into the bush and hunted about till past midday, and although we saw plenty of elephants there seemed to be a scarcity of other kinds of animals. However, a guide who had a gun, and who had accompanied me from Mawambi, managed to kill a wild pig, and this provided us with plenty of meat for two days.

On the way back to our camp I had another encounter with a snake. It was lying right across my path and I thought it was the green branch of a tree, and very nearly stepped over it, when I saw its little head turn round, and its sparkling evil eyes fix upon me. I had in my hand a buffalo-hide stick, which I usually carried when my boy carried my gun, and with this I hit it across the head and it seemed to stun it, and then gave it another, which finished it off. It was rather a large one, about five feet, and was a most beautiful bright green colour.

Reaching camp, we went down to the river to try and catch some fish, and I was greatly surprised to find how easy it was with a bent pin for a hook and a cane for a

A ROCK ELEPHANT SO STYLES THE CACIQUE.

rod and without a float; I was able to catch what provided me with a good, substantial meal. After having caught my fish, I fell into the river myself. I was trying to cross it, walking along the trunk of a fallen tree; it was only a small one, and was like walking the tight-rope, and beneath me was the rushing river several feet deep. When I got into the middle my foot slipped, and in I went. After floundering about a little I reached the shore in safety and then retired for the night, a little crestfallen.

The next day the guide who shot the pig again showed his prowess. He was some hundred yards ahead of us all, when we heard him fire a shot, then another and another and still another, then all was quiet. We rushed up to see what had happened, and there we found, a few yards from the path, an elephant stone dead and the guide calmly cleaning his gun, which was of course a breech-loader. I was very proud of my guide, he was certainly a very expert marksman. By nationality he was a Wanyema, and had been trained for a soldier by the Belgians, and had taken part in several big battles. I did not wait while some of the men cut up the meat, but pushed on to camp, as I was tired after all my exertion of the day before.

In the middle of the night, hearing a strange sound close to camp, I got up and went out of my tent to see what caused it; I found that it was only a porter snoring in a curious sort of way, but as I turned to retrace my steps the light of my lantern fell upon an object crouching down a few yards from the peaceful sleeper. In a moment I realised that it was a panther; the boy who was with me saw it too, and cried out to the porter, who, when he awoke, yelled, and I seized from the fire a burning faggot and flung it at the beast, and it slunk off into the forest again. Fires were then banked up and kept blazing the rest of the night.

Then came a miserable experience. For two whole days we were tramping through water, sometimes to our waist, often to the armpits. It was great toil and seemed to wear one out. The first day we absolutely could not find a dry place on which to camp, everywhere was water. It was evidently a flood—there had been an abnormal quantity of rain during the previous week. We searched everywhere until we were tired of searching, and finally put up the tent in three or four inches of water. The boys climbed up a tree, and then tried to find a place where they could sleep, but dare not trust themselves, being afraid of falling in the night. The insects also that they met with while trying the experiment helped them to decide against it. It was a most miserable business, and I shall not soon forget it. Fortunately the water was not deep enough to reach my bed, but for all that it must have been a most unhealthy position to be in all night. The poor boys had to pile up a lot of logs and branches in the water until they were able to make a platform sufficiently raised from the water and upon which they could sleep. My loads also were stacked up in a similar fashion, but not before many of them had been completely submerged, and clothes and food were ruined.

At the close of the second day we got free from the water and arrived at a place called Pengi, where we found a native soldier of the Belgians in charge, named Baruti, a very fine fellow, who was extremely kind to me. He had a letter for me from an officer who was then at Avakubi, which is on the confines of the primeval forest, the area inhabited by the Pygmies. This gentleman had most kindly sent two canoes for me, which were to take me from Pengi to Avakubi by river, and in his letter most warmly greeted me, asking me to make it convenient if possible to stay a few days with him at Avakubi. At Pengi I was able to pay off all my porters and to send them back to Mawambi; now no longer did I need porters; joy to tell, the whole way to dear old England I should not have to walk another mile.

Baruti was a man of about 6 feet 3 inches in his socks, and when I say socks I mean it, for so great a swell was he that he possessed both boots and socks. In the course of the evening he came to me, bringing a large

A RIVER PEEP IN THE FOREST.

native-made knife of most curious shape with two or three different blades. I believe it is used as a throwing knife in the same way as the aborigines of Australia use the "boomerang." For this knife he wanted me to give him a pair of stockings. He pointed out to me that socks were not quite the thing, evidently being intended only for children. "See, all this part of my leg has nothing to cover it," said he. I gave him an old pair, and this delighted him and he immediately donned them, and began strutting about the place as large as life.

The next day's journey was a most enjoyable one; we got into our canoes at 6 a.m. and were paddled downstream by a number of natives who had been brought with the canoes from Avakubi for that purpose. In the canoe in which I sat was a nice awning made to keep off the sun's hot rays, and my hammock chair was put beneath this, and one could recline or sit up at leisure. The change of motion was a little difficult to get used to, and the strong light on the river, after the many days in the forest shades, made the first few days by water rather trying, and I consequently suffered from headache. We had not long been in the boat before we came to some rapids. The men called them small ones, but I certainly thought them very terrible and wondered what they would have been like had they been worse. The boat seemed to spin through the water, and was tossed about by the current at will and yet at the same time the men were most skilfully guiding the tiny craft between hidden rocks. In less than ten minutes we were again in smooth water.

At midday we put into the shore and cooked some food, then on again for another two hours. It was most exhilarating to be passing through the air at such a speed. The boatmen who stood up to paddle were dwellers on the banks of the Aruwimi river and were able with but little exertion to make the boat go along at a good seven miles an hour aided as they were by the current. The river Aruwimi, had a fall of no less than 750 feet from Mawambi to Avakubi; no wonder, therefore, that we found the current strong.

We camped again on the bank, at a little settlement where Belgian soldiers were in charge; a nice little cottage built on the river-side was pointed out to me as the house in which the European might sleep. Here I spent the night.

We had hoped to reach Avakubi the next day, but a chapter of accidents occurred which made it impossible. We left at 6 a.m., and after shooting some more rapids we came to a station where there was a native soldier in charge. Here I was told there was rather a bad rapid, and that it would be best for me to get out and take out all my things, that the boat might go over alone with the men. I was half inclined to remain in the canoe, as it did not seem necessary to take everything out; however, the boatmen pleaded so hard that I consented, and glad I am that I did so. No sooner had the boat started with three men on board, to guide her through the rapids, than she was caught up by the current and dashed about in a terrible fashion. The boatmen held on for dear life, and did their best to keep her in the proper course, but about halfway through the boat turned broadside on to the stream, and the next moment was sent with tremendous force into a rock, and smash it went into two pieces. The three poor fellows were of course whirled about in the stream and soon lost to view, and we gave up hope of seeing them again. I sent the other boat out to look for them below the rapids, and ran along the bank myself to try and find them. One was seen hanging on to the rocks near the shore and was rescued first, the other two were eventually rescued, having been swept down the river some long distance. One, however, was senseless and half drowned, but after trying all sorts of methods to restore him he came round and was soon all right again, and scarcely any the worse for his very severe ducking.

We procured another canoe, and again started off. but the rain came down in such floods that we were glad enough to put up in a little deserted village, where there was a miserable hut, into which I went for the night. All my things were wet, including blankets, bed, and clothes; the hut was full of vermin, and all sorts of other unmentionable horrors. Rats were everywhere, and had not the common decency to keep off one's bed. There was no firewood, so the porters told me, everything was wet, no chance even of getting a cup of tea. There seemed to be nobody about, the whole place was desolate. Everybody got angry with everybody else, nothing seemed to go right.

In the middle of the night, while trying vainly to sleep, a rat actually got on to my pillow, and squealed close to my ear. I made a dash at him, and missed him of course; he had got under my mosquito netting and could not get out. I chased him all round the bed, now and then I would just feel him, but I could not catch the little tease. I got desperate, and jumped out of bed to be immediately seized by millions of the most bloodthirsty little mosquitoes I ever encountered. I struck a light; there was the rat calmly sitting on my blanket, evidently quite content since it had been successful in turning me out of bed. I charged down upon that rat in such a way that I am sure if he had had a little more sense it would have had the effect of causing him to escape. Not he! I never saw such impudence! But I doubt if he will be so naughty again, for a boot made a deep impression upon him.

Worried to death with mosquitoes that seemed to get more determined every moment, I again rolled myself up in my blankets: but not for long—a gale of wind, a crash, and the rain came pattering down upon me; half the roof had gone, and there I lay, exposed to all the fury of the storm. At first I made up my mind I would not move, but it became too awful, and once more I dragged myself out of bed, and put the bed on the other side of the room, and then, worn out with the troubles of this wicked world, I went to sleep.

No wonder I was a bit stiff the next day; we could not get away till 9 a.m., and by that time, owing to the great heat of the sun, most of my things were dry. It was then only about three hours to Avakubi, and right glad we were to get there.

CHAPTER XVII

AVAKUBI TO BASOKO

Houses Gardens Coffee Rubber Ivory—Another start—A struggle for dear life—A great loss—Cannibals of the Upper Aruwimi—An anxious night—Another canoe swamped—Among the cannibals—Their dress—Their habits—The kola nut—Iron work—Panga Falls—Our warrior boatmen—We make rapid progress—"The European is coming"—Bangwa weapons—Choosing a tender spot—Mukopi—Gymnastics in the forest—A cannibal dance—Mupe—Cannibals and the bicycle—Banalya—A headstrong Belgian—I visit the cannibal chief—An eye opener—What it will lead to—Basoko.

I WAS very heartily welcomed by the Belgian officer in charge, and throughout my stay was most kindly treated.

Avakubi is a beautiful place, quite an ideal station. Fine, lofty buildings constructed of good sun-burnt bricks, and the whole place was most compactly arranged. The Europeans' houses, built four square, with an open quadrangle in the centre, and a high brick wall surrounding the back part, which contained the servants' quarters and outhouses. The doors and window-frames were made of well-planed wood, so very different from the reed work that we are so accustomed to in Uganda.

I was shown into a room where I was told I might sleep, and I was asked to stay for as many days as I possibly could. There was indeed a great temptation to make a long stay here, where everything seemed so nice and homelike after the roughness of camp life. A very luxurious meal was prepared, and the hungry traveller did ample justice to it. I was then shown round the grounds. The gardens at once took my fancy, for here not only was there every kind of European vegetable, but also the most beautiful flower-beds, arranged with great taste, and which cast a brilliance upon the scene that is lacking in most Mission gardens. This garden was no doubt the hobby most indulged in by the officer in charge, and a very useful one too. When in Central Africa one can get fine English potatoes, pineapples, mangoes, and grapes, besides a host of other things equally tempting, there is not much left for one to desire to make life pleasant. The greatest care had been taken to shield the products of the soil from the heavy rains, without shutting out the morning and evening sun.

Coffee, also, was growing everywhere, although, as my friend told me, it did not come to much perfection on account of a strange worm which seemed to take up its quarters in every berry. The production of coffee is of great importance to each officer of the Congo Free State. It is to his advantage to have as many coffee-plants as possible, because for every plant over a given height he is paid a certain sum, which, when he has a few thousands, makes a very considerable addition to his income. This applies also to cocoa. The coffee when ripe and ready for picking is packed up in sacks, and sent down the river to Leopoldville, and for every pound weight a percentage is given; this also applies to rubber and ivory. And it is here, it seems to me, that the evils of native oppression come in. The officer, whose salary fluctuates according to the amount of coffee, ivory, and rubber produced, is naturally very keen to get the natives to work with might and main on the coffee plantations, and in the forest to procure rubber and ivory. These he must and will have at almost any cost.

A young sergeant, for instance, goes out from Europe to the Congo, and is immediately put into a responsible post, with a few thousand black men at his beck and call; he very soon finds that the ordinary African is afraid of the European, and will do almost anything rather than incur his displeasure, and the European discovers that by bringing a little pressure to bear, occasionally, he is able to get a little more out of the "nigger." But there is a "thus far" even with the poor ill-used black man, and if pressed beyond that he turns; and what wonder that in an unexpected moment he wreaks his vengeance upon his oppressor. Alas! not before he has himself suffered most bitterly.

A chief of a district, where some European officer of the Congo Free State is stationed, is called up by the officer and told to send his people out for rubber, so many pounds' weight are required, and *must* be brought in. The chief perhaps has but a small following, and cannot produce what is asked of him; he is given another chance to get it, and again fails, and he must be punished. A native officer is instructed to take a number of soldiers and destroy the chief's village. Then follows the most bloodthirsty wickedness that is anywhere recorded; men, women, and children ruthlessly murdered, and the whole place destroyed. Such cases as the above are now, thank God, less frequent, and one hopes that they will ere long be entirely unknown. A large number of the Belgian officers whom I had the pleasure of meeting at the various stations were thoroughly good fellows, and quite incapable of instigating such bloodshed as mentioned above, but there are men, and not a few, still holding positions of trust and of great responsibility whose actions are a standing disgrace to a white man, and that make the white man a veritable demon in the eyes of the natives.

Ivory is in great abundance on the Aruwimi, and its value is little known to the natives; they will kill the elephants for the sake of the meat, but the ivory is often left in the forest. The Belgian officer therefore gives instructions that all ivory is to be brought to him, and he will buy it with brass wire. The ivory appears to be quite a different quality from that which is procured in the

BELGIAN OFFICER, AVAKUBI.

more open country. Forest ivory can nearly always be distinguished by its dark colour, while the ivory obtained from the elephants that roam about the plains is quite white and of greater commercial value. In the earlier days the Manyema were the great ivory hunters of the Aruwimi, and still are to be found there, but usually working in conjunction with the officers of some Belgian outpost. These men sometimes shoot and sometimes trap the elephants with pits, or heavily weighted spears suspended above the track, and which fall when the elephant knocks a creeper with its foot, to which the spears are attached.

I saw several tons of ivory lying at the various Belgian stations on the Aruwimi and Congo, waiting to be taken down to the coast.

At Avakubi were stationed about two companies of soldiers, comprising all kinds of nationalities, chiefly Manyema and Bangala. They were a very fine set of men, who were well equipped, and whose houses were of

HOUSES, AVAKUBI.

quite a model character. They were fine mud buildings, in long rows, each house occupied by about five men, excepting the native officers, each of whom has one to himself. The whole place, however, is but a clearing in the forest, and one only has to walk for about ten minutes to get right into the forest again. There exists excellent communication between Avakubi and the lower Aruwimi, as the whole distance can be traversed by canoe, and with good boatmen it should only take twelve days to reach Basoko, which is at the mouth of the Aruwimi, or rather at its confluence with the Congo. The return journey takes much longer on account of the current, usually about twenty-two days, but in low water it can be done in less time. At Avakubi my aneroid registered an altitude of 1,800 feet, and at Basoko, 1,350 feet; the fall therefore was about 450 feet in about 320 miles.

There are no cows at Avakubi, or rather I should say there is one, a bull, but it seems to be kept more for ornament than use. There was a good flock of sheep and

BUYING IVORY FROM THE CANNIBALS.

goats attached to the station, and these supply the Europeans with butter and milk, as well as occasionally a little meat.

I stayed there two days, enjoying the kind hospitality and the benefits of a rest, to straighten up my things and to dry my wet clothes. As there are some strong rapids a little below the station I walked for about half an hour before embarking again in the canoe that had been prepared for me through the kindness of the officer in charge; but a disagreeable experience awaited me. The boats were moored in a place just below the rapids, where the current was still very strong. I packed all my boxes into the canoe and then got in myself. As is usual, a large awning had been put up for my comfort, and under this was my deck chair. I got in as soon as all was finished, and waited for the boatmen to do the same, but they had still a great deal to do in gathering together food, &c., that they would require for the journey, and in the meantime I went off to sleep in my chair.

My next sensation was an alarming one; it was that of being pitched over to one side and then more forcibly still to the other and right into the water, the boat turning upside down. Being underneath the awning I was entrapped like a rat in a cage, and could not get my freedom. I thought my last moments had come, the water rushed into my head, for I was completely submerged, and it was not until I had had a very severe ducking, and the boat had been swept along for some considerable distance, that at last I got free from it, and with my fast failing strength struck out for the shore. The boy who was in the canoe with me was still hanging on to the upturned boat, and the men, as soon as they saw the boat upsetting, jumped out, and were soon safely on the bank. I had on large Wellington boots, which of course soon filled with water, and in addition to the weight of my other clothing it was as much as ever I could do to get to the bank. When I finally reached shallow water I turned round and saw the boy still clinging on to the boat, while the current was rapidly taking him down-stream. After recovering my breath a little I ran along the shore to where there was a horseshoe bend in the river, and then jumped in and struck out for the boat and managed to catch hold of a rope that was hanging from it, and by this I pulled it in to shore once more. How I was able to do all this I cannot tell, I only know that when

I had finished I was completely knocked up, and sat down upon the bank in an utterly exhausted condition. The boxes that were in the boat were, of course, precipitated into the water, but only one was lost. The others were all filled with water, and many valuable things were utterly ruined, chief amongst these were my photographic plates. At least four dozen unexposed negatives were spoilt, and two dozen exposed ones. The latter were of even greater loss to me than the former, for

CANOEING ON ARUWIMI.

there were plates among them that could never be replaced. I had always been so careful to try and get good results, and photos that would be of real interest; some that I took in the forest were especially valuable to me, and to lose all in one day was almost heartbreaking. It might have been much worse, however, for another moment under water and I should have lost consciousness and been drowned, but thank God He once more mercifully preserved my life, and indeed the lives of all of us, for we all had a very narrow escape.

We righted the canoe and cut down the covering so kindly put up for my comfort, and which had so nearly cost me my life, for it was undoubtedly the cause of the upset, and once more packed in the boxes, and tried again; and this time we were more successful.

We reached a large village called Bazibangi about three in the afternoon. It was here that we met with the first real cannibals of the Upper Aruwimi.

PASSING THROUGH CANNIBAL LAND.

I was not at all charmed with their personal appearance; dirty and degraded they seemed to be, and some of their evil habits which I witnessed were too awful to mention. They were almost nude, both men and women. They seemed to me to be the remnants of various tribes. Manyema were again to the front, and the chief himself claimed to be of that nationality, but had undoubtedly been placed there by the Belgians, and was not the real chief of the country. Numbers of the villages round about were utterly deserted, the inhabitants, I was told, having gone further inland so as to be out of the reach of the Europeans, that they might carry on their cannibalism unchecked. The old chief gave us plenty of food, and was kind enough to turn out of his house to make room for me. It was a nice clean little cottage overlooking the river. The whole of that night I spent trying to dry my photographic plates, spreading them about the floor in all directions, upon old newspapers, and even upon my bed, sitting myself in my chair, waiting and waiting for the films to dry; but it was a hopeless task, and the rats were a great nuisance running over the plates as they gambolled with each other. I was glad enough when morning came and I could pack away all that were dry, a very small percentage.

The following day we had another river mishap; fortunately I was not in it myself this time. We had arrived at some more rapids and the men told me to get out and take out all the boxes, &c.; this we did, and then the canoes went down the rapids with two men in each. Two got through all right, but the third was swamped in the middle and over it went, but the men did not seem to mind at all; both were expert swimmers and quickly reached the shore and then set off after the overturned boat in a small canoe. Soon after this the rain came down in torrents and we had to camp.

The next few days we passed through the wildest cannibal country to be found anywhere, and every day we saw dozens of villages inhabited by the Bangwa. They are a splendid race of people; I was very much taken with them. I have seldom seen such physical development and such symmetry of figure; they are upright as a dart, with heads erect, and bright, intelligent faces. These men came up to me with the greatest confidence—not as the cringing savage who will grovel at your feet before your face, and put a spear into you when your back is turned. The cannibal was straightforward and brave, and his character could be read in his actions and bearing, and one could see at once that here were the materials for the making of a fine race of people. And yet they were the most advanced cannibals, who lived on human flesh. The men all wore a bark cloth about their loins, not wound round the body, but fastened back and front with a hide strap, or a cord of plaited grass. The chiefs all wore a belt of hippopotamus hide, studded at the ends with brass nails, and into this were fixed their terrible knives: upon the ankles they wore solid iron rings, some weighing 2 lbs. each; these were also worn upon the wrists. In addition to these they all seemed to wear leg ornaments, half-way up the calf, of bright spiral iron wire, shaped to the leg, and the same thing on a smaller scale upon the arms. A ring or two of beads round the neck and a curiously shaped headdress completed the most ornamental attire of the Bangwa warrior. The headdresses were of various kinds, those made of monkey-skin predominating; the fur being worn on the outside. Others were of prepared hide with the fur removed, and some were made of a kind of straw worked into most fantastic shapes. Others are made with the bright plumage of birds. The warrior, when dressed for evening, is a most obnoxious being, having smothered himself from head to foot, particularly on the head, with palm oil. He smears a kind of red paint over his face and chest and looks a most hideous character. His hair is long, for it is never shaved, and either hangs in a tangled mass or is fixed up in a kind of leather nightcap, tied under his chin with leather thongs. His cannibalism is most pronounced, and, unlike many others, he does not seem to mind being known as a cannibal; generally speaking, he devours the bodies of his enemies, but a woman is seldom, if ever, eaten by the Bangwa. The women, however, join in the feast, not sitting with the men, but in a separate group by themselves.

It would be difficult to say whether the cannibalism of the Bangwa is practised merely from pleasure or from some superstitious idea about the strength of the enemy entering into themselves. As far as I could make out this latter is the more general belief. It is for the same reason that some tribes of Eastern

A BANGWA VILLAGE.

Africa will eat the liver of a dead leopard that they may imbibe its strength—as the Bangwa warrior devours his enemy. On several occasions I saw them engaging in their feasts, and most ghastly were the sights, too horrible indeed to mention. Sometimes one would see part of a limb roasting over the fire, or else in a cooking pot, boiling, while the warriors sit round watching eagerly until it was cooked. But still, notwithstanding the fact of there being a superstitious idea in connection with this cannibalism, there is no doubt a depraved appetite. I have seen the wild, exciting feast, where spirit dances and invocations have been the principal items, and I have seen the warriors in all soberness sit down to a "joint of man" in exactly the same way as they would do to a piece of forest antelope. Once, when told by a European that the practice of eating human flesh was a most degraded habit, the cannibal answered, "Why degraded? you people eat sheep and cows and fowls, which are all animals of a far lower order, and we eat man, who is great and above all, it is *you* who are degraded!" Thus will the cannibal defend the practice.

Another usual accompaniment to the feast of the Bangwa is the drinking of a concoction of the kola nut. The nut, being dried, is pounded up to powder and mixed with a pot of palm wine and then boiled upon the fire for some hours; more wine is then added to the other ingredients until a very strong concoction is made. Then when cool the chief and his head-men, or any others who may be asked, will sit round the pot with long hollow reeds in their hands, and with these they suck up the terrible poison.

I have several times sat by them as they indulged in this dangerous practice, and watched the effects of the drug. First a kind of hilarity comes over them, and this in time gives place to hysterical laughing, and their eyes seem to stand out from their heads, and utter wildness is stamped upon their faces: gradually the effect becomes so great as to cause temporary madness, and they will jump up and down, waving their awful knives above their heads, and then they rush off into the wood thirsting for human blood. I was told that when the Bangwa want to go on some raiding expedition they first have a great revel round the kola-nut pot, and when worked up into a state of frenzy, they rush off to attack their foes in order that they may afterwards drink their blood, should they be victorious. The women are not allowed to drink this poison, it being reserved for the warriors only.

Another custom that has to do with the kola-nut drinking is as follows: When a man has lost his wife, either by death, or his enemies having stolen her, and when he wishes to obtain another, if he drinks the kola-nut concoction night after night it is supposed to bring

BANGWA WARRIOR CHIEFS.

him good luck in seeking another wife. It is a fact I believe that many of the men succumb to the influence of this drink.

As iron-workers the Bangwa are among the foremost of all Africans. Their spears, knives, and ornaments surpass any I have ever seen; their spears are of two kinds, the long lance and the short throwing-spear.

The lance is, of course, used at close quarters or when

repulsing a charge by the enemy; they will hide themselves in the grass or undergrowth, with their long lances fixed in a slanting position and upon which their foes rush. The throwing-spears are beautifully made, being in shape quite a work of art. At the end of the shaft, which is ornamented in various ways, with copper and brass bands, is a long iron ferrule, hectagonal in shape, and tapering down to a fine point; this end is used for spearing the women and children; they are not considered worthy to be killed with the same blade as the men.* Their knives are of great variety; I collected and brought home with me about thirty of them, and all are different; most of them are double edged, with a dagger-like point at the extremity. Some are longer than others, and one particular kind is much like a sickle: this is the execution knife, with one cut of which they will decapitate an unfortunate victim for the feast, tying his neck to the bough of a tree which has been bent down for the purpose, and which, when the head has been severed from the body, springs back into its original position, pitching the head into the air. This is the method adopted for decapitating the prisoners of war, and a more ghastly spectacle could not possibly be seen anywhere. All the knives have various geometrical designs upon them, which show that the Bangwa, although cannibals, are by no means lacking in capabilities for better things. The iron for making these knives, &c., is procured from the iron ore found in the forest; they smelt it and forge it themselves, and with the most primitive tools turn out most excellent work.

At Panga, on account of the very heavy fall of about 30 feet, we had to change canoes and boatmen, and I was able to get a large company of the Bangwa to accompany me in the capacity of rowers. It was rather

* This is a custom which is also observed by the Waganda, and many other African tribes.

CAMBRAI.

a new experience, to be spinning along down-stream with a boat-load of the wildest cannibals, and to be completely at their mercy. I tried to show them that I trusted them implicitly to help me in every way. I chatted to them as best I could by interpretation, using doggerel Kiswahili, and made all sorts of fun to please them and gain their confidence; and I confess that a jollier set of black men I never in all my life had to do with; they were brimful of fun, and entered most heartily into all my jokes.

My English concertina, my dog Sally, camera, and binoculars, to say nothing of my bicycle, all tended to create the most hearty feelings of good fellowship possible. With such stalwart fellows as these to run the boat we simply sped along at a tremendous pace, and the banks seemed to whirl past us, and village after village, with crowds of its inhabitants eagerly watching us from the shore, was passed in the few days between Avakubi and Basoko. The houses of the Bangwa are curiously built, being cone-shaped. They are not more than 10 feet in diameter at the base, but are at least 15 to 20 feet high; they are thatched with leaves from the forest and give the general appearance of a lot of huge palm cones set in rows.

The Bangwa (like most of the Aruwimi and Congo tribes) have a most wonderful means of communicating the one to the other. Telegraphic messages, *i.e.*, *wireless telegraphy!* are sent by means of curiously shaped drums which are made from the solid trunk of a tree some 5 feet in diameter, which is hollowed out most cleverly, and from it can be produced two distinct notes, and by varying these two notes they can convey messages to a neighbouring village. The sound travels like magic along the river, and so at almost incredible distances these drums can be heard. It therefore came about that long before I got to a village, the people knew of my approach; and as I came in view they communicated the news to the next village by means of the drum, and so on right down the river. "The European is coming!" I was told that from one village to another, a distance of over a hundred miles, a message could be sent in less than two hours, and I quite believe it possible to be done in much less time. The Belgian officers use this method of communicating with the natives, always keeping a

CANNIBAL FISHERMEN.

drum on the station, and a man that can beat it. Thus, when the supply of rubber is getting small, a telegraphic message is at once despatched to the village chief to acquaint him of the fact and to remind him that he must bring in some more.

Several times upon landing at the various villages I had rather unpleasant experiences, and often such as made me feel a little uncomfortable. For instance, upon our arrival at a large village, I would at once be surrounded by some fifty or sixty great fellows, each with his terrible knife in his hand, and they would walk all round looking me up and down, in a most careful manner, and often I wondered if they were choosing a tender spot upon which to commence. It would have been fatal, however, if I had shown the least sign of fear or suspicion, and so I had to look pleasant, although I felt quite the reverse. When I explained to them that I was an Englishman, and belonged to a great and powerful nation, which loves the black men and wishes to try and do them good, I was always able to establish a friendly

FLEET OF CANOES.

spirit amongst them; it was really wonderful that these great fellows, with a defenceless Englishman completely in their power, should have acted in so friendly a manner. I usually made the chief a present of some kind, and all sorts of little trinkets, such as a tin whistle, looking-glasses, &c., gave great delight.

As huntsmen the Bangwa are noted for their prowess, and at Mukopi, a large village, I thought I should like to go off into the forest to hunt, taking a Bangwa warrior with me as a guide. But after almost standing on my head, and twisting myself into all kinds of positions and performing many other extraordinary feats, I thought it was time to return to camp; the forest was truly awful, and as to hunting—well, all I could do was to look after myself and leave the game to do likewise. He who wishes to hunt in this forest must be both an athlete, an acrobat, and a strong man with plenty of control over his temper; if he is not the first he will soon come a "cropper" over some fallen tree; if he is not the second he will get hopelessly tied up by the creepers; and if he is not the third, and goes into the forest, he will never come out again. Of course *I* saw nothing to shoot, I was too much taken up with my athletics even to look for anything. I am ashamed to say that every now and then I was angry, and a lot of good it was; a creeper with terrible thorns wrapped itself round my neck in loving embrace, and thinking to gain my freedom, I tried the "strong-man" trick, and found that instead of getting liberated, I not only got more firmly fixed up than ever, but in addition I was nearly strangled, not to mention having my nose frightfully lacerated with the thorns. A stream of water 12 feet wide presented itself and I jumped, coming down splash in the middle into deep water. All these and many other incidents of a similar character befell me that day when I required a little exercise. True I got the exercise, with a few bruises given in.

At another very large village of the Bangwa I had an opportunity of witnessing a midnight dance performed by the natives. It was a bright moonlight night when the people began to collect in the clearing in front of the chief's house; in all about two hundred men and women, alike nude, gathered in this spot for the national dance. A huge fire was built in the midst of the open space, and around this they all arranged themselves, men and women on opposite sides, forming a circle, and when the circle was complete the chief gave the word and the dancing commenced. Words fail me to depict the utter strangeness of the scene—the attitudes into which they wriggled themselves, all keeping time like a trained troupe of acrobats, the weird sounds made by hands and mouth, and the ghastly grimaces; all this, in the dim, uncertain light of the moon, baffles description. Presently the noise of murmuring made by the dancers as they wriggled

CANNIBAL POTTERY.

round the fire became louder and louder, and the contortions to which they put themselves more violent, quicker and quicker, until they all burst forth into a terrible yell, and seemed veritably to fly round the fire, still keeping time with hands, and feet, and voices. I have never seen anything so strange in all my travels, and as I looked at the distorted features of these people, working themselves up into a state of madness, and realised that they were all the fiercest of cannibals, and at any moment might change the scene into one of bloodshed, I admit to a creepy feeling stealing over me, and I wondered if I should ever get through the country alive. This dance was kept up for nearly two hours, and then suddenly there was a hush. Not a sound disturbed the stillness of the night. The dance was over, and in the twinkling of an eye the crowd dispersed in all directions. Noiselessly every one crept back to his hut, and I was left alone by the fireside, wondering at the weirdness of the scene just enacted.

The more I saw of the Bangwa the more I liked them, and it seems strange to me that a race of people of such great depth of character and superiority, should be left so utterly neglected, in as gross a state of darkness as it is possible to imagine. Surely the time has come when we in this civilised land of ours, possessing as we do all the privileges of a Christian country, should stretch out our hands to these poor ignorant cannibals, and seek to lift them out of their darkness and gross superstition into the light of the gospel of Christ. Their blood will surely be upon us as a nation if we, knowing their state, seek not to break their age-bound chains of heathenism, and " proclaim liberty to the captives, and the opening of the prison to them that are bound."

At Mupe, a large village of some thousands of people, I put my bicycle together—which I still had with me, and had brought right through the forest—and suddenly appeared in the village street riding my "bike." I shall never forget the sight of those yelling savages, racing after me in the wildest excitement, knocking each other over in their eagerness to get out of the way. Some ran off into their houses and barred the door, others took flight into the forest, only to return most cautiously one by one, when they found that it was a harmless thing. Some with their eyes starting wildly raced across my path, shouting, " The white man on a snake!" Children

THE BICYCLE AND THE CANNIBALS.

screamed, and men and women yelled; never was such a sight witnessed before. I hardly knew how to ride for laughing. After a while they got more used to it, and then all joined in the fun and scampered round their village in the greatest state of excitement. Presently I dismounted and called the chief to come and look at it. "It is a snake," he said; I tried to assure him it was not, but it was no use, he pointed to the track, and with a knowing shake of the head said, "And you tell me that's not a snake track?" In the midst of all this excitement my dog Sally, thinking the crowd had congregated quite unnecessarily, turned round and made for them, scattering them right and left, barking most furiously. Altogether, I think that was a red-letter day for the people of Mupe.

At Banalya I saw many things that upset me. The officer in charge greatly annoyed me by his ill-treatment of the natives. All day long some poor native was being scolded, and at night, in a state of intoxication, I saw what I could hardly believe. The European was sitting in his house, when some little noise occurred outside, an argument between two natives. The Belgian jumped up, and swinging a knife slashed about at the native in a most abominable fashion, and I was obliged to interfere, and afterwards reported the case to the Commandant. Such men ought never to be allowed to hold places of responsibility, and these are the men who have brought the Congo Free State into bad odium with the civilised world, and the great wonder is that proper investigation has not been made, and such men removed at least from positions of power.

At this same place I visited the Bangwa chief, a very big man in the district, and of great power, and he very soon told me many of his grievances relating to the treatment he and his people received at the hands of the Belgians.

There is a smouldering fire at the heart of these people, and by and by, if greater care and justice be not exercised amongst them, it will burst forth, and I would not like to be a European in the district if once the Bangwa rise. Of course in the end the fight would be one-sided, as it always is where breechloaders meet spears and bows and arrows; but a desperate fight it would be, and many would lose their lives, and a fine race of people, born for better things, would be smashed up, and

YAMBUYA.

made more degraded than they are to-day with all their cannibalism. They are cowed for the present, and will sit and listen quietly to the insults and the harsh words of the headstrong Belgian a little longer, but severe trouble will come if there be no improvement. While talking privately to the chief above mentioned, he catechised me most closely as to my nationality, &c. I told him that I was an Englishman, and he asked if the English ruled anywhere over the black people. I told him about the Uganda Protectorate to the east, and he then said, "Is there rubber in Uganda?" When I replied in the negative he said, "Then why do the English rule the people?" I said, "To do the black man good, and to make peace in his country." He was greatly interested, and asked me several questions about the government of Uganda, letting out many "trade secrets" with reference to his masters, and finally said

BASOKO.

that he wished his country were governed by the British also.

On November 1st I reached Basoko, the convict station of the Congo, situated at the confluence of the two rivers, the Congo and the Aruwimi. Mr. Hoffman, the officer in charge at Basoko, was most kind to me, and helped me in every way possible. One of my first questions was, " When will the next steamer start for the coast?" Unfortunately, one had just gone, and I was advised to cross over to Barumbu on the left bank of the Congo, where Captain Burrows, the commandant of the Aruwimi district, resided, and there to await the next steamer.

CHAPTER XVIII

BASOKO TO ENGLAND

Captain Guy Burrows—Ten days' rest The palm grove -Shooting our dinners- The steamer arrives Mode of progress Missionary friends at Upoto The captain drunk - Stanley Pool - Leopoldville—Kind friends—Catching the train -The saloon car—A strange sensation—Matadi Kind hospitality- Boma—The Governor-General's compliment— Cabenda The mail-boat arrives The lazy Portuguese—Getting passport signed—On board the *Loanda*—Lisbon Sud express to Paris— Home at last Conclusion.

CAPTAIN GUY BURROWS, Commissioner of the Aruwimi district, is a man who has had a great deal of experience, both as an officer in the British army, serving in India and Egypt, and also as an officer of the Congo Free State, in which he has laboured since 1894, first in the Wellé Mobanghi district, and then in the Upper Wellé, and finally in the Rubi-Wellé district. He received me very kindly, and I soon found him to be what others have found before me, a good friend, and a Briton to the core. My first difficulty upon my arrival at Barumbu was, how to book for myself a passage on the State steamer. I had no gold with me at all, it being unnecessary in Central Africa, but to my dismay I found that on the Congo, gold, and nothing but gold, would procure me a passage on the steamer and by rail. Previous to my leaving Toro I had armed myself with a letter from the Right Rev. Bishop Tucker of Uganda, but I found that the Belgians merely read it through, and handing it back, said that the Congo Free State does not care for bishops' letters. I took my difficulty to the captain, and he, like a true fellow-countryman, ever ready to help a lame dog over a stile, unhesitatingly advanced the money to me, and I procured my passage on the steamer. However, I had to wait at Barumbu ten days before it arrived.

Barumbu is very prettily situated, about two hundred

BARUMBU.

feet above the level of the river, and about a mile from its banks. The houses are built in the midst of a palm-grove, and give a most enchanting appearance to the station. The greatest difficulty in these places is to procure fresh meat; occasionally a wild pig is shot by one of the soldiers sent out for that purpose, or a forest antelope, but sometimes even these are not obtainable. Several times we were obliged to go out and shoot our dinners—parrots, pigeons, and suchlike. The native houses are by the river side, and are quite different from the Bangwa houses. They are low structures built with bamboo cane and thatched with pine-tree leaves. They are not so fine a race of people on the Upper Congo as on the Aruwimi, but seem to have great ability both as workers in pot and in iron; as fishermen they are quite expert.

The arrival of the steamer at Barumbu always causes the greatest excitement among the natives. They collect in great crowds along the bank and await its approach, and many are the queer notions they have with respect

CANNIBAL HOUSES ON UPPER CONGO.

to it. Captain Burrows procured for me the use of the largest cabin on the boat, which is usually kept, so I was told, for the exclusive use of any State official who might be requiring a passage. I was therefore highly favoured, and although there were ten other Europeans on board, I was able to keep my cabin to myself the whole way, and had the further privilege of taking my meals with the captain of the boat in his private cabin. These steamers form a startling contrast to the very wild state of affairs in Central Africa, and it seems almost incredible that they can penetrate no less than 1,300 miles inland from the Atlantic. They are well built with about eight small cabins for the use of Europeans, besides a spacious compartment as a saloon in addition to engineer's and captain's quarters.

I parted with my two faithful Waganda boys, Elisa and Alberto, and also the one Toro boy who had journeyed with me all the way. They had a long tramp before them, but I am glad to know that they arrived quite safely back

ARRIVAL OF THE STEAMER.

into their own land, being helped very considerably by the officers in charge of the various stations.

Our mode of procedure on the river was not of a particularly exciting kind. In the morning we started off, usually about 6 a.m., calling at each State post on the way, and stopping at some fuel station for the night. On account of the sand-banks and other obstructions in the river it was not safe to travel by night, although at high water it is sometimes done. All day long one would sit on the deck reading, or else spend the time examining the banks as we sped along. It was not at all possible to make many observations of native life, or to find out the customs of the people. I must leave this for others to write about who have spent years on the Congo, and have had opportunities of studying these things. I simply passed through the country on my way home, and therefore am not able to give many details. There is no coal at present found in the Congo State, and wood is the fuel used on the steamers. There is, of course, an

UPOTO.

unlimited supply of this article, and many little stations have been built at intervals along the river bank, where a good quantity is always found ready chopped.

I met many missionary friends on the Congo, at Upoto, Bolobo, Matadi, and Bomba, but we did not stop at the numerous stations of various missions. I was much surprised to find that really beautiful houses are built by the missionaries, no better than they are absolutely needed, but one hardly expected to see such neat, painted bungalows, with European furniture, &c. The natives are set to work and are taught how to do ordinary carpentering work and house-building, and very clever they are, and soon learn to use their hands.

The captain on our steamer was quite a character, a

FUEL STATION, UPPER CONGO.

Norwegian. He spoke fair English, however, but seemed quite incapable of entering into conversation, except when he had taken a glass or two of absinthe, then there was no stopping him. The traders at various places at which we stayed seemed well acquainted with this peculiarity of the captain's, and generally brought a bottle or two of this stuff on board when they visited him. Alas, one day the absinthe got into the captain's head, and then he became so very merry that we were much afraid that in his exuberance he would run the boat into the bank. It was therefore necessary to stop and anchor for the rest of the day. I was much annoyed, as I was anxious to catch the mail boat at Matadi, and a day's delay meant my missing it. The next morning, therefore, I gave the captain a little

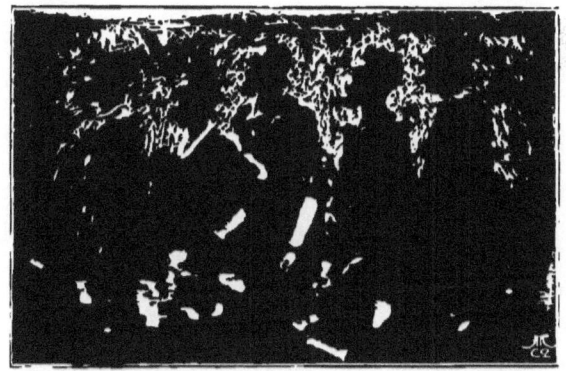

NATIVE TYPES, UPPER CONGO.

bit of my mind; not only had I missed my boat at Matadi, necessitating, as I thought, another month's delay there, but he had endangered the lives of all on board. He was most profuse in his apologies, and promised not to drink absinthe again, and it will be good for him if he does not.

But my journey was drawing near its close, and one day, about 12 noon, we found ourselves in Stanley Pool, steaming away to its most westerly point, where is the town of Leopoldville. The Cliffs of Dover, as they are called, on the north of the Pool, looked very beautiful as we passed. They are white chalk cliffs, and most strongly resemble those of Dover.

It was the 24th of November when I once more set foot on dry land, at Leopoldville. From here the river is not navigable on account of the rapids, and the rest of the journey to the coast must either be done by land, the ordinary caravan route with carriers, or else by rail, for the new railway was finally opened in 1896 from Leopoldville to Matadi.

DOVER CLIFFS, STANLEY POOL.

Upon my arrival I began to look about for friends and I was not long in finding some. I had been strolling about for a few minutes when I saw over the door of one of the houses the three letters C.B.M., and I knew that this stood for "Congo Balolo Mission." I went in and was not mistaken. Two young fellows were in charge, and welcomed me heartily. I found that a train left the following morning for Matadi, so I decided not to wait a day longer than was necessary, but to keep on the move as long as I could, trusting to Providence

to catch a boat at the coast, in spite of having missed the Belgian mail boat, which had left Matadi on the 23rd. The evening was spent in chatting with my friends at the Mission, who very kindly rendered me much assistance in procuring a ticket for me on the railway, and in the early morning I started off to *catch the train!*

What an anomaly! Catching a train in Central Africa! For we were still three hundred miles from the actual coast line. After tramping about Africa for

LEOPOLDVILLE.

a few years it seemed almost absurd to go off to *catch a train*. Presently I heard a most unmistakable train whistle, and in a few moments I was in the station and saw the train—two carriages, one for passengers and the other for luggage and black men, and the engine. The saloon carriage, in which I very soon seated myself, was most comfortable, being fitted up with cane chairs and small tables; there was also a lavatory at one end. But the motion was anything but nice. I had only just seated myself when, with another shriek and a terrific jerk, that almost sent me through the window, away we went. I tried to look out of the window, but was soon so covered with a thick deposit of soot, that I sat down and tried to look as if I enjoyed it. We were travelling at the rate of fifteen miles an hour, and I thought every moment would be our last; in fact, so nervous did I get by the sudden change of motion, and of the awful possibility, as I thought, of being precipitated down one of the yawning gullies over which we raced, that I got

OLD CARAVAN ROUTE TO COAST FROM LEOPOLDVILLE.

up to change my seat for one nearer the door, and was on the point of calling out to the driver to stop, when the train gave a lurch to the left, and over I went on to the floor at the bottom of the car. Here, however, where I had almost made up my mind to stay, the rumbling of the wheels was so great that I again struggled to my feet. Oh! the rocking, and the pitching! it was far worse than being on a really first-class ocean liner, and the squealing of that terrible little engine very nearly drove me out of my senses for the first hour. And I have it on the very best authority, that one of the passengers had a bad attack of *mal de mer*, and I am not at all surprised. After a while we got used to it, as one does to most things in life, and I settled down more comfortably, and determined to make the best of it. After all, the scenery

THE NEW WAY.

made up for a lot, it was simply exquisite. We were winding round and round the hillsides, sometimes overlooking a precipice hundreds of feet deep, then madly rushing at a breakneck speed down an incline, then turning round a sharp corner at the bottom, and over a bridge across some deep gully. It was quite an unique experience, to be rushing through Africa without any exertion save that of keeping the perpendicular. All day we kept on our way, each passenger having provided himself with food, and at 6 p.m. we steamed into Tumba, where we stayed for the night. In the early morning we were off again, the latter part of the journey being more beautiful as far as scenery is concerned. The whole distance is 230 miles to Matadi, but it takes nearly two days, and we reached there at 4 p.m.

VILLAGE ON CONGO.

The Congo railway is undoubtedly a masterpiece of modern engineering skill, and I imagine there are few stretches of country that present so many difficulties to the engineers as were met with in the construction of this railway. Such a work, however, was not carried on without the loss of numbers of lives; whole gangs of men were struck down by the ravages of malarial diseases. A great many Europeans, too, went out for this work who were quite unfitted to stand the climate, and many went there with the idea that they could indulge in their lowest passions, away from restraint, without harm to themselves. How sadly were they mistaken! I was told that a party of six men went out, and, arriving at Matadi, they, imagining they could do just as they liked, participated in all kinds of evil habits, with the result that in less than six months not one of them was left. It is just the same anywhere on the Congo; it is well-nigh

RAPIDS ON LOWER CONGO.

impossible to live a gay and reckless life without injuring the health; good, nourishing food is absolutely necessary, and in addition to this comfortable, well-built houses. On one of the Aruwimi stations I met a young American, who, in the company of nine others, had gone out in the service of the Congo Free State only three years before, and only two were left, and one of these invalided home soon afterwards. It was most pathetic to hear him say, "Well, I guess I shall be the next!"

At first sight Matadi seemed to consist of dirty streets,

bare rocks, and broken gin bottles, with a blazing sun overhead, but I found out afterwards that there were some pleasant spots even in Matadi.

Up the hill above the station is the house of Mr. and Mrs. Forfeitt, of the Baptist Missionary Society, and it was cheering to get into the well-built house with its kind and genial occupants after wandering about the streets for an hour or so. These good people gave me hospitality

STOPPING FOR WATER.

during my stay at Matadi, and none could have been more kind.

But my time was short, for I received information that the Portuguese mail boat was to leave Cabenda on the 2nd of December and the boat from Matadi to Boma on the 28th of November. Another two days were spent at Boma, and Mr. and Mrs. Cramer, of the American Christian Alliance, hospitably entertained me. They have a very nice house situated on the rising ground overlooking the sea. There seemed to be but little mission work going on at Boma, Mr. and Mrs. Cramer and a Miss

Villars being the only Protestant missionaries. The Roman Catholics have a fine iron church.

The European population of Boma is about 300; it is the seat of the local Government. The Governor-General's house is a very fine one indeed. The town is divided into two parts, the lower part by the seashore, with hotels, general stores, post-office, and Government offices, and the Boma plateau, with the house of the Governor-General, and the soldiers' barracks, hospital, &c. A steam tram runs between both parts. Before I left I

RAILWAY SHEDS.

called upon the Acting Governor-General. After waiting a little while I was shown into one of the spacious rooms and he soon after came in. He received me kindly and proceeded to ask me many questions concerning the journey I had accomplished, and when I told him that I had crossed the Continent from east to west he asked me how many troops I had with me. I told him I had journeyed without escort, and he was at first disposed to doubt my word, and then asked if I went through the forest and the cannibal districts of the Aruwimi, and when I said, "Yes," he politely said, "Well, if you went without an escort you are a fool." I thanked him for the compliment, adding that whether a fool or not, I *had* passed through, and had never any occasion to fire a single shot in self-defence, nor had I been stopped by natives anywhere, but had undoubtedly made friends with many of the chiefs. He did not mean any insult, and I did not take it as such, but he certainly seemed very surprised. Personally, I believe that any one who has a little knowledge of native character and customs, and a smattering of Swahili, could accomplish the same journey in as comfortable a manner as I did, providing that he act honourably and with strictest justice towards the natives; not harshly, without considering the ignorant state of the offenders, but making due allowances for them; and, above all, letting them see that they are recognised as fellow-men, and not as creatures of a lower order.

But I do not attribute my safety throughout this perilous journey to any wisdom of my own in dealing with the natives, or to any "good luck," for I am bound to believe that a stronger Arm than my own defended me in dangers, and that where good fortune seemed to favour me it was the evidence of a watchful Providence. In short, I believe that as I trusted myself into the hands of God, when I left England in 1894, going out as a Christian missionary to do His will, and day after day, in spite of weariness and sorrows, relied upon His mercy, although so very imperfectly, so He, in His love, has helped me, and through Christ has heard my prayers, and the prayers of many of my friends.

On the 30th of November I left Boma and arrived at Cabenda about 3.30 p.m. Here I expected to see the Portuguese mail, but as I looked up and down the coast no mail boat could I see; just as I was about to go ashore, however, a big steamer hove in sight, and this proved to be the mail. How thankful I was now to see the boat that would take me to Europe!

When I got on shore I asked what time the boat would leave, as I had to get my passport signed by the Portuguese Governor in the morning, and if it started too early I should not be able to catch the boat. I waited till ten o'clock, and then news came that the mail would leave at twelve noon the following day. I put up at a small hotel belonging to a trading establishment in Cabenda, and in the morning went off to try and get my passport signed. I first went to the chief secretary and found him in bed; I sent in word that I must see him on business, and he then appeared in his night apparel, looking very much astonished to see a foreigner. I told him my business, and he then seemed very angry and said that he would see me in an hour's time at the office. And so I waited, and the time crept by, and I knew the mail would not wait for me. At the end of an hour I called again at the office; he was not there; I sent in my card and said that I must see him immediately, and then at last he came. I produced my passport and he looked at it and said, "This is no good, it only takes you to Cabenda." I told him that I was a subject of Her Most Gracious Majesty, Queen Victoria of Great Britain, and my passport was signed by Her Majesty's consul at Boma, and would take me anywhere. After this speech the gentleman bowed and signed without another word. I was only just in time. To reach the mail boat was a big undertaking, as it was five miles out at sea; and the only boat available was a small surf boat hardly large enough to take myself and my luggage, but by dint of hard rowing and at some risk it was accomplished, and as soon as I was on board up went the steps and away we steamed.

The *Loanda* was the name of the mail boat, and I was most agreeably surprised to find her quite an elegant little boat, fitted up in really good style. There was excellent accommodation for passengers, the cabins being large and airy. The food, certainly, was a little trying to one's digestive powers after forest fare. Oil and onions seemed the accompaniments to every dish, especially the former.

There were about two dozen passengers, mostly Portuguese, and two Frenchmen. I was the only Englishman, and none of the others could speak English. The engineers, however, were all British, and this made things much pleasanter for me. The captain was a curious old fellow, and was always talking, either to himself or some poor unfortunate sailor or passenger. In addition to this weakness, he had an immoderate affection for cod's head, and as this fish and others often appeared on the festive board, he had this curious appetite frequently satisfied.

We had a most delightful voyage in the *Loanda*, with charming weather the whole way. Touching at St. Thomas' and Princes' Islands, and then right on to the Cape Verde Islands, stopping at Santiago and St. Vincent, and thence to Madeira, from there to Lisbon.

I disembarked at Lisbon, and found that a train left the same evening for Paris, the Sud express. What a change after the Congo railway! This was luxury indeed, sleeping and luncheon cars, saloon and smoke-room, all of the latest improved style. Coming from the wilds of Africa, all seemed very strange, but very nice. We reached Paris on Christmas morning, and home in England on Christmas night.

And so I bring this brief record of my journey to a close, conscious of its many imperfections of style as a literary work, and of the brevity of its scope.

As I have before remarked, in a journey such as this it was impossible to really study the native races, or even the country, and I have merely related passing impressions and hastily-made observations. I can only hope that these records may create a little deeper sympathy in the minds of the people of England for the sable sons of Africa who have suffered much, and are *still* suffering. The doors of this dark continent are wide open for the reception of Christianity and of righteous government, which alone shall drive away the darkness, alleviate the sufferings of the people, and bring peace to the land.

[NOTE.—The author is much indebted to Rev. Lawson Forfeitt and Mr. R. H. Leakey for some of the photographs herein produced.]

The Gresham Press,
UNWIN BROTHERS,
WOKING AND LONDON.

BOOKS FOR RECREATION AND STUDY

PUBLISHED BY
T. FISHER UNWIN,
11, PATERNOSTER
BUILDINGS, LON-
DON, E.C. . . . .

T. FISHER UNWIN, Publisher,

THE STORY OF THE NATIONS

A SERIES OF POPULAR HISTORIES.

Each Volume is furnished with Maps, Illustrations, and Index. Large Crown 8vo., fancy cloth, gold lettered, or Library Edition, dark cloth, burnished red top, **5s.** *each.—Or may be had in half Persian, cloth sides, gilt tops; Price on Application.*

1. **Rome.** By ARTHUR GILMAN, M.A.
2. **The Jews.** By Professor J. K. HOSMER.
3. **Germany.** By the Rev. S. BARING-GOULD.
4. **Carthage.** By Professor ALFRED J. CHURCH.
5. **Alexander's Empire.** By Prof. J. P. MAHAFFY.
6. **The Moors in Spain.** By STANLEY LANE-POOLE.
7. **Ancient Egypt.** By Prof. GEORGE RAWLINSON.
8. **Hungary.** By Prof. ARMINIUS VAMBERY.
9. **The Saracens.** By ARTHUR GILMAN, M.A.
10. **Ireland.** By the Hon. EMILY LAWLESS.
11. **Chaldea.** By ZENAIDE A. RAGOZIN.
12. **The Goths.** By HENRY BRADLEY.
13. **Assyria.** By ZENAIDE A. RAGOZIN.
14. **Turkey.** By STANLEY LANE-POOLE.
15. **Holland.** By Professor J. E. THOROLD ROGERS.
16. **Mediæval France.** By GUSTAVE MASSON.
17. **Persia.** By S. G. W. BENJAMIN.
18. **Phœnicia.** By Prof. GEORGE RAWLINSON.
19. **Media.** By ZENAIDE A. RAGOZIN.
20. **The Hansa Towns.** By HELEN ZIMMERN.
21. **Early Britain.** By Professor ALFRED J. CHURCH.
22. **The Barbary Corsairs.** By STANLEY LANE-POOLE.
23. **Russia.** By W. R. MORFILL.
24. **The Jews under the Roman Empire.** By W. D. MORRISON.
25. **Scotland.** By JOHN MACKINTOSH, LL.D.
26. **Switzerland.** By R. STEAD and LINA HUG.
27. **Mexico.** By SUSAN HALE.
28. **Portugal.** By H. MORSE STEPHENS.
29. **The Normans.** By SARAH ORNE JEWETT.
30. **The Byzantine Empire.** By C. W. C. OMAN, M.A.
31. **Sicily: Phœnician, Greek and Roman.** By the late E. A. FREEMAN.
32. **The Tuscan and Genoa Republics.** By BELLA DUFFY.
33. **Poland.** By W. R. MORFILL.
34. **Parthia.** By Prof. GEORGE RAWLINSON.
35. **The Australian Commonwealth.** By GREVILLE TREGARTHEN.
36. **Spain.** By H. E. WATTS.
37. **Japan.** By DAVID MURRAY, Ph.D.
38. **South Africa.** By GEORGE M. THEAL.
39. **Venice.** By the Hon. ALETHEA WIEL.
40. **The Crusades:** The Latin Kingdom of Jerusalem. By T. A. ARCHER and CHARLES L. KINGSFORD.
41. **Vedic India.** By ZENAIDE A. RAGOZIN.
42. **The West Indies and the Spanish Main.** By JAMES RODWAY, F.L.S.
43. **Bohemia.** By C. E. MAURICE.
44. **The Balkans.** By W. MILLER.
45. **Canada.** By Dr. BOURINOT.
46. **British India.** By R. W. FRAZER, LL.B.
47. **Modern France.** By ANDRÉ LE BON.
  The Franks. By LEWIS SERGEANT, B.A.
48. **Austria.** By SIDNEY WHITMAN.
49. **Modern England before the Reform Bill.** By JUSTIN MCCARTHY, M.P.
50. **China.** By Professor DOUGLAS.

11, Paternoster Buildings, London, E.C.

T. FISHER UNWIN, Publisher,

BUILDERS OF GREATER BRITAIN

EDITED BY

H. F. WILSON

A Set of 10 Volumes, each with Photogravure Frontispiece, and Map, large crown 8vo., cloth, **5s.** *each.*

The completion of the Sixtieth year of the Queen's reign will be the occasion of much retrospect and review, in the course of which the great men who, under the auspices of Her Majesty and her predecessors, have helped to make the British Empire what it is to-day, will naturally be brought to mind. Hence the idea of the present series. These biographies, concise but full, popular but authoritative, have been designed with the view of giving in each case an adequate picture of the builder in relation to his work.

The series will be under the general editorship of Mr. H. F. Wilson, formerly Fellow of Trinity College, Cambridge, and now private secretary to the Right Hon. J. Chamberlain at the Colonial Office. Each volume will be placed in competent hands, and will contain the best portrait obtainable of its subject, and a map showing his special contribution to the Imperial edifice. The first to appear will be a Life of Sir Walter Ralegh, by Major Hume, the learned author of "The Year after the Armada." Others in contemplation will deal with the Cabots, the quarter-centenary of whose sailing from Bristol is has recently been celebrated in that city, as well as in Canada and Newfoundland ; Sir Thomas Maitland, the "King Tom" of the Mediterranean ; Rajah Brooke, Sir Stamford Raffles, Lord Clive, Edward Gibbon Wakefield, Zachary Macaulay, &c., &c.

The Series has taken for its motto the Miltonic prayer :—

"𝕿𝖍𝖔𝖚 𝖂𝖍𝖔 𝖔𝖋 𝕿𝖍𝖞 𝖋𝖗𝖊𝖊 𝖌𝖗𝖆𝖈𝖊 𝖉𝖎𝖉𝖘𝖙 𝖇𝖚𝖎𝖑𝖉 𝖚𝖕 𝖙𝖍𝖎𝖘 𝕭𝖗𝖎𝖙𝖙𝖆𝖓𝖓𝖎𝖈𝖐 𝕰𝖒𝖕𝖎𝖗𝖊 𝖙𝖔 𝖆 𝖌𝖑𝖔𝖗𝖎𝖔𝖚𝖘 𝖆𝖓𝖉 𝖊𝖓𝖛𝖎𝖆𝖇𝖑𖊊 𝖍𝖊𝖎𝖌𝖍𝖙𝖍, 𝖂𝖎𝖙𝖍 𝖆𝖑𝖑 𝖍𝖊𝖗 𝕯𝖆𝖚𝖌𝖍𝖙𝖊𝖗 𝕴𝖘𝖑𝖆𝖓𝖉𝖘 𝖆𝖇𝖔𝖚𝖙 𝖍𝖊𝖗, 𝖘𝖙𝖆𝖞 𝖚𝖘 𝖎𝖓 𝖙𝖍𝖎𝖘 𝖋𝖊𝖑𝖎𝖈𝖎𝖙𝖎𝖊."

1. **SIR WALTER RALEGH.** By MARTIN A. S. HUME, Author of "The Courtships of Queen Elizabeth," &c.

2. **SIR THOMAS MAITLAND;** the Mastery of the Mediterranean. By WALTER FREWEN LORD.

3. **JOHN CABOT AND HIS SONS;** the Discovery of North America. By C. RAYMOND BEAZLEY, M.A.

4. **EDWARD GIBBON WAKEFIELD;** the Colonisation of South Australia and New Zealand. By R. GARNETT, C.B., L.L.D.

5. **LORD CLIVE;** the Foundation of British Rule in India. By Sir A. J. ARBUTHNOT, K.C.S.I., C.I.E.

RAJAH BROOKE; the Englishman as Ruler of an Eastern State. By Sir SPENSER ST. JOHN, G.C.M.G

ADMIRAL PHILIP; the Founding of New South Wales. By LOUIS BECKE and WALTER JEFFERY.

SIR STAMFORD RAFFLES; England in the Far East. By the Editor.

11, Paternoster Buildings, London, E.C.

T. FISHER UNWIN, Publisher,

WORKS BY PROF. PASQUALE VILLARI

THE LIFE AND TIMES OF GIROLAMO SAVONAROLA

Translated by LINDA VILLARI

New and Cheaper Edition in one volume. Fully Illustrated.
Cloth, large crown, **7s. 6d.**

"No more interesting book has been issued during the present season."
— *Pall Mall Gazette*
"The most interesting religious biography that we know of in modern times."
— *Spectator.*
"A book which is not likely to be forgotten." — *Athenæum.*
"By far the best book on Savonarola available for English readers." — *Standard.*
"Is perhaps *the* book of the publishing season." — *Star.*
"Sincere, complete, and, upon the whole, well-balanced and candid." — *Yorkshire Post.*
"A work of very great value." — *Scotsman.*
"No more graphic view of the ecclesiastical and social life of ancient Italy has been opened up for us than this of Linda Villari." — *Morning Leader.*
"As complete and trustworthy as care, judgment, and the fullest investigation can make it." — *Dundee Advertiser.*
"A credit to the publisher." — *Independent.*

THE LIFE AND TIMES OF NICCOLÒ MACHIAVELLI

New and Cheaper Edition. Fully Illustrated. Large crown 8vo.,
cloth, **7s. 6d.**

"Indispensable to the serious student of Machiavelli, his teaching and his times."
— *Times.*
"The fullest and most authoritative history of Machiavelli and his times ever given to the British public." — *Glasgow Herald.*
"May be regarded as an authority on the times of which it treats. . . . The book is enriched with rare and interesting illustrations, and with some valuable historical documents." — *Daily Telegraph.*

BY FRANK HORRIDGE

LIVES OF GREAT ITALIANS

Illustrated. Large crown 8vo., cloth, **7s. 6d.**

Opinions of the Press.

"A poetical, romantic, and charmingly written book, which will be popular with all who love their Italy." — DOUGLAS SLADEN in *Literary World.*
"Able, eloquent, and interesting." — *Queen.*

11, Paternoster Buildings, London, E.C.

CUBA AND PORTO RICO

WITH THE OTHER ISLANDS OF
THE WEST INDIES,
BY ROBERT T. HILL,
Of the United States Geological Survey.

BAHAMAS,
JAMAICA,
HAITI,
SAN DOMINGO,
ST. THOMAS,
ST. KITTS,
ANTIGUA,
MONTSERRAT,
GUADELOUPE,
MARTINIQUE,
ST. LUCIA,
BARBADOS,
ST. VINCENT,
GRENADA,
TRINIDAD.

A valuable Work of Reference.
A Scientific Presentation.
An indispensable Guide.
A readable Narrative.
500 Pages.
160 Illustrations.
Price 16s.

Flora,
Climate,
Soil,
Products,
Minerals,
Agriculture,
Scenery,
Topography,
Sanitation,
People,
Transportation,
Statistics,
History,
Routes of travel,
Administration,
Accessibility,
Possibilities.

"His book is a very good example of its kind, carefully written, full of the information that is required."—*The Times.*

"He has written the most important book that has been published on the subject."—*Chicago Tribune.*

"His volume of 429 pages, with profuse Illustrations and an index, forms a little condensed library of reference."—*N. Y. Times.*

"The book is well and ably written ... is brightened by a truly magnificent series of photographs ... beautifully reproduced on fine paper."—*Edinburgh Scotsman.*

Tourists to Cuba, Porto Rico and the West Indies will find this a most reliable and the only General Handbook.

T. FISHER UNWIN, PATERNOSTER SQUARE, LONDON.

3 GREAT ART BOOKS
EDITED BY JOSEPH PENNELL.

Lithography and Lithographers:
SOME CHAPTERS IN THE HISTORY OF THE ART.

With Technical Remarks and Suggestions by JOSEPH and ELIZABETH ROBINS PENNELL. Together with 154 Illustrations, besides a Frontispiece Portrait of Joseph Pennell by JAMES MCNEILL WHISTLER, and other original lithographs by A. Legros, W. Strang, C. H. Shannon, A. Lunois, J. McLure Hamilton and T. R. Way. (13½ × 10½ inches, xiii + 279 pp.) £3 13s. 6d. net. Also, a Fine Edition signed by JOSEPH PENNELL; on Japan paper, £15 15s. net.

"The selection is done as admirably as the reproduction, which is saying much.... The authors .... present, in fact, the first complete and intelligent historical survey of the art in the different countries of the world."—*St. James's Gazette.*

"The present volume contains a great number of admirably-reproduced examples by many artists, and these illustrate in a very complete manner, not only the growth of ideas in regard to lithography, but also the varied possibilities of the stone in different hands."—*Morning Post.*

"*The Greatest English Artist since Hogarth.*"
The Work of Charles Keene.

With Introduction and Comments by JOSEPH PENNELL, and numerous Pictures illustrative of the artist's method and vein of humour; to which is added a Bibliography of Selected Works and Notes by W. H. CHESSON. The Edition is limited to 750 copies (250 of these for America), an Ordinary Edition at £3 13s. 6d. net., and 15 copies of a Fine Edition at £15 15s. net.

"This work .... will be a revelation even to those who are beginning to estimate this consummate artist at his true merit."—*Literature.*

"Mr. Pennell's is the fullest critical appreciation of Keene we have yet had."—*Daily News.*

"Extraordinarily good and well worth having .... we thank Mr. Pennell very warmly for the thorough performance of a task that called out to be accomplished."—*Daily Chronicle.*

"The bibliography by Mr. W. H. Chesson .... is a labour of real merit and value, carried out in a thorough and workmanlike manner." *Graphic.*

"*The Masterpiece of a Great Spanish Artist.*"
PABLO DE SEGOVIA:
The Adventures of a Spanish Sharper.
BY FRANCISCO DE QUEVEDO.

Illustrated with over 100 Drawings by DANIEL VIERGE. With an Introduction on "Vierge and his Art," by JOSEPH PENNELL; and "A Critical Essay on Quevedo, and his Writings," by H. E. WATTS. Super royal 4to, parchment, old style (limited edition), £3 13s. 6d. net.

London: T. FISHER UNWIN, PATERNOSTER SQUARE.

www.ingramcontent.com/pod-product-compliance
Lightning Source LLC
Chambersburg PA
CBHW032143010526
44111CB00035B/987